The Galapagos Islands

A Natural History Guide

To Mei Fang,
who had to get up every
morning to type the book
on the computer, instead of
sleeping until noon, as usual.

THE GALAPAGOS ISLANDS

PIERRE CONSTANT

Nothing gets lost,
nothing is created,
everything transforms
—Lavoisier

Copyright © 1997, 1995 The Guidebook Company Ltd, Hong Kong
All maps copyright © 1997 The Guidebook Company Ltd, Hong Kong
Odyssey Guides, an imprint of The Guidebook Company Ltd,
G/F 2 Lower Kai Yuen Lane, North Point, Hong Kong
T 852 2856 3896 F 852 2565 8624 E mail odyssey@asiaonline.net

Distributed in the United Kingdom, Ireland and Europe by
Hi Marketing Ltd, 38 Carver Road, London SE24 9LT, UK
ISBN: 962-217-505-8
British Library Cataloguing-in-Publication Data
A catalogue record of this book is available from the British Library

This edition first published in North America in 1997 by
Passport Books, 4255 W. Touhy Avenue,
Lincolnwood (Chicago), Illinois 60646-1975, USA
T 847 679 5500 F 847 679 2494
ISBN: 0-8442-4755-3
Library of Congress Catalogue Card Number: on file

PASSPORT BOOKS
a division of NTC/*Contemporary Publishing Company*
Lincolnwood, Illinois USA

(This edition first published in 1994 in French by Calao Life Experience, under the title
Archipel des Galapagos)

Co-ordinating Editor: Stefan Cucos
Editor: Mark Morris
Cover Concept: Aubrey Tse

Production by Twin Age Ltd
Printed in China

CONTENTS

FOREWORD

I shall never forget the vision of the stone arch, emerging slowly above the surface of the Pacific Ocean at first light, after a long night on a sailingboat in Galápagos waters. This monumental arch, made of volcanic tuff—a haven for snow-white masked boobies—is the Great Arch of Darwin Island, at the extreme northwest of the archipelago. Swept by surf and foam, which roll at its foot, and looking like an oceanic Arc de Triomphe, Darwin Arch, oriented east-west, is the symbol of the 'Gate'. Silent witness of time forgotten, it shows the direction from which the first unsuspecting discoverers of history came: an archbishop from Panama, drifting with the currents, lost on an ocean in the middle of the XVIth century.

The first name given to the islands, Las Islas Encantadas or 'the Enchanted Isles', evokes the magical aura that has always surrounded the Galápagos. Since I first came to the archipelago in 1980—as a a young trainee of an Ecuadorian tourism company but soon to become a naturalist guide for the Galápagos National Park—the islands have changed, under the influence of man. The human population has increased fourfold in 15 years, and has doubled in the last five years. Today, the population is estimated at 20,000 people, scattered on four main islands. Tourism has been booming tremendously on this chain of volcanic isles, and the number of visitors, about 17,500 people in 1980—though limited to 25,000 visitors by the 'Master Plan' of 1981—eventually passed the record mark of 60,000 persons at the end of 1997. Souvenir shops multiply in Puerto Ayora, and hotels are sprouting like mushrooms after the rain (of dollars).

The fire on the slope of the Sierra Negra volcano in 1985 not only devastated hundreds of hectares of vegetation but, following a worldwide ad campaign, provoked a blaze of tourism, which saw a dramatic boom in 1986. The same year, a second airport was inaugurated on San Cristóbal Island, and the Reserve of Marine Resources was created by presidential decree. Since then, a lot of ink has been spilt; this includes my book, *Marine Life of the Galápagos*, a guide to the fish, whales, dolphins and other marine animals, published in 1992. Even though it stimulated the development of scuba diving, it also invited all sorts of abuses. Among these are the intensive plundering of the submarine riches and schools of sharks by Japanese commercial fishing boats, which first became interested in shark fins, then in *pepinos*, or sea cucumbers. The scandal broke in 1992, despite laws passed by the Ecuadorian government for the protection of sharks and *pepinos*, but illegal fishing continued in 1996, under the very noses of the authorities.

The economic stake for Galápagos fishermen is enormous. They went knocking on the door of the president in Quito to lift a ban on fishing. Eventually they won in July

1994, and the government gave them the go ahead to fish lobsters for three months, sea cucumbers for three months, and even sharks for three months. The number of tourism boats, which was limited in the Galápagos to avoid a 'tidal wave', was soon exceeded. Nowadays, about 100 boats operate in the archipelago. Will the hen that lays the golden eggs be exploited to the point of exhaustion? There are profits to be made, but the economic pressures that they bring are so unavoidable that one may fear that the Galápagos have already lost their sacred aura, their image of a lost, unviolated, natural paradise. UNESCO became ultimately concerned in 1995-96, and now puts pressure on the Ecuadorian government to bring a change and to effectively protect the Marine Reserve, already 'Whale Sanctuary' and newly declared a 'Biological Reserve' by INEFAN, (Instituto Ecuatoriano Forestal, de Aereas Naturales y de Vida Silvestre) in November 1996.

Nevertheless, the Darwin Station goes on with its research programme as if everything were fine, and the Galápagos National Park continues with programmes of protection, conservation, environmental education and the breeding of giant tortoises. Not to mention the training of multilingual naturalist guides, who are, to some extent, the 'arrowhead' of integrity in the Galápagos National Park. It is pleasant to imagine the Galápagos as a kind of Noah's ark in the middle of the deluge.

But I do not wish to darken the picture more than I should. The magic and the spell of the Enchanted Isles really do exist. They are found in the inquisitive look of the blue-footed boobies; in the sweetness and the frolic of the sea lions on land or in the water; in the peaceful and detached somnolence of marine iguanas flat on the rocks under the equatorial sun; in the enigmatic smiles of the land iguanas under the opuntia cacti; in the eternal immobility of the giant tortoises in their centenarian shells, overlooking the world from the rim of the volcanoes; in the mystical contemplation of the pelican standing on its rock, facing the glowing ocean at sunset; in the grace and innocence of the flightless cormorant during the courtship display; in the comical duel of the albatrosses fencing with their beak in the mating season; in the joyful gamboling of the bottlenose dolphins, for which each boat is a pretext to play; in the wave that crashes against the Great Arch and turns into one thousand drops of iridescent light...

For all that, I pay my respects to these islands. The Galápagos must be safeguarded as the innocence of the world. For the sun rises east on Noah's ark or on the arch of Darwin, and glows west on the great blue yonder of the Pacific. The magic of 'Las Encantadas' may one day disappear under the surface of the waves, but until then, men would have gone long before.

Pierre Constant
Paris, May 19, 1997

If I was asked to give advice to someone about to undertake a long journey, my answer would totally depend on that traveller's liking for one science or another, and on the advantages that he found for his own studies. Doubtless, one experiences great satisfaction in contemplating such diverse lands, and to review, so to speak, the variety of human races, but this satisfaction far from compensates for all the hardship one is likely to endure. Therefore, one must have an aim, and this aim should be a study to complete, a truth to unveil. In short this aim must support you and encourage you.

If life is but a dream, as poets say, I am sure that the visions of a journey are among those which would best help get one through a long night. Over the last 60 years, long journeys have become much easier. In the time of Cook, a man would leave his home to undertake such expeditions, and expose himself to the hardest privations. Nowadays, one can go around the world in a yacht in the greatest of comfort. If one is subject to seasickness, one should think twice before undertaking a long voyage. This is not an alment which you can be rid of in a matter of days; I speak from experience.

In conclusion, it seems then that there can be nothing more profitable for a young naturalist than a journey to distant countries. It heightens, and partly satisfies, one's eagerness to know what captures all men. Travel teaches patience and erases all traces of selfishness. It teaches one to make choices for oneself and to adapt to all things; in a word it gives one the kind of qualities that may be found in mariners. Travel also teaches one a bit about suspicion, but one discovers at the same time that there are many men with an excellent heart, always ready to help, although one has never seen them before nor will one ever see them again.

Charles Darwin, Voyage of a Naturalist (1859)

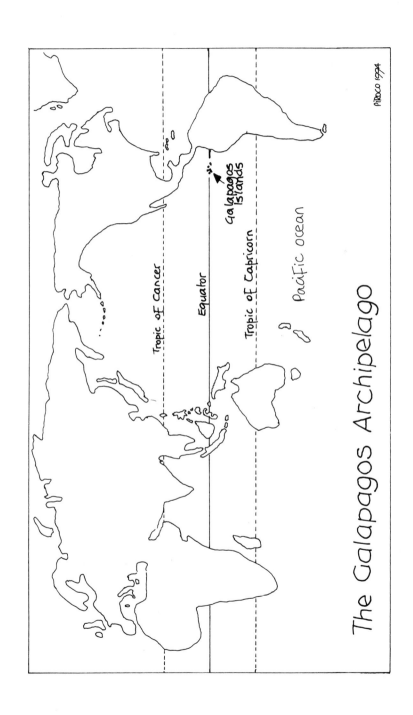

The Galapagos Archipelago

PART ONE

SCIENTIFIC AND HISTORICAL DATA

CHAPTER ONE

GENERAL SETTING OF THE ISLANDS
GEOLOGY AND ORIGIN OF THE GALÁPAGOS
VOLCANISM; GLACIAL AGES

The Galápagos Islands stretch over a 320-kilometre (174-mile) axis from east to west, and the equator passes precisely across the crater of Wolf volcano in the north of Isabela Island. The archipelago is made up of 19 islands and 42 islets or surfacing rocks. San Cristóbal, the easternmost island of the Galápagos group, lies about 1,100 kilometres (600 miles) west of the mother country, Ecuador, on the South American mainland.

The total land surface of the archipelago is just over 8,000 square kilometres. Isabela, the largest island, has an area of 4,588 square kilometres; Santa Cruz, the second in size and the most central, is only 986 square kilometres; James is 585 square kilometres; San Cristóbal is 558 square kilometres; Floreana is 173 square kilometres. Among the tiniest islands, with a land surface between one and five square kilometres, are Rábida, Seymour, Wolf, Bartolomé, Tortuga and Darwin. Forty-two islets have a landmass smaller than one square kilometre, and 26 emerging rocks are numbered.

OCEANIC ISLANDS

The islands are purely oceanic, which means that they have never been connected to the mainland by any sort of land bridge. In the past, it was assumed that the Cocos and Carnegie ridges, underwater mountain ranges rising up to 2,000 metres above the sea floor, once connected the islands to the mainland of either Central America or South America, but this has been disproved, because of the sheer drop of the Peru-Chile trench. The conspicuous absence of land mammals in the Galápagos also helps to confirm the oceanic island theory.

The islands rise on the Galápagos Platform, a basaltic submarine plateau located between 200 and 500 fathoms (ie, between 360 and 900 metres; 1 fathom being equal to 1.82 metres) under the surface of the ocean. The archipelago is entirely volcanic, and Isabela Island alone is made up of six volcanoes side by side. Five of them are typical shield volcanos, the craters of which are huge 'calderas'.

CALDERAS

Caldera means 'cauldron' in Spanish. This geological name is used to define the aging of a shield volcano. This huge craterlike depression is formed by the subsidence of the

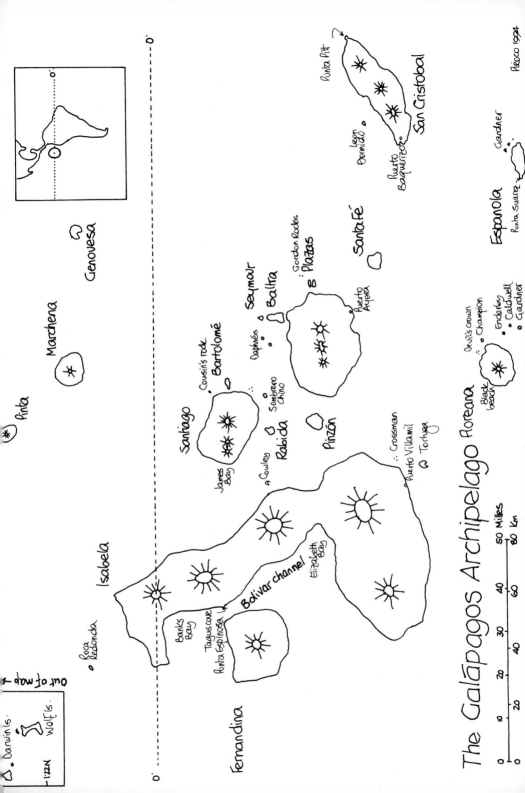

The Galápagos Archipelago

upper part of the volcano when the inner walls of the central crater fall in, widening the cross section of the crater over time.

Following repeated eruptions and regular volcanic activity, the magma chamber gets larger and swells up each time the magma rises. As magma creates pressure on the roof of the magma chamber, circumferential fissures form around the crater. Sometimes the lava spreads out through the cracks and creates parasitic cones on the slopes of the volcano. When the eruption comes to an end, the level of the magma subsides. The roof of the magma chamber is no longer supported and it collapses. Through successive collapses of the crater, the caldera is formed.

The most recent example was the collapse of the Fernandina volcano in 1968. The crater floor—800 metres deep at first—collapsed another 350 metres after a violent explosion. Ashes were launched 25 kilometres high into the sky and spread over an area of a few hundred square kilometres. Fernandina is the youngest caldera in the Galápagos, with a diameter of 6.5 kilometres. Sierra Negra, the oldest caldera of Isabela Island, measures 10 kilometres across. Santa Cruz and the southern part of San Cristóbal are also large shield volcanoes, whose summits have been eroded.

GEOLOGICAL ZONING

A deep oceanic trench, 3,000 metres under the ocean surface, separates the small northern islands of Darwin, Wolf, Marchena, Pinta and Genovesa from the rest of the archipelago to the south. MacBirney and Aoki (1966) show that the Galápagos are divided in three zones, comprising islands of like structure and of similar petrography.

The first zone to the southeast is made of Fernandina, Isabela and Floreana Islands. The second zone is made up of the northern islands mentioned above, adding Cerro Pitt, the northeastern tip of San Cristóbal Island. The third zone is made of the central islands of Santiago, Rábida, Santa Cruz, Pinzón, Baltra, Santa Fé, Española and the south of San Cristóbal.

PLATE TECTONICS

According to the theory of plate tectonics, the Galápagos archipelago is located in the north of the Nazca Plate, just under the Cocos Plate, and east of the South East Pacific mid-oceanic ridge, also called the East Pacific Rise (see map of Tectonic Plates, page 15). The islands are connected by two submarine ridges: the Carnegie Ridge to the east and the Cocos Ridge to the northeast.

The S E P mid-oceanic ridge (SEPMOR) stretches roughly north-south from California (San Andreas fault) to Easter Island and farther west into the southwestern Pacific. It spreads magma on the ocean floor, westward and eastward, pushing the oceanic Nazca

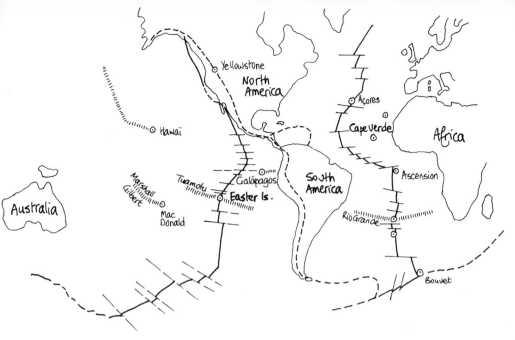

Hot Spots and Mid-oceanic ridges

⊙ Hot Spot   ⌐ Transform Faults   / Mid-oceanic ridge

Tectonic situation of the Galápagos

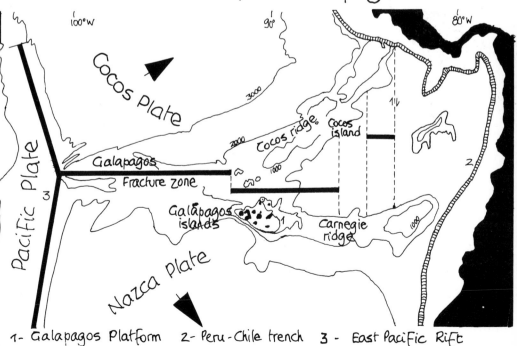

1- Galápagos Platform   2- Peru-Chile trench   3 - East Pacific Rift

Plate east, towardss South America. At the same time, we have an extension of the SEP-MOR from west to east, called the Galápagos Fracture Zone (GFZ) or Galápagos Rift, which eventually evolves in a transformation fault* between the Carnegie and Cocos ridges. The GFZ also expands magma on the ocean floor, northward and southward, thus pushing the Nazca Plate southward.

We understand now that the Galápagos are located on an oceanic plate that receives pressure from the west (SEPMOR) and from the north (GFZ). What happens next? Well, think of a window pane on which you exert pressure from two adjacent sides. Crack. Get the picture?

HOT SPOT

The archipelago is a 'hot spot', an area of high thermic flux* and intense seismic and volcanic activity, subject to almost annual eruptions. A hot spot is related to a weakness of the oceanic crust, a zone of remarkable fragility in the tectonic plate, which leads to fissures on the ocean floor. In the Galápagos there is a system of parallel and orthogonal fractures*, which resemble a checkerboard. Under the Nazca Plate, the hot magma is always in motion due to convection currents. The hot spot, being a more sensitive area, creates a magmatic plume which pierces the oceanic crust in a weak part of the plate. The magma rises upward into the ocean (see figure Hot Spot, page 15). Upon contact with the cold ocean water, the lava cools off rapidly, builds a platform and keeps rising. It eventually creates a volcanic cone, which in a few years reaches the surface of the ocean. We then have an 'aerial volcano', a volcanic island born of the ocean. The base of the volcanic construction of the Galápagos could be 10 to 15 million years old. The hot spot is now responsible for the making of an archipelago, ie, a chain of volcanic islands more or less aligned. Hawaii is a classic example which is much older than the Galápagos, with an age of about 20 million years.

The magma rising up from the SEPMOR creates the expansion of the oceanic floor and the migration of the Nazca Plate to the southeast at a rate of five centimetres per year. The Nazca Plate will be forced under the continental plate of South America. The point of contact between the two plates (continental and oceanic) forms a trench, which is called the subduction zone. The Nazca Plate will then be in subduction under South America, and the Cocos Plate will migrate northeast and dive in the subduction zone of Central America (see Appendix 1).

If the hot spot does not move, the tectonic plate will shift. An island is created, then the oceanic plate moves east. A second island will be made later on, when the plume pierces the oceanic crust again, which in turn will migrate eastward with the plate. And so on, forming a chain of islands, that is to say, an archipelago.

The Age of the Galápagos

The consequence of this phenomenon is that, logically, the eldest islands will lie to the east and the youngest to the west. That is where the volcanic activity is resumed nowadays in the archipelago, mainly on Isabela and Fernandina islands. This brings us to determining the age of the Galápagos.

Various methods, including potassium-argon (P A) and paleomagnetism, have been used to date the age of volcanic rocks, essentially basalts. The first dating technique, P.A., shows that the Galápagos have a maximum age of three million years. The oldest basalts analyzed, using the radioactivity of the elements gave the following results: 3.2 million years (+/- 0.2) on Española; 2.7 million years (+/- 0.1) on Santa Fé; 4.2 million years (+/- 1.8) on South Plaza.

Many of the analyzed rocks come from submarine lava like Santa Cruz (1 million years), basalts of Wolf volcano (0.72 million years) and San Cristóbal (0.66 million years). Isabela Island was dated at about 700,000 years, and so are the islands of Fernandina, Santiago, Genovesa, Marchena and Darwin (Culpepper).

Wolf, Santa Cruz, Baltra, Rábida, Pinzón and Floreana are between 0.7 and 1.5 million years old, while the age of San Cristóbal is between 2.4 million years (Cox) and about 4 million years (Paul Colinvaux).

Former studies on magnetism also proved the young age of the islands. Most samples analyzed were dated in the period of Bruhnes (between 0 and 0.7 million years) and the period of Matuyama (0.7 to 2.4 million years). The age of the archipelago stands of course for the aerial part of the islands, ie, the date when the volcanoes surfaced above sea level. The islands' submerged bases could be of Miocene geological times, about 15 million years.

The Galápagos archipelago is one of the largest and most active groups of oceanic volcanoes in the world. The islands, never connected to the mainland, were built on a large but shallow platform 2,000 kilometres east of the SEPMOR. The localization of the main volcanoes seems to have been controlled by two systems of quite orthogonal fractures: one has a north-northwest direction; the other is rather east-west.

Uplifts

Numerous examples of island uplift have been observed on Santa Fé, Española and Santa Cruz. Cerro Colorado, facing Plazas Islands, is a rocky hill east of Santa Cruz Island which was uplifted in the past, bringing up tuff formations bearing fossils of Miocene times. Most recently, in Urvina Bay, on the west coast of Isabela Island, a tectonic uplift in 1954 brought coral heads and marine life five metres above sea level. It was followed a few months later by an eruption on the slope of Alcedo volcano.

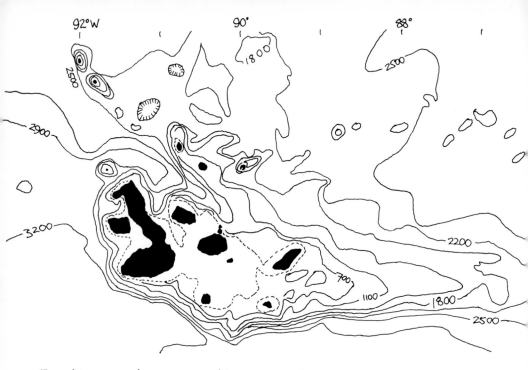

Bathymetry of the Galapagos
(after "Bureau of Commercial Fisheries", 1962) - Soundings in metres - Dotted line < 360 m.

The submerged islands
(source: "Nature" magazine and New York Times News s.)

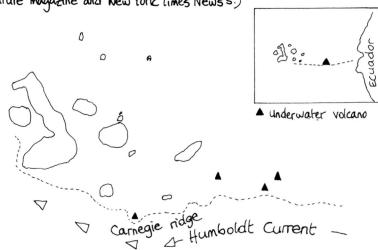

▲ underwater volcano

Carnegie ridge

Humboldt Current —

▲ Supposed sites of the submerged islands.

THE SUNKEN ISLANDS

In the beginning of 1992, in an issue of the English magazine *Nature,* American scientists from Oregon, California, Cornell University and the NOAA (National Oceanic and Atmospheric Administration) on a 26-day expedition discovered submarine mountains along the Carnegie Ridge, to the south and southeast of the Galápagos, in the direction of South America. David Christie and his colleagues gathered samples of volcanic cobblestones (typical of the shoreline) resulting from aerial and marine erosion. This demonstrated the existence of a chain of islands that were once above sea level and which were later submerged. The submarine mountain closest to the continent, only 590 kilometres away, had an estimated age of nine million years. Obviously, there should be even older sunken islands of the Galápagos group, which, according to the latest thinking, could now be as old as 90 million years (see drawing, page 18).

PETROLOGY

Chemically speaking, the petrology of the Galápagos is different from Hawaii's, for the magma of our archipelago is typical of the southeast Pacific ridge. The plutonic rocks and the effusive tholeïtes (subalkaline basalts, ie those rich in silicon) follow similar modes of differentiation, being enriched in iron and magnesium, in alkaline products and with an excess of silicon.

The islands are composed of basaltic lava, rich in iron and magnesium. Black at first, the lava becomes gradually brown, then brick red after alteration when iron becomes oxidized over time. This erosion process is typical of the 'basic' kind of lava; in the 'acid' kind, it is totally different.

VOLCANISM OF THE GALÁPAGOS ISLANDS

If the Galápagos Islands are well known for their extraordinary fauna, let us not forget that their appearance depends first on volcanic phenomena. A few elements of vocabulary will be essential for the proper understanding of the volcanic activity. Let us consider, first of all, volcanic activity in general, then the volcanic materials or volcanic products and, finally, where the magma comes from.

VOLCANIC ACTIVITY

It is divided into the aerial and the submarine activities. The aerial eruption depends on two factors: the viscosity of the magma and the quantity of liberated gases. Four major types of volcanoes are usually distinguished:

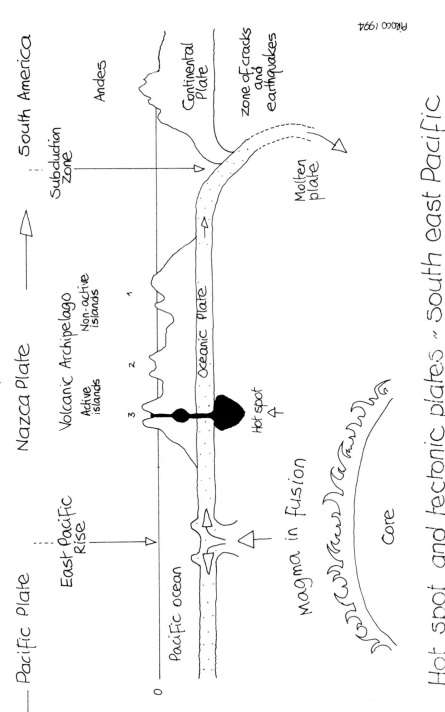

Hot spot and tectonic plates ~ South east Pacific

Ritoco 1994

- the explosive or Vulcanian type: where the gas phase is predominant.
- the explosive or Domean type: where the magma is viscous and acid.
- the effusive or Hawaiian type: where the magma is fluid and basic. This is precisely the case of the Galápagos.
- the mixed or Strobolian type: the eruption is rich in gases, liquids and solid products.

This can be represented in a triangular diagram, where the three poles would be gases, fluid magma and acid viscous magma.

In submarine activity, the magma coming out of the ocean floor explodes violently when it contacts the cool water. Pieces of lava are torn apart and pulverized. Vitreous fragments spread over the ocean floor, cement and form submarine volcanic tuffs or 'hyaloclastites' (a Greek word meaning 'broken pieces of glass'), which can build real mountains. The submarine tuff cones thus formed are called 'guyots'. Their summit is flat, for the crater is soon to be filled by marine sediments.

The submarine lava flows come from aerial flows which have reached the shore. Steaming at the point of penetration, these flows once underwater are known as a 'giant's highway', for their surface is made of blocks (resembling tiles) with a polygonal structure. This is true when the slope is mild. When the slope is steep at the point of entry, however, the flow gives way to 'pillow lava', or lava cushions, which roll downhill and pile up at the bottom of the ocean.

VOLCANIC MATERIALS

FUMAROLES

Gas emanations are called fumaroles. These are seen on the slope of the crater and within the crater itself. Gases are important, as they help the magma to come out, pushing upward and acting on the viscosity of the lava. The two main components of fumaroles are water and carbon dioxide (CO_2). Nevertheless, their classification is based on chemical composition and temperature, which can rise up to 500° C. Thus we may distinguish chlorated, chlorhydrated, ammoniacal, sulphurhydrated, 'mofettes' (CO_2), thermomineral waters, geysers (H_2O) and 'soffionis' (sprays of steaming water). Sulphurhydrated fumaroles can be seen on Isabela Island, in the craters of Alcedo and Sierra Negra volcanoes.

LAVAS

Lavas are molten materials which pour out of the crater. The movement of a flow depends on the viscosity, the push-up action of the magma in the chimney of the volcano, and the substratum. The speed of the flow, a few kilometres per hour at the exit of the vent, can be reduced to a few metres per hour at the bottom of the slope. The cooling action is quick at the surface of the lava flow, in which two types are distinguished:

- the 'aa' type: (Hawaiian word, meaning 'to hurt'), where the chaotic aspect of the surface of the flow is due to the gas explosions, having torn apart the external crust. We have there a fluid lava, rich in gas. This can be seen when climbing volcan Alcedo.
- the 'pahoehoe' type: or ropey lava (after the Hawaiian word meaning 'ropey'). Here the surface is smooth, and shows 'ripple marks', 'intestinal figures', waves in the directions of the flow, and 'ropes'. The lava progresses by tongues; it is not as fluid and has lost its gas (eg on Sullivan Bay, Santiago Island). The hardening of the basalts is generally quick under the crust. The cooling process often generates prismatic figures in columns. These are the organ pipe basalts, with four, five or six faces.

LAVA TUBES
These tunnels are frequent in the Galápagos. When lava spreads out of the crater, the surface of the flow cools off rapidly, while the inner flow rushes downhill quickly. When no more lava comes out of the crater, an empty tube is often left behind, surrounded by a solid outside crust. These natural tunnels, usually five to six metres wide and up to ten metres in height, can be seen at Puerto Ayora and Bellavista, on Santa Cruz Island.

TEPHRAS
Also called 'pyroclastites' or broken fire pieces (from the Greek), tephras are volcanic projectiles, mainly bombs, shapeless fragments or ashes. In the shapeless fragments, we have 'pumice', pieces of acid magma, viscous and grey-white in colour. These are ejected following violent explosions (eg Alcedo volcano, Isabela Island).

The 'scoriae', pieces of fluid magma with no set shape, are the most common volcanic projectiles. The red-purple colour is due to iron oxidation. Cinder cones are frequent in the Galápagos. Among 'bombs', we may distinguish 'spindle bombs' (rotated in flight), or 'spatter bombs', formed by the ejection of fluid magma. Spatter cones are seen on Bartolomé Island. Ashes appear because of violent volcanic projections up in the air. These consist of pieces of crystal or glass. The white colour of the ashes persists in acid lava, but in basic lava, the black ash may turn to red or orange-brown with time.

'Lapilli' and volcanic sands are scoriae fragments, which vary in size from 2 to 20 millimetres in 'lapilli' and from 0.2 to 2 millimetres in sands. Little bombs, drops of glass, are part of the same family, and may form hardened layers of crystals.

'Volcanic tuffs' (0.2 to 20 millimetres) are lapilli and sands cemented by ashes. 'Cinerites', or hardened ashes, form distinct, stratified layers.

PARASITIC CONES

Frequent in the Galápagos (James Bay, Santiago Island, or Bartolomé Island), tuff cones are always found near the coast or on the shoreline, for they are created in shallow sea water. Magma is blown up in small grains and ashes, which cement later on. Spatter cones are formed on firm land by projections of fluid magma patches, lava fountains (Bartolomé Island). Cinder cones are made of light small volcanic bombs cooling off in the air, after a dry explosion.

WHERE DOES MAGMA COME FROM?

If we consider the chemical composition of magma, we could simply say that they differentiate into two main groups: the acid and the basic.

The 'Basic Group' (basalts, gabbros)

Also called basaltic magma, it is black in colour, poor in silica (SiO_2) and alumina (Al_2O_3), with mean contents of 60-70 per cent, but rich in iron (Fe), magnesium (Mg), calcium (Ca), sodium (Na) and potassium (K). Thus, when the content in 'bases' is superior to the amount of silicon, we talk about 'basic' rocks.

The 'Acid group' (rhyolites, granites)

Comes from the granitic magma, rich in silica and alumina (80 to 90 per cent of the contents) and poor in bases: Na, K, Fe, Ca, Mg. When the silicon content is greater than the base content, the term used is 'acid' rocks.

Theory of Bimagmatism (last century)

According to this theory, there are two sources from which magma comes. In the crust is the acid magma (SiAl), at a depth of less than 20 kilometres. In the mantle is the basic magma (SiMg), at a depth between 35 kilometres and 100 kilometres.

The MOHO or 'Mohorovic discontinuity line' separates the crust and the mantle at a depth of 15 to 35 kilometres. The theory of bigmagmatism explains simply where the magma comes from, be it in the crust: SiAl (silicon-aluminum) or SiMa in the mantle (silicon-magnesium).

Later on, as the process became better understood, it was theorized that there is a common origin for the magma ('monomagmatism'). Furthermore, a more recent theory was posited by Yoder and Tilley (1962), based on the differentiation of the basalts.

SUMMARY OF MAGMAS

CHEMISTRY	BASALTIC	ANDESITIC	GRANITIC
	Basic	Calco-alkaline	Acid
Depth of Formation	35-100 Km	10 to 35 Km (mantle)	less than 20 Km (crust)
Temperature of Formation	1200-1500°	C1200-1300° C	550-750° C
Effusive Products	Frequent	Frequent	Rare
Petrography	(+) Basalts (-)Gabbros	(+) Andesites Diorites (-)Rhyolites	(+) Granites (-)Basalts

(+)= more of (-)= less of
* Basalts and rhyolites are eruptive rocks (surface); granites and gabbros are plutonic rocks (deep).

Glacial ages in the Galápagos
It has been proved that the age of the Galápagos is between three and five million years. For the last two million years, glaciations have been important on earth and have contributed to modifying the geography of the continents. Today, ice covers 10 per cent of the planet's surface. Twenty thousand years ago, in Pleistocene times, that ice surface was three times as extensive as it is now. Ice comes from the ocean. If the ice of the poles should melt today, the sea level would rise up as much as 65 metres. In the Pleistocene, the ice cover had a volume of 77 million cubic kilometres, which means that the sea level then was at least 120 metres below its present level. Many islands in the Galápagos would have been joined together then.

The glacial ages of the Galápagos have been studied by Paul Colinvaux (1984) and measured by the study of sediments in ancient lakes. The Galápagos appeared to be more arid in glacial times. Four lagoons were investigated:
- Darwin Lake: in Tagus Cove (Isabela Island) had a bottom of salt and lava. No sediment, so quite young in age.
- Beagle Lake: (Isabela Island) possesses a 15-centimetres deep sandy bottom. The age is not significant.
- Arcturus Lake: (Genovesa Island), 30 metres of salt water cover a muddy sediment five m in depth. The age was estimated to be 4,000 to 6,000 years.
- El Junco: (San Cristóbal Island) was the most interesting. With a diameter of 273 m, this sweet-water lake, only six m in depth, had a sediment depth of 16 metres, which was aged 40,000 years. A red clay sediment was also found which had a core more than 48,000 years old. This lake seems to have existed for at least 100,000 years. It was protected from evaporation by the cloud layer and the annual March rains.

CHAPTER TWO

OCEANIC CURRENTS
SEASONS AND CLIMATE
TEMPERATURES

Oceanic currents and trade winds have a determining action on the Galápagos, for they influence not only the climate but the two resulting seasons, which are:
- The *garua*, or dry season.
- The hot season, or wet season.

Even through they are located on the equator, the islands are classified as 'subtropical' rather than tropical. Nevertheless, the northern islands are almost tropical, because they are less affected by the cold waters of the south. The southern islands are more affected by the cold ocean stream of the Humboldt Current.

OCEAN CURRENTS

The confluence of many ocean currents in the Galápagos turned the islands into an unusual geographical spot on the world map. Even though on the equator, they do not have a characteristically equatorial climate and are therefore considered to have a micro-climate.

Logically, the ocean currents are a key to this phenomenon. The oceanic masses come primarily from the southeast, the northeast and the west. Some are cold, such as the Peruvian Coastal Current and the Peruvian Oceanic Current, with a mean temperature of 15° C. Upon arrival in the Galápagos, they surface from a depth of 100 metres.

Another important cold-water current is the Cromwell Current, also called the Sub-equatorial Countercurrent. With a front of 300 kilometres, it comes from the western Pacific, exactly under the equator and under the South Equatorial Current, which in turn flows west. The Cromwell Current is 150 to 200 metres thick, with a temperature of 13° C in its core, and flows at a speed of 25 centimetres per second. It upwells to the west of Fernandina and Isabela islands, then goes around these two islands towardss the center of the archipelago, where its action gradually fades away.

From the east, the South Equatorial Current flows at a speed of 50 centimetres per second. This water mass is influenced by the cold waters of the southeastern Pacific (Humboldt Current) and by the warm waters of the northeast coming from Panama (a flow sometimes called 'El Niño'). The border between the subtropical waters of the south and the tropical waters of the north is known as the 'Equatorial Front'. This diagonal line, southeast to northwest, stretches between 4° south latitude and 1° to 3° north latitude.

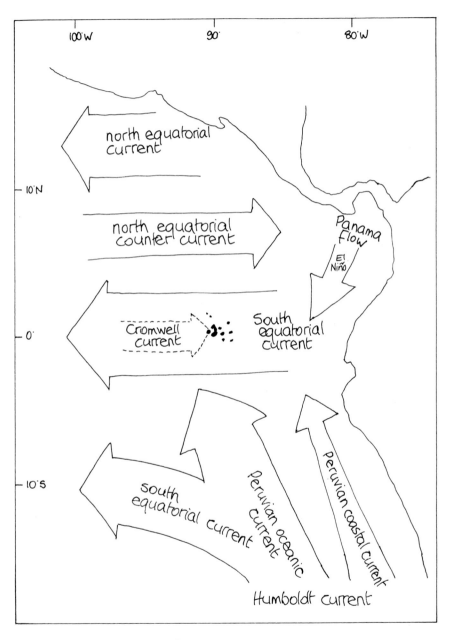

100°W   90°   80°W

north equatorial current

10°N

north equatorial counter current

Panama Flow

El Niño

0°

Cromwell current

South equatorial current

10°S

south equatorial current

Peruvian oceanic current

Peruvian coastal current

Humboldt current

Distribution of the currents ~ Tropical East Pacific.

There is also a convergence of the trade winds, more or less parallel to the Equatorial Front. This is the Intertropical Convergence Zone (ITCZ), where the southeast trade winds and the northeast trade winds meet. This ITCZ is located at 10° north latitude in the dry season, and migrates down to 3° north latitude in the wet season.

Another important current, associated with the Panama flow or El Niño, is the North Equatorial Countercurrent (NECC), which places itself between the South Equatorial Current (SEC) and the North Equatorial Current (NEC), at about 5° north latitude. This superficial current brings warm tropical waters from the western Pacific and ends in the Gulf of Panama, where it splits in two. One part flows up north, along the coast of Central America towardss California. The other part flows south, where it meets the SEC. The NECC is the main conveyor of organisms coming from Asia and from the Panama-Colombia area.

THE GARUA SEASON

This cool and dry season lasts from May to December. Temperatures are lower than during the rest of the year, and the season brings a subtropical climate, when cold waters come up from the antarctic region.

A frequent mist covers the top of the islands, with some sort of fine rain or 'garua', which is more infrequent on the coast. During the garua season, the cold Peruvian Oceanic Current and Peruvian Coastal Current (known as the Humboldt Current) are dominant. This cold-water mass comes up from Antarctica along the western coast of South America, then heads west to the Galápagos upon reaching the equator. The southeast trade winds, very strong during the garua season, contribute to the process. The temperature of the water is about 18° to 20° C, with a salinity of 35 ppm. The marine fauna is rich. The Humboldt Current is strongest in September, and the sea surface rather rough (see map of Ocean Currents, page 26).

HOW IS THE GARUA FORMED?

The Intertropical Convergence Zone (ITCZ) is well north during the dry season. The southeast trade winds drive the waters of the Humboldt Current north. Warm air migrates over a cold-water current, at an elevation of a 100 or 200 metres, cools off upon contact, and becomes bottom heavy and loaded with humidity. An inversion is formed, with hot air above and cold air below. An equilibrium is reached, and the lower layer is saturated with condensed water. A stratus cloud is formed, which will travel horizontally above the ocean surface, with little precipitation.

If this layer meets an elevated island (eg Santa Cruz), an orographic elevation is created, with lower pressure. Hot air will cool off (since cold air cannot hold moisture as well as warm air), and precipitation will pour down in the form of garua.

THE WARM SEASON

It stretches from December to May. The annual rains occur during the first three months of the year. Nevertheless, the temperature is higher, and the sunny days are more numerous than during the garua season. The southeast trade winds vanish, as does the action of the Humboldt Current. The northeast trade winds become dominant, and warm waters head south from Panama and Colombia. Sea surface temperatures range from 24 to 27° C, with a low salinity of 33.5 ppm, and the waters are poor in organisms. The ITCZ migrates south, to a few degrees north of the equator. The warm waters again meet the Humboldt Current and form the South Equatorial Current, which flows across the Galápagos archipelago.

The climatic 'inversion' created during the garua season disappears, allowing for the formation of cumulus clouds. During the wet season, precipitation occurs as conventional rains—strong, but of short duration.

THE 'EL NIÑO' PHENOMENON

Some years the warm-water flow coming from the north is considerably increased. Since it happens around Christmas, it has been named 'El Niño' (after the infant Jesus). It is not a real current. Its action is mainly on the South American mainland, where it triggers heavy rains and disasters in the fishing industry. In fact, it doesn't really affect the Galápagos, where it is manifest every four to seven years.

In 1982-83, an exceptional Niño in the Galápagos brought nine months of continuous rain, an abnormal rate of ambient humidity, suffocating heat and a sea surface temperature of 30° C, followed by tremendous animal mortality. The climatologic effect of that Niño was felt worldwide. Scientists had to study the case seriously. What factors induce such an imbalance? After investigation, it seemed that the phenomenon simply resulted from the dynamics of the Pacific Ocean, and the displacement of considerable oceanic water masses.

During the dry season, the preponderant southeast trade winds push surface waters towardss the west, away from the South American mainland. In the Pacific Ocean, the wind action does the same. This brings a conspicuous upheaval of the ocean level in the western Pacific, which means that the water column is higher in the west than it is in the east. Part of the 'return' system is made through the NECC and the Cromwell Current. With the start of the Galápagos' wet season in December, the ITCZ moves south. The water temperature rises with the arrival of warm waters coming from Panama. An enormous amount of warm water returns from the western Pacific towardss the east. It is believed that this is what triggered the 1982-83 Niño. These unusual conditions are associated with variations in pressure in the Pacific, allowing equatorial west winds to blow east. This would create surface waves that move across the Pacific, draining warm waters. Thus the floods in Ecuador, the abundant rains and the elevation of the ocean level in the Galápagos by 22 centimetres.

To conclude, the position of the ITCZ is slightly north of the equator, because the dominant winds come from the southeast. Since these bring humidity to the islands, the windward side of the islands is wetter than the leeward side. That is easily seen in the vegetation zones. The arid zone will rise up higher on the leeward side than on the windward side. Let us take the example of Santa Cruz Island, where the windward side is to the south: the arid zone stretches up from 80 to 120 metres maximum. On the north, leeward face, the arid zone rises up to 200–300 metres. The same applies to the transition zone. This phenomenon is called the 'rain shadow effect'. Fernandina Island is .another example, lying in the 'rain shadow' of Isabela Island (see drawing of Vegetation Zones, page 69).

ANNUAL TEMPERATURES AFTER SIX YEARS OF READINGS AT THE DARWIN STATION

	JAN	FEB	MAR	APR	MAY	JUN	JUL	AUG	SEP	OCT	NOV	DEC
Max Temp.° C	28	29.6	30.6	29.5	27.9	26	24.6	24.2	24.3	25.3	25.8	26.7
Min Temp.° C	22.8	23.2	22.7	22.7	22.1	19.1	19.8	19.1	19.6	19.5	20.4	20.9
Hours of sun	5.3	7.5	6.0	7.5	5.2	4.4	2.8	3.3	2.9	3.8	3.5	4.0
Sea Temp.° C	24.4	25.2	24.9	25	24.5	23.1	22	21.5	21.8	22.3	23	23.3

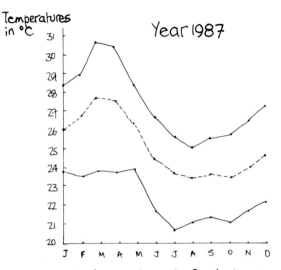

Temperatures
in °C

Year 1987

Month of the year

Air temperatures in Puerto Ayora
(Santa Cruz), equal to a "Niño"
[after "Carta Informativa", CORS 1988].
Sea surface temperatures
Year 1987, for a possible "Niño".
[after CORS, 1988].

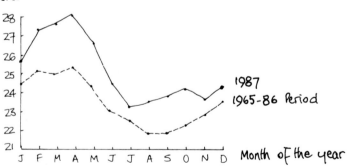

Temperatures
in °C

1987
1965-86 Period

Month of the year

CHAPTER THREE

HUMAN HISTORY OF THE GALÁPAGOS ISLANDS

Well before the Incas—that they ever visited the islands is doubtful—it seems that the first visitors to the islands were Indians who came from Ecuador on balsa rafts. Probably of Mantena or Huancavilca culture, they did not stay long. Pieces of pottery have been found on Santiago Island, on Santa Cruz (Whale Bay) and at Black Beach on the island of Floreana.

Around 1485, Tupac Inca Yupanqui, a prince from Cuzco (who would become the tenth inca), heard rumors about two uninhabited islands far to the west. He was then near the present site of Guayaquil with his army, and decided to build a fleet of balsa rafts equipped with sails. The expedition was gone for nine months to a year. The Inca Yupanqui returned with gold, a bronze seat, and the skin and jaws of a 'horse'. These trophies were kept in the fortress of Cuzco until the arrival of the Spaniards (after Cabello de Balboa, 1586). The two islands were called Nina-Chumbi (Fire Island) and Hahua Chumbi (Outer Island). According to Thor Heyerdahl, the Norwegian explorer, the trophies and the black men could have come from a raid on the mainland, north of the starting point. The skin and jaws of the so-called 'horse' could well have been that of a male sea lion.

The Galápagos bear no archeological remains of dwellings or other structures, so it is quite unlikely that a colony was ever established there, even in remote times.

After the discovery of the Americas by Christopher Columbus in 1492, and the liberation of Spain from the Moors by the Catholic King Ferdinand and Queen Isabela, trips beyond the Atlantic became popular. Conducted with the blessing of the Spanish kings, who were eager to discover new territories, the adventurers' declared aim was the conversion of pagan souls, and their exploits were undertaken under the high authority of the Borgia pope, Alexander VI, who divided the New World for that purpose between Spain and Portugal.

The year 1519 saw the conquest of Mexico by Hernan Cortez. Then in 1532 came the conquest of Peru by Francisco Pizzaro, who subdued the Inca empire. Far away from the kingdom of Spain, the conquistadors made their own laws in these new lands and without mercy enslaved all the Indians. Gradually, their thirst for gold and riches (one-fifth was given to the Spanish Crown) brought the conquistadors to quarrel among themselves for supreme power.

It was at that time that Fray Tomas de Berlanga, archbishop of Panama, was given a mission by King Charles V, to report on the anarchic situation in Peru. He and his crew set sail in a caravel for Lima on February 23, 1535. After seven days of navigation along the coast of South America, the wind dropped for six days. The vessel drifted 800 kilometres west into the Pacific Ocean, carried by the South Equatorial Current. Fray Tomas de Berlanga officially discovered the Galápagos archipelago on March 10, 1535. The bishop wrote to King Charles V, describing the giant tortoises, the iguanas, and the tameness of the birds. To him, the islands appeared very inhospitable.

Eleven years later, in 1546, a Spanish renegade named Diego de Rivadeneira, having deserted the army of Francisco Pizarro, fled with a dozen men on a stolen boat. He got lost just as the bishop had, and drifted away to the islands, where he eventually found water and turtles. He is the first visitor to mention the Galápagos hawk.

After their discovery, the islands still remained without a name. It was much later, during the second half of the XVIth century, that quite a number of navigators named them Islas Encantadas or 'Enchanted Islands', for they seemed to appear and disappear on the surface of the ocean by magic. The phantom silhouettes of the volcanoes were always bathed in fog, which made the islands hard to distinguish.

Nowadays, the official name is Archipelago de Colon, and was given to the islands by Ecuador in 1892 to commemorate the 400th anniversary of the discovery of the Americas by Christopher Columbus. The usual name, however, remains 'Galápagos'.

The first marine charts mentioning the islands date to 1570. In 1574, the 'Enchanted Islands' appeared on the map of Abraham Ortelius, with the name 'Archipelago de los Galopegos'. The pirate William Cowley, in 1684, followed by Captain Colnett, in 1793–94, brought English names to the islands. All the names, in English or Spanish, honor kings, admirals, pirates and numerous visitors of the islands.

In 1577, the English pirate Francis Drake cleared Cape Horn and arrived in the Pacific Ocean, where the situation becomes suddenly explosive. 'There is no peace beyond the line,' said he, referring to the boundary line drawn by Pope Alexander VI, which stretched north to south, 1,800 kilometres west of the Cape Verde Islands. Hostilities were declared between England and Spain. These would last from 1593 to 1710.

In the 17th century, English, French and Dutch pirates waged a war against Spain and used the Galápagos as a refuge. From there, they could easily attack the Spanish galleons sailing from the South American coast and sack the coastal ports of Guayaquil and Lima. Buccaneer's Cove and James Bay, on Santiago Island, became favourite hideouts of the pirates. There, they would collect water, wood and giant tortoises. The unfortunate reptiles that were piled in the hulls of the boats could survive a year without drinking water. The most famous of the English pirates were Cowley, Dampier, Davis, Wafer, Cook and Eaton. Among the French were Groguiet, l'Escuyer, Desmarais, Le Picard and Rose. The most visited islands were Santiago and Floreana, where volcanic caves served as primitive dwellings as well as a place to hide bounty and food.

TABLE OF THE NAMES OF THE ISLANDS

Spanish	English
Pinta	Abington
Isabela	Albemarle
Baltra	South Seymour
Santa Fé	Barrington
Beagle	Beagle
Marchena	Bindloe
Tortuga	Brattle
Bartolomé	Bartolomew
Caldwell	Caldwell
Champion	Champion
Floreana, Santa Maria	Charles
San Cristóbal	Chatham
Cowley	Cowley
Crossman	Crossman
Darwin	Culpepper
Wolf	Wenman
Daphné	Daphné
Pinzón	Duncan
Eden	Eden
Enderby	Enderby
Gardner	Gardner (Charles)
Gardner	Gardner (Hood)
Guy Fawkes	Guy Fawkes
Española	Hood
Santa Cruz	Indefatigable
Santiago, San Salvador	James
Rábida	Jervis
Sin Nombre	Nameless
Fernandina	Narborough
Onslow	Onslow
Plaza Sur	South Plaza
Genovesa	Tower
Watson	Watson

Another famous man who came to the Galápagos was 'Robinson Crusoe'. Alexander Selkirk was his real name. He was freed in February 1709 from his lone island—Juan Fernandez, off the coast of Chile—by Captain Woods Rodgers, another pirate. After four years and four months, Robinson Crusoe, who had been master of the ship *Cinque Ports*, was taken aboard Woods' ship. Three months later, he was in the Galápagos. There, he was given the command of a ship, and later on, he took part in the sack of Guayaquil, a port on the coast of Ecuador. Two years later, in 1711, he returned to England, where he became famous, thanks to *Robinson Crusoe* by Daniel Defoe.

Between 1780 and 1860, the waters of the Galápagos became a favourite place for British and American whalers. During the 19th century, thousands of fur sea lions were butchered. Captain Benjamin Morell confessed to having skinned 5,000 sea lions in two months. Thousands of turtles left the islands at that time, piled alive in the hulls of the boats, from which they were extracted periodically for their meat and their fat. In 1793, a strange barrel was erected on Floreana Island to facilitate communication between boats and the land. The barrel was put there by Captain James Colnett of the British Royal Navy, and officially marked the beginning of the era of the whaling industry. It is still in place today, at Post Office Bay.

The first man to live in the archipelago was Irish, and his name was Patrick Watkins. Nobody knows whether he was a castaway or if he deliberately chose to live on Floreana, in 1807. Anyway, he survived by growing vegetables, which he traded for rum with the passing whalers. His only wish was to drift permanently in the vapor of alcohol. Captain Porter of the navy frigate USS *Essex* described Watkins as a monster with devilish looks:

> *The most dreadful that can be imagined: ragged clothes, scarce sufficient to cover his nakedness, and covered with vermin; his red hair and beard matted, his skin much burnt from constant exposure to the sun, and so wild and savage in his manner and appearance that he struck everyone with horror.... But this man, wretched and miserable as he may have appeared, was neither destitute of ambition, nor incapable of undertaking an enterprise that would have appalled the heart of any other man; nor was he devoid of the talent of rousing others to second his hardihood.*

Two years later, in 1809, Watkins seized a whaling ship, the *Black Prince*, while the crew was on land in search of fresh water and turtles. He took with him five sailors that had landed on Floreana. Unable to find a way out without Watkin's help these five men became his 'slaves'. Watkins eventually made his way to Guayaquil on his own and no one ever discovered what became of his companions, whether he ate them or threw them overboard.

In 1813, the famous Captain David Porter of the USS *Essex*, who hated the English, captured the British whaling fleet in the Galápagos, taking 12 ships in five months. Porter wrote many interesting notes on the Galápagos environment. After Watkins, the islands were more or less uninhabited until 1832, when Ecuadorian General José Villamil founded a prosperous colony on Floreana. The population was mainly composed of convicts, political prisoners and other unwanted people, who traded meat and vegetables with the whalers. In February 1832, two years after the creation of the young republic, Colonel Ignacio Hernandez took official possession of the archipelago in the name of Ecuador. Spanish names were given to the islands, in addition to existing English names. After Villamil departed to San Cristóbal, the colony of Floreana was turned into a penitentiary and fell into chaos. In 1869, a cruel and tyrannical man named Manuel Cobos founded the penal colony of El Progresso on San Cristóbal Island. He regularly abused the wives of his men, and was eventually murdered with a machete by a Colombian convict in 1904.

Many colonies were established over the years, and nearly all collapsed. One succeeded, founded in 1893 by Don Antonil Gil, an honourable citizen of Guayaquil, in Puerto Villamil, on the southern coast of Isabela Island. People survived by selling cattle and by the exploitation of the sulphur mine of Sierra Negra volcano. A Norwegian colony settled on Floreana Island in 1926. Just like its predecessors, the attempt quickly went awry and the island was deserted.

Some years went by. In 1929, a strange German doctor, Friedrich Ritter—dentist, vegetarian and philosopher—arrived on the island with his female assistant, Dore Strauch. They built a house named 'Friedo' in the highlands of Floreana, near a freshwater spring, then created a cosmogonic orchard, following the elaborate theories of Dr Ritter. For the next three years, he wrote many articles for the press, which became well known in Europe. In 1932, the Wittmer family decided to settle on the island too, to practice agriculture and to lead a peaceful life. Floreana became so fashionable that luxurious yachts used to call in, and rich Americans dropped anchor at Black Beach to pay a visit to the 'Robinson Crusoes' of Floreana.

This was tremendously pleasing to the Baroness von Wagner de Bosquet, a young German woman who had a notion to build a hotel for 'millionaires' on the same island. With her two lovers, Lorenz and Philipson, she disembarked in 1932 and built the 'Hacienda Paraiso', a mere shack of planks and corrugated iron. Soon after, she proclaimed herself the 'Empress of Floreana' by virtue of the gun and the whip. Of course, this was not to the liking of Dr Ritter or the Wittmer family. Tensions rose.

The story ended in 1934, after the disappearance of the baroness and Philipson, and the tragic death of Lorenz, who was caught in a storm in a small boat and cast away on the shore of Marchena Island, where he died of thirst with a Norwegian sailor. Dr Ritter died, too, poisoned by tainted chicken. Dore Strauch left the island and returned to

Germany, where she wrote a book entitled *Satan Came to Eden* before she fell to the curse of Ritter some years later. At present, only Margret Wittmer has survived this untold drama, and the mystery lives on. She still lives at Black Beach on Floreana, and turned 90 on July 12, 1994. Her book, *Floreana, Poste Restante,* an extraordinary adventure tale of life at the end of the world, was published in 1961 and became a bestseller.

During the Second World War, an American Air Force base was built on the strategic island of Baltra (north of Santa Cruz Island), from where it was possible to defend the Panama Canal (see the Historical Index, in Appendix). Nowadays, Floreana and Isabela islands are inhabited, and bigger communities have been established on Santa Cruz and San Cristóbal. On Santa Cruz, the most central of all, two villages are occupied with agriculture in the tropical highlands. Puerto Ayora, in Academy Bay, is the touristic capital of the Galápagos. Puerto Baquerizo Moreno, on San Cristóbal, is the administrative capital and Ecuador's second naval base.

In 1981, the population of the islands was estimated at about 5,000 people. It reached 10,000 people in 1988, and was around 20,000 people in 1994 (see Appendix 3, page 292).

DARWIN AND THE GALÁPAGOS

Without any doubt, the most famous visitor to the Galápagos is Charles Darwin. His short stay in the archipelago has proved enormously significant for science and for the study of evolution (see map: the Route of Charles Darwin, page opposite). At the age of 26, the young British naturalist travelled around the globe on the HMS *Beagle* with Captain Fitzroy. Towardss the end of 1835, he sailed from Tierra del Fuego, along the coasts of Chile and Peru, and arrived in the islands for the most unforgettable five weeks of his life. One morning, after dropping anchor in a cove at San Cristóbal, he disembarked and would later write:

> *The surface of this part of the island seems to be punctured like a skimmer by subterranean steam; here and there, the lava, still soft, has puffed up in giant bubbles; elsewhere, the roof of the caverns thus formed has collapsed and one can see in the middle a well with perpendicular sides. The common shape of these numerous craters gives an artificial aspect to the land which reminds me of the furnaces of Staffordshire. It was incredibly hot. I felt extremely tired to walk on this rough surface, but the strange scene of this cyclopean country compensated far beyond my tiredness. During my wandering, I met two giant tortoises, each could have weighed at least 200 pounds; one was eating a cactus pad. When I approached, it stared at me conspicuously, then moved away slowly. The other one whistled formidably and retracted*

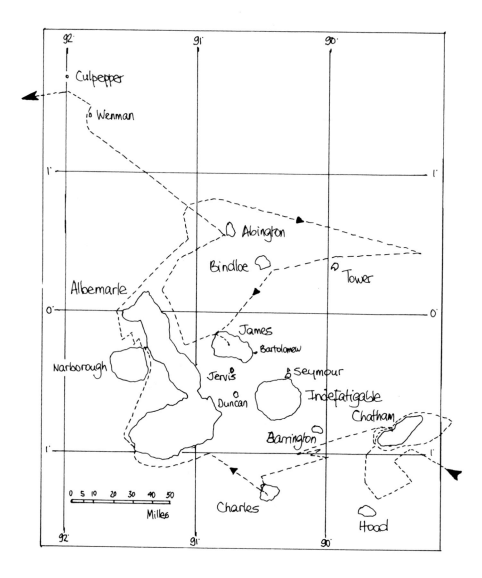

The Route of Charles Darwin
aboard HMS Beagle [Sept.17 ~ Oct. 20 1835]

her head under the shell. These huge reptiles, surrounded by black lava, by shrubs with no leaves and tall cacti, looked like real antediluvian beasts. The few birds with dim colours than I met here and there, could not bother less about me than they would of the giant tortoises.

As he observed the fauna of the archipelago, one of Darwin's major discoveries was to realize that the species were not 'unchangeable', but that they were exposed to the irreversible process of evolution. Natural selection, adaptation to the environment and genetic mutation, became keywords that helped him to elaborate—thanks to the finches mainly—the celebrated theory of 'Evolution of the Species', which came to light in 1859, 24 years after his journey to the enchanted islands. A new revolution in the scientific mind was born.

CHAPTER FOUR

ARRIVAL AND ESTABLISHMENT OF THE ORGANISMS

The first thing to consider is the difference between two fundamental concepts: 'continental island' and 'oceanic island'. A continental island is an island that has, at some time in the past, been connected to the continent by a land bridge, and which, therefore, possesses flora and fauna typical of the continental mass from which it originated. By contrast, an oceanic island is born from a submarine volcano which has emerged from the ocean without any life on it. The great distance between an oceanic island and the continent make if difficult for land organisms to reach it, even those having good means of dispersal. Logically, groups of plants and animals having an easy means of dispersal have a greater chance of reaching an oceanic island and thriving, if the conditions are favourable.

The consequence of this phenomenon is an unbalanced flora and fauna in comparison to the continental mass. The word 'disharmonic' is used to define this condition. The Galápagos Islands are therefore a good example of biotypic disharmony. The vertebrates are well represented by birds and reptiles; native mammals are poorly represented, while amphibians and freshwater fishes are totally absent. Among insects, only butterflies and beetles are well represented. A good number of land birds are totally absent in the archipelago.

Among plants, lichens, ferns, grasses, sedges and the Compositae family are well represented, whereas gymnosperms and palm trees are absent, and monocotyledons almost nonexistent. Very few trees are native to the islands. Orchids (11 species), Labiatae (mint family), Acanthacae (grasses, shrubs) are appreciated by the pollinating insects.

Groups of animal and plants well represented in the archipelago are therefore those most likely to cross an ocean frontier of hundreds of kilometres. Such a crossing could be made in three different ways:
- free floating on the sea, or on a natural raft.
- dispersal by wind, or in the air.
- transport in the body of another organism, by air or by sea.

ARRIVAL

Let us consider first transport by sea. Seeds can be carried away passively by flotation. Legumes, even though intolerant of immersion, have an empty space between the embryo and the external shell of the seed. The Galápagos cotton (*Gossypium darwinii*) can withstand a lengthy stay in salt water, and may float for 10 weeks or longer (Stephens, 1958). The Humboldt and South Equatorial currents may carry these cotton seeds from the coast of Peru in less time than that.

Turtles have also a great capacity for flotation, for they have a pocket of air between the upper back and the shell. The second type of passive transport is 'rafting', by natural raft. These vegetation rafts have been seen drifting hundreds of kilometres from the coast, pushed by the sea winds towardss the Galápagos from Peru to Ecuador by the Humboldt or Panama currents. Even palm tree logs can carry various insects: ants, larvae, beetles. In 1892, Agassiz saw large rafts drifting from Panama to Cocos Island and the Galápagos, at a speed of about 130 kilometres (75 miles) a day. Such a raft could reach the archipelago in two weeks. Reptiles have a completely waterproof skin, and drink very little water. In 1880, a boa constrictor was seen (alive) in the Caribbean, coiled around the log of a cedar tree, floating 300 kilometres from Trinidad. Sea lions and fur sea lions also travel with the help of the currents. They came from the north (California) and from the southeast (Antarctic), and colonized the archipelago after a group migration.

The second type of transport is transport by air. Aerial dispersal is the best means by which insects reach the islands. It can be passive, as with spiders taken in air currents at an elevation of about 3,000 metres. Likewise, the seeds of orchids and spores of ferns, mosses and mushrooms, which can resist very low temperatures, are dispersed this way. When they arrive above the islands, the spores drop with the condensation of the air. The poor representation of butterflies in the Galápagos is due to the fact that adults have fragile wings, and the larvae are very sensitive.

Transport via other organisms, or active transport, is mainly carried out by birds. Seagulls for example, come from areas with abundant vegetation. They carry seeds in their stomachs, between their feathers or under their wings, even in the mud stuck to their feet. Seeds collected from riverbanks or swamps can be carried away in such a fashion.

Among 607 species of plants found in the Galápagos, it has been estimated that 59 per cent of them were transported as seeds by birds, 32 per cent by the wind, and nine per cent by ocean transport. If one considers the influence of man, then 40 per cent were transported by birds, 32 per cent by man, 22 per cent by wind and 6 per cent by flotation.

ESTABLISHMENT AND SURVIVAL

Once on the island, the organism has to establish itself, and before anything else it must find food to survive. Reproduction of the species comes later. The establishment is as vital as the arrival in order to colonize the island with success. Two major reasons explain why a group of animals or plants can be absent from an island:
- The organism has not reached there at all.

- After arriving, the organism has not been able to establish (importance of the season).

An airborne organism—unlike one carried by sea—is not conditioned to land on a particular island. It can drop on the soil of any habitat, and therefore has a greater chance to become established. Once the difficulties of arrival are overcome, the living being has to reproduce to ensure the survival of the species.

Hermaphroditic plants have no problems in reproducing, for the male and female principals are located on the same flower. By contrast, in dioecious plants, male and female principals are on different plants, as is the case with most animals, for whom reproduction is possible only if the complementary individual is present.

In the Galápagos, three plants are dioecious: Castela and Croton, which are shrubs of the arid zone, and Bursera, also called palo santo, which is a tree with white bark.

Lindsay (1966) thinks that the first plants introduced to the islands were self-reproducing. Later on, the presence of a wasp, as well as of some other pollinating insects, was important in the reproductive process of the plants. To illustrate the action of the wind in reproduction, studies have shown that 32 per cent of the flora are pollinated by the wind in Hawaii, 34 per cent in Juan Fernandez in the southeastern Pacific and 29 per cent in New Zealand.

Some factors are essential for a plant to establish. The majority of land plants need a soil rich in humus, and will not establish on an island where the soil is poor. Exceptions include the lichens Archicera, which can fix themselves upon lava on the shore.

Finally, animals are dependant on plants for food, therefore the plants must be established before the animal. We may talk about the vegetarian vertebrates, such as turtles, or marine iguanas, which need a good cover of vegetation to survive. Some sea birds need material to build their nests. The optimum moment chosen by an organism (eg a bird) to arrive is important when related to the arrival of another competing species. The 'ecological niche' (that is, all conditions necessary for survival and reproduction) of an arriving species may be already occupied by another organism which established itself earlier in the community. A morphological transformation will then take place. Otherwise, one of the two species is doomed to extinction. The arrival of an organism in an already overpopulated island is only possible if another species is going extinct or has already disappeared. The island reaches equilibrium when immigration is balanced by extinction. When they are near to the mainland, big islands have a high immigration rate and a low extinction rate, which means that they are soon saturated. Faraway islands, with a low immigration rate (even more if they are small), will be saturated less quickly. This is also due to a faster extinction rate.

MacArthur and Wilson (1963), authors of the equilibrium theory, take the example of Krakatoa Island, where fauna took 36 years to reach equilibrium after the devastating volcanic eruption. As a matter of fact, Krakatoa is very interesting, for it is a similar example to the Galápagos.

Krakatoa, a volcanic island of Indonesia, between Sumatra and Java, emerged from the ocean after a memorable explosion in 1883. In 1886, three years later, there were 11 species of ferns, two species of *Compositae* and two grasses. In 1894 (11 years later), the interior of the island was bedecked with grassy vegetation and a few shrubs. The year 1903 saw luxurious vegetation on the island. In 1908, 25 years after the eruption, one could find 13 species of birds, a species of monitor lizard, one gecko, 192 species of insects, ants, flies, beetles, dragonflies and butterflies; spiders and scorpions were also present.

The Galápagos followed the same pattern of population, and are today the home of unique organisms, including land and marine iguanas, giant tortoises, mockingbirds, lava gulls, Darwin's finches, the Galápagos dove, the flightless cormorant, the albatross and the Galápagos penguin, which are found nowhere else in the world.

GEOGRAPHIC AFFINITIES

Logically, most of the animals in the Galápagos originated from North, Central and South America and the Caribbean.
- from North America: some land birds like the 'yellow warbler' and the California sea lions.
- from the Caribbean: pink flamingos, Darwin's finches (the ancestor on Ste Lucie Island was transported by winds to Costa Rica, and later on to Cocos Island, before reaching the Galápagos).
- from South America: land iguanas, giant tortoises, pelicans,
    flightless cormorants, vermillion flycatcher.
- from the Antarctic: fur sea lions and penguins.

CHAPTER FIVE

THE THEORY OF EVOLUTION AND THE GALÁPAGOS

The Galápagos archipelago has been called the 'showcase of evolution', and truly, for the biologist, the islands are a living laboratory for the study of evolution. The closest example to the Galápagos is perhaps Hawaii, which, at 20 million years old, is six times older than the assumed age of our archipelago.

Evolution is the central topic of biology. Before Darwin, the creationist theory declared that life appeared on earth on Sunday 23 October 4004 BC, at nine in the morning. Darwin had been brought up to become an Anglican clergyman. He left England for a five-year journey around the planet, questioning himself for a long time, testing his ideas. He recognized variation within species and also that a gradual change was sometimes affecting a species. The world means change in the characteristics of living beings, which cannot be inherited. A living being is recognized by five essential characteristics, which are:
- the ability to reproduce.
- the ability to memorize information in their genes (in a molecular sense).
- control of their environment.
- excitability, or ability to respond to a stimulus.
- excitability by/in producing energy.

A living organism knows how to adjust to specific conditions and is able to 'modify' itself. These evolutionary changes may be an answer to natural selection. Those which fail are doomed; those which succeed must change and evolve. 'The survival of the fittest', said Darwin. According to the theory of evolution, all living organisms have a phylogenetic heritage, in other words, a genetic heritage linked to the development of the group (Grzimek, *Encyclopedia of Evolution*, 1972). This phylogenetic process is stimulated by two factors:
- genetic variation
- natural selection

If organic evolution is a change in genetics, natural selection should not be mistaken for evolution. Evolution refers to temporal changes of all sorts, whereas natural selection brings about a particular way through which these changes are made (E.R. Pianka, 1974).

Another definition of evolution is: non-cyclic changes in the genetic pool (sum of the allele genes in a population). Two ideas come up next: the 'genotype' and the 'phenotype'. The genotype is the genetic asset of an individual as inherited from its parents' DNA. The phenotype is its morphology, physiology and real behavior after interaction of the genotype with the environment.

The evolutionary space-time (or time-free) frame of evolution is the mutation. Mutations within a population, and within a given time, play an important role in the future evolution of this population. Evolution is induced by mutations and natural selection. Mutations favor genetic variety. Natural selection, on the contrary, limits the genetic variety. Evolution is a continuum; it is not a number of species following one another. 'Speciation', or multiplication of the species, occurs when a genetic pool is divided in two isolated parts. This is to say that members of a given population become reproductively isolated from the other members of that population. Once evolution reaches such a level, where two populations cannot mate, then each turns into a unique species. The evolution process is so unique that the complex relationship between an organism and its environment changes with time. Three examples will bring some light to this idea:
- Evolution may occur when the biological entity (animal) stays within its habitat and does not substantially change its lifestyle.
- Organisms, having gone through mutations, even minor ones, may conquer a new habitat (a new ecological niche) by modification of their behavior, but still keeping their old structure. In other words, structures may accomplish new functions.
- Another possible evolution links the two cases mentioned above. Anatomic changes and new functions may occur simultaneously in the evolution of an animal group.

The original organism, having gone through the effects of natural selection, is transformed in such a way that its body is able to meet the functional demands of the environment. It evolves so that the last forms of individuals have more chances of survival and a higher rate of reproduction success than the earlier forms.

To conclude, let us quote Haeckel: 'Ontogeny recapitulates phylogeny', which means that the development of the individual within the egg sums up the development of the animal group to which it belongs. In the Galápagos, one important factor to consider is insularity. Islands differ from the continental landmass by their isolation, which implies not only the role of selection, but also that of the 'chance' factor in the evolutionary process. Mayr (1963) has shown the extreme importance of geographic isolation in speciation. Darwin is known for his famous saying: 'The survival of the fittest', which can be compared with 'the death of the weakest'. Considering fitness or adaptability, natural selection stresses an answer to the conditions of the environment.

For an animal, a change in behavior brings about a change in physiology, therefore a morphological change. Natural selection is the means through which organisms become gradually better adapted to their environment. Even though the majority of the species are doomed to extinction without the creation of a new evolutionary way, it is not impossible that a particular species can become a pioneer of evolution. Without differentiation of the species, there would not be any diversity in the organic world, and very little progress in evolution. The species is then the 'key' to evolution.

For insular populations, two common factors induce fragmentation and speed up speciation:
- the tendency for a well-established population to move out of the marginal habitats towardss more central habitats, therefore minimizing the capacity of dispersal of the population.
- the fact that island organisms have a tendency to form restricted and localized populations.

DARWIN'S FINCHES

Archipelagos are ideal for geographic isolation and speciation. In the Galápagos, 13 species of finches (in fact 14, counting the one on Cocos Island) have evolved from one original species, which migrated from Costa Rica. *Melanospiza richardsoni*, on Ste Lucie Island in the West Indies, is the nearest species.

For populations in isolation, various selective pressures on different islands lead to evolution and divergent adaptations. Occasional interactions between islands favour 'competition' which promotes the diversity of the 'niches'. (Niche: all the necessary conditions for an animal to survive and to reproduce in a given environment.) The competition may be 'interspecific', ie, between different species, or 'intraspecific', within the same species. The more individuals, the greater the competition. For the niches of the original island, the increasing population leads to the departure of a number of individuals towardss other habitats. Each newly colonized island will later yield as many unique species, adapted to a specific environment with adequate functions. The 'adaptive radiation' of the finches in the Galápagos has created four distinct genera, which differ by the following factors:
- where they feed
- how they feed
- what they feed on

For the Darwin finches, the morphological changes are seen in the size and shape of the beak: ground finches, tree finches, cactus finches, vegetarian finch, warbler finch, sharpbill ground finch, carpenter finch... Some of these individuals migrate in the opposite direction, towardss islands already colonized by their ancestors, and live in perfect harmony with other species, each with its specific function and proper habitat. There would be no more competition for food. The 'allopatric' model of speciation (Peter Grant, 1981) explains the 'adaptive radiation' in four successive steps:

1) Colonization of an island in the Galápagos by a population coming from the continent (Central America), after crossing an oceanic barrier.

2) The population develops on the initial island. Some individuals migrate to nearby islands. Genetic changes occur in the new environment. The second step

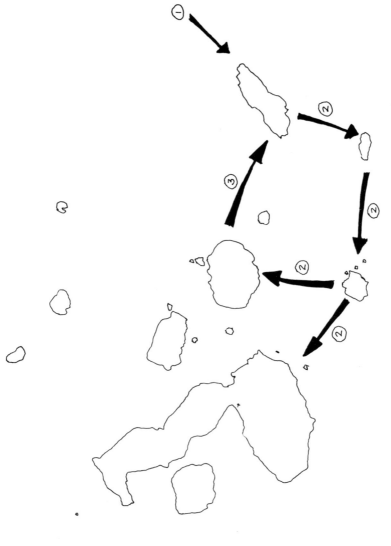

Allopatric model of the distribution of the species
e.g. the speciation of Darwin's Finches [after Peter Grant, 1981].

may be repeated many times, resulting in the establishment of allopatric populations of one single species on many islands.

3) A secondary contact between the original population and the second population occurs. It is important to know how different the two groups are at the time of contact. If the differences are minor, the interaction goes freely and the two groups fuse. If the differences are moderate to wide, the individuals of the two groups may show a slight tendency to mix, and those which do so will leave offspring less fit than those which mate within the same group. Natural selection will favour those which reproduce in the tradition.

Differences between the new groups will be greater in the signals and responses related to mating. The result is that the reproductive isolation between groups initiated in 'allopatry' (ie, on different islands) will be perfected in 'sympatry' on the same island. In the end of the third step, two species have been produced out of one. Their coexistence is dependent on sufficient ecological differences: the selective process is similar to the one mentioned above. Selection acts against individuals of the two incipient species, which look so alike that they will certainly develop a competitive spirit for resources such as food. The consequence will be the divergence between the characters to exploit the resources.

4) The final step is the simple repetition of this cycle of events. This is how the 13 species of Darwin's finches were made (see the 'Allopatric model', page 46).

ENDEMISM

An organism, species or group, living and evolving in a specific place, which is found nowhere else is called endemic. It is important to remember this word, since it will be used frequently in the description of the flora and fauna of the archipelago. Oceanic islands have a high rate of endemism because of their isolation. If the island is small, such as Cocos Island, northeast of the Galápagos, speciation will not be as great as in an archipelago. The Cocos finch is endemic, but that is the only species. On bigger islands, where possibility for isolation is greater, differentiation may occur. In the Galápagos, 14 endemic races of tortoises, distinct and subspecific, have evolved on 11 islands. On the island of Isabela alone, five races were distinguished—one on each volcano. It is quite likely that these five volcanoes have been separate islands in the past, since in the Quaternary ice ages the level of the ocean rose and fell considerably.

Land iguanas have evolved on the central islands of the archipelago, and one distinct species has been recognized on Santa Fé Island. The lava lizard has distinct forms on Floreana, Española and San Cristóbal, as well as on the northern islands such as Marchena and Pinta. One single species is found on the central islands, with the exception of Pinzón, which has an endemic species.

The four species of mockingbirds have an easier dispersal ability than reptiles. They inhabit all islands, except on Floreana where they are extinct.

EXAMPLES OF ADAPTATION TO THE ENVIRONMENT

The flightless cormorant—whose ancestor came from equatorial America—lost its ability to fly. Without any predators, its wings became useless. The flightlessness is also due to the action of strong winds, which may take birds far away from the islands against their will. For those which keep their wings, the flight technique is to fly low above the ground. Marine iguanas feed on chloropyllian algae encrusted on the rocks, and may dive to a depth of 20 metres without breathing for half an hour. Some finches on Wolf Island suck blood from the wings of masked boobies. At first, finches were probably interested in the parasites on the boobies (such as horseflies) hidden between the feathers and around the neck of the seabirds.

In the tropical forest of the islands, the carpenter finch uses a wooden stick as a tool to dig larvae out of old stumps. Well-known reptiles such as tortoises and land iguanas feed on vegetation and not on insects. On the islands where these reptiles are found, opuntia cacti, with conspicuous pads, grow up like trees and develop a trunk, as tall as possible, to avoid being eaten by the reptiles. On islands where these reptiles are absent, opuntia grow close to the ground. It is amazing to realize that the cactus has developed an ability to 'think'—no more than a survival reaction—that some may call a 'conservation instinct'.

THE UNCERTAINTY OF THE FUTURE

Living organisms in the Galápagos are doomed to possible extinction. Islands deteriorate due to the erosion of wind, rain, sea. The worst factor, though, has been the arrival of man, who introduced unwanted species into the fragile ecosystem of the Galápagos: goats, rats, pigs, dogs and cats. These animals, at first domestic, turned feral and became a threat to the native species of the archipelago. Goats are very competitive and eat the food of the reptiles; dogs prey on iguanas; wild pigs on tortoise nests and young; fire ants destroy the population of invertebrates and become a plague.

Aerial view of Punta Pitt, San Cristobal 1992

Aerial view of the crater of Beagle Lake, Isabela 1990

Bartolomé and Sullivan Bay 1990

Spatter cones, Bartolomé 1993

The "pahoehoe" lava field of Sullivan Bay, Santiago 1990

Ropey lava on a "pahoehoe" surface, Sullivan Bay 1982

Hornito, Sullivan Bay 1990

Aerial view of Bartolomé 1990

Bartolomé at Sunset 1981

The garua on the rim of Sierra Negra volcano, Isabela 1988

Sulphur fumaroles, Sierra Negra, Isabela 1986

Punta Vicente Roca, the sea lions' lagoon, Isabela 1990

Tuff cliffs, Punta Vicente Roca 1988

Volcan Ecuador, Isabela 1992

The blowhole of Punta Suarez Espanola 1989

Lava tube, Santa Cruz 1988

Darwin's Arch, Darwin Island 1993

The "Grottos", James Bay, Santiago 1990

Cathedral of tuff, "Leon Dormido" Cristobal 1992

Volcan Fernandina 1990

Salt mine and tuff cones, James Bay, Santiago 1992

Mangroves in "Divine's Bay", Puerto Ayora, Santa Cruz 1984

Opuntia *cacti and* sesuvium *flowerbeds in the dry season, Plaza 1993*

Giant opuntia *cactus, Buccaneer's Cove, Santiago 1990*

Flower of the opuntia *cactus, Punta Moreno 1986*

Jasminocereus *cactus, Pta. Moreno 1988*

Sesuvium *flowerbeds, Punta Pitt, San Cristobal* 1992

Red mangrove, Santa Cruz 1980

Jasminocereus *cacti, Darwin Station 1988*

Brachycereus *(lava cactus), Punta Espinosa* 1990

Nolana galapageia, *Floreana 1993*

Parkinsonia aculeata, *Floreana 1993*

Arid zone of the palo santos, Genovesa 1993

Agriculture zone of Santa Cruz, Santa Cruz 1993

Scalesia *forest, Los Gemelos, Santa Cruz 1993*

Scalesia *forest, Santa Cruz 1993*

Tree ferns, Sierra Negra, Isabela 1988

Lava lizard (female), Espanola 1992

Lava lizard (male), Punta Pitt Cristobal, 1992

Lava lizard (female), Punta Pitt 1992

CHAPTER SIX

FLORA AND VEGETATION ZONES

We mentioned earlier that the disharmony of the flora in the Galápagos is supported by the fact that the islands have never been connected to the continent. There are no native gymnosperms (cone-bearing trees), and 'monocotyledons' are poorly represented. Ferns represent a high percentage of the flora. Lichens are pioneer plants, which do not need any soil to grow.

Orchids, with only 11 species in the archipelago (as opposed to 3,000 species on the continent), are poorly represented. Their survival is limited by elevation, and they require a pollinating insect to ensure reproduction. The absence of such a pollinating insect considerably reduces the number of families and plants present on the islands.

In the Galápagos, 607 species of plants are found (or 736 taxa, if one considers species, subspecies and varieties). Out of that number, 412 species are native, and 195 species were introduced by man (32 per cent). Among natives, 242 species are indigenous and 170 species are endemic (34 per cent). If we consider the taxa, 312 taxa are indigenous, 229 are endemic, 195 are introduced. The number of introduced species rises with immigration of Ecuadorian settlers. In 1986, the new number of introduced plants was 240 species.

The distribution of plants on various islands is influenced by climate and soil. Larger islands, high in elevation, have many vegetation zones and therefore a greater number of species. The number of species depends therefore on surface and elevation, but more on elevation.

	PINTA	MARCHENA	ESPAÑOLA	SANTA FÉ
SURFACE	60 km2	30 km2	58 km2	24 km2
ALTITUDE	650 m	343 m	213 m	244 m
NUMBER OF SPECIES	200	60	110	70

Ninety-nine per cent of the flora of the Galápagos originated in South America, and only one per cent comes from Central America and Mexico. As we said earlier, the transport of seeds is carried out by birds (60 per cent), wind (31 per cent) and rafting (nine per cent).

Ferns, with spores dispersed by wind, are best represented in the archipelago (but endemic species are few). Lichens, grasses and mosses are also important due to their dispersal ability. Flowering plants, of the *Compositae* family, are very well represented (daisies and sunflowers belong to that family). With an excellent dispersal, they are pioneer plants in the colonization of faraway islands. In taxonomy, one considers:

- Phylum
- Class
- Order
- Family
- Genus
- Species
- subspecies   } Taxa
- variety

Seven endemic genera of plants are found in the Galápagos:

- *Scalesia*	(16 species)	
- *Lecocarpus*	(3 species)	
- *Darwiniothamnus*	(3 species)	Compositae family
- *Macrea*	(1 species)	
- *Jasminocereus*	(1 sp., 3 ssp.)	
- *Brachycereus*	(1 species)	Cactae family
- *Sicyocaulis*'	(1 sp. of vine)	Cucumber family

SCALESIA

This genus is spread out and adapted to different zones: arid, humid, and cliffs. It is distinguished by the shape of the leaves, and flowering heads.

- *Scalesia pedunculata* (central islands) is a tree of the humid zone (ex: Santa Cruz). Branches have small flowering heads (see photo, page 63)
- *Scalesia dentatae*: shrub with large flowering heads (*Scalesia affinis* on Santa Cruz).
- *Scalesia lobatae* (*Scalesia helleri*) : shrub of the arid zone on Santa Cruz Island.
- *Scalesia foliosae*: shrub with flowering heads and arrow-shaped leaves.

CACTI

Two endemic genera: *Jasminocereus* and *Brachycereus*, and one endemic species: *Opuntia echios*.

- *Jasminocereus thouarsii*, also called the candelabra cactus, is a tall cactus found in the arid zone, and resembles Mexican organ pipe cacti. (see photo, page 59).
- *Brachycereus*, is a small cactus with white spines, 50-60 centimetres high, which grows directly on lava surfaces (see photo, page 60).
- *Opuntia* is the most common species of the arid zone. Rather small like a shrub, or tall like a tree with a trunk rising up to five metres, and spines at the base to discourage herbivores. The most impressive *Opuntiae* are found on Santa Fé Island, where the circumference of one trunk reached three metres (see photo, page 59).

VEGETATION ZONES

Seven vegetation zones are distinguished in the archipelago, but only big islands like Santa Cruz have them all (see drawing, page 60). From the bottom to the top, we may consider :

> 1) the Coastal or Littoral Zone
> 2) the Arid Zone
> 3) the Transition Zone
> 4) the Scalesia Zone
> 5) the Brown Zone
> 6) the Miconia Zone
> 7) the Pampa or Fern Zone

THE LITTORAL ZONE

A very narrow stretch a few metres wide, which is found on the coast or around saltwater lagoons. The vegetation is influenced by salt, and is made of shrubs and small trees. Mangroves are dominant, with four species:

- Red mangrove	*Rhizophora mangle* (see photo, page 60)
- Black mangrove	*Avicennia germinans*
- White mangrove	*Laguncularia racemosa*
- Button mangrove	*Conocarpus erecta*

The four mangroves are easily recognized by the shape of the leaves: oval in the white mangrove, elongated and pointed in the black mangrove. The red mangrove has bigger, arrow-shaped leaves and has stilt roots sticking out of the water. The button mangrove is distinguished by conspicuous white buttons at the base of the leaves, at the end of the branches.

The saltbush: *Cryptocarpus pyriformis* is a bush with fat, green leaves, very common in the islands, which may reach two metres in height. Local name: *monte salado*.

Sesuvium edmonstonei or *Sesuvium portulacastrum*, of the succulent family, are very colourful annual plants which may cover large areas of the ground. Leaves are small sugar-almond type, red or green according to the dry or wet season. Flowers are pink or white, according to the species: *Sesuvium portulacastrum* (pink) or *Sesuvium edmostonei* (white).

THE ARID ZONE

This rather large zone spreads up to an elevation of 80–120 metres. Dominant vegetation is represented by three cacti: *Opuntia, Jasminocereus* and *Brachycereus*. Most of the plants have a xerophytic adaptation (ie, adaptation to dry land), which is characterized by small leaves, a high rate of photosynthesis, spiny shrubs (eg *Scutia pauciflora*), deep roots (eg *Parkinsonia aculeata*), and leaves that may orient themselves towardss the sun (eg *Maytenus octogona*).

The arid zone is also the country of the palo santo, *Bursera graveolens* (see photo, page 62), a tree with white bark which has leaves only during the wet season. It is characteristic of the arid zone and found everywhere. Acacia are also seen, as shrubs or small trees (*Acacia rorudiana*), with tiny leaves, flowers like small yellow balls and a fruit like a brown bean. The almost identical *Prosopis juliflora* has bigger oblong leaves, typical of the acacias.

Chala: *Croton scouleri* is a shrub with grey stems, leaves are orange to yellow-green, and the fruit looks like a capsule. The sap of this plant stains clothes.

Manzanillo: *Hippomane mancinella* is a tree that develops at first near the ground, then grows quite tall. The fruit, green or yellow, resembles a small apple, but it is highly toxic, and may burn the skin and the eyes. If eaten, very painful stomach cramps may result.

Muyuyo: *Cordia lutea* is a nice tree with yellow flowers which is found frequently in Academy Bay, Santa Cruz Island.

During the wet season, the arid zone blooms with 'annual plants'. These plants are ephemeral.

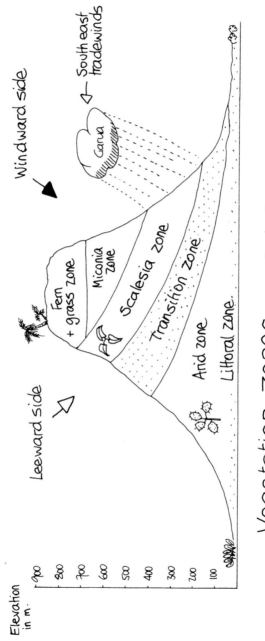

Vegetation zones   e.g. Santa Cruz
[after Van Straelen Hall, Darwin Station].
Aloco 1994

Windward side

← South east tradewinds

Garua

Leeward side

Fern + grass zone

Miconia zone

Scalesia zone

Transition zone

Arid zone

Littoral zone.

Elevation in m.

900
800
700
600
500
400
300
200
100

THE TRANSITION ZONE

This zone climbs up between 100 and 200 metres in elevation, but may rise up to 500 metres on the leeward side. There again, palo santos are found. The characteristic plant of this zone is pega pega (*Pisonia floribunda*), a tree with a short stem and spread-out branches. The coarse bark is covered with lichens. The local name pega pega means 'stick stick', because the leaves of this tree will 'grab' your fingers.

Guayabillo: *Psidium galapageium* is also spread out and conspicuous. The bark of this tree is soft and pinkish grey. Leaves are leathery and the fruit is similar to the guayaba (*Psidium guayava*) introduced to the islands, yellow and round with a pink flesh. The transition zone is intermediate between the arid and the humid zone.

THE SCALESIA ZONE

From 200 to 400 metres. A very humid zone with constant precipitation. This is where the garua concentrates during the dry season. Ferns, grasses and mosses are abundant, but the predominant species is *Scalesia pedunculata* (local name: *lechoso*). This sunflower tree may reach ten metres in height, and concentrates in dense forests, with mosses hanging from the branches and with flowers looking like white daisies. The scalesia forest climbing up the slopes of Santa Cruz volcanoes is a beautiful sight.

THE BROWN ZONE

This part ends the scalesia zone. Liverworts are the characteristic plants. Liverworts are epiphytes, which cling to the tree but do not depend on it. These brown mosses fall from the branches of scalesia, thus the name 'brown zone'.

THE MICONIA ZONE

Above the former zone, it rises up to 1,000 metres. This zone is represented by miconias, leafy bushes two to four metres tall. Leaves are long, rather oval shaped, and distinguished by three parallel central ribs. *Miconia robinsoniana* is also called 'cacaotillo', because the leaves resemble cacao. Flowering heads are pink or violet. The species is endemic, and is found only on Santa Cruz Island (Media Luna) and on San Cristóbal, towardss San Joaquin volcano.

THE PAMPA ZONE

The pampa finishes the scale of the vegetation zones and ranges from 650 metres' elevation up to the summit of the island. This windy and misty land with no trees is represented by ferns, grasses, sedges and other plants adapted to water; swamps and peat bogs are common. Waterholes within small collapsed lava tubes are often like greenhouses, where mosses, ferns and four species of orchids grow. The only tree present is the tree fern, *Cyathea weatherbyana*, which may reach three metres in height. The moist pampa is a microclimate in itself (see photo, page 63).

THE INTRODUCED SPECIES

By 1986, 240 species of plants had been introduced by man to the Galápagos. These were found in the colonized, agricultural zone. The arrival of farmers and settlers on Santa Cristobal, Floreana and Santa Cruz, as well as in the south of Isabela, has created a few ecological disorders in the scalesia and miconia zones. As a matter of fact, many introduced species are taking over the native species.

Twenty per cent of the introduced species originate from North America or Europe. At least 10 species are aggressive in their active dispersal ability, ie, the ease with which they invade vegetation zones, to the detriment of the indigenous or endemic species. This is a major concern of the Galápagos National Park Service, in its efforts to protect and conserve the islands.

For two years the SPNG has used herbicides against guayaba, but the problem remains. No one knows exactly how much poison should be used to eradicate it efficiently. An attempt has been made to plant fast-growing teck or scalesia to counteract the slow-growing guayaba.

THE TEN PRINCIPAL INTRODUCED SPECIES OF PLANTS

FAMILY	SPECIES	LOCAL NAME	USE
Agavaceae	*Furcraea cubensis*	Cabuya (cactus)	Hedges
Crassulaceae	*Kalanchoe*	Pinnata	Ornamental
Lauraceae	*Persa americana*	Avocado, aguacate	Fruit
Mytaceae	*Psidium guayaba*	Guayaba	Fruit
Mytaceae	*Eujenia jambos*	Pomarosa	Fruit
Rustaceae	*Citrus spp*	Limon, Toronja	Fruit
Verbenaceae	*Lantana camara*	Lantana	Hedges
Poaceae	*Digitaria decumbens*	Pangola	Pasture
Poaceae	*Pennisetum purpureum*	Pasto elephante (elephant grass)	Pasture

"fou à pattes
bleues."

PART TWO

FAUNA

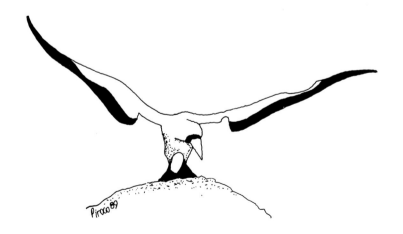

CHAPTER ONE

Reptiles

In the Galápagos archipelago, the dominant quadrupeds are reptiles. This is the reason that the islands were long considered a refuge for prehistoric, antediluvian beasts. These reptiles, related to South American forms, are represented by iguanas, lava lizards, geckos, snakes, and of course giant tortoises, which gave fame to the Galápagos. Sixty three per cent of the reptiles (17 species of 27) are endemic to the Galápagos.

Geckos

Geckos are small lizards of the Geckonidae family. Three genera are found in the archipelago, and six species are endemic, all of the genus *Phyllodactylus*:
- *Gonatodes caudiscutatus* (1 species, on San Cristóbal only.)
- *Phyllodactylus* (6 endemic species, on Santa Cruz, Isabela, Baltra, Floreana, San Cristobal)
- *Lepidodactylus lugubris* (1 species, on Santa Cruz, Isabela, San Cristóbal).

The gecko is five centimetres long, with sand-coloured skin, and may climb smooth and vertical surfaces (such as windowpanes) thanks to the adhesive pads on its toes. With a vertical slit in its black eye, it is an essentially nocturnal reptile, but it may be seen during the daytime under rocks and in cracks. One or two eggs are laid in October and November. Geckos have permanent eyelids, like contact lenses. After eating, they lick their eyes with their tongue. They also swallow their dead skin after moulting. Some species change colour, like chameleons. Geckos have the ability of autotomy, ie they are able to part from their tail if necessary. Geckos are found in the central islands of the Galápagos.

Snakes

Two snake species, a land snake and a sea snake, are found in the Galápagos:

The Galapagos Land Snake

This small, diurnal constrictor may catch prey up to 1.5 metres in length. Posteroglyphous, hardly venomous, it belongs to the family Colubridae and to the genus *Philodryas*, originating from the West Indies (Caribbean). Eight species were identified in the Galápagos:
- *Philodryas biserialis* (Española, Cristobal)   3 spp.
- *Philodryas slevini* (Central islands, except for Santa Fé)   2 spp.
- *Philodryas dorsalis* (Central islands)   3 spp.

Brown with yellow stripes, or grey-black with yellow spots in a zigzag pattern, it measures about 1.2 metres in length. It feeds on lizards, insects, small birds and young marine iguana hatchlings. The Galápagos snake is found on all islands, except in the five northern islands.

The Yellow-bellied Sea Snake (*Pelamis platurus*)
Belongs to the family Hydrophiidae. Dorsally black, ventrally yellow, with spots on the tail section. It measures up to 85 centimetres in length. Its venom is stronger than the cobra's. Rare, except during the Niño years when waters are warmer. Common from the west coast of Central America westward.

LAVA LIZARDS

family: Iguanidae
genus: *Microlophus*

This genus is found only in South America and the Galápagos. Seven species are endemic to the archipelago (one on each island). The biggest lizard is found on Española island, where it grows up to 25 centimetres. The smallest is half that size and is found on Floreana (south of the archipelago) (see photo, page 64). The male is bigger than the female, greyish black in colour with specks. The female has a conspicuous red-orange throat; sometimes, on Española, for example, the whole head is red.

Lizards feed on insects, seeds, flowers and leaves, and show a preference for vegetarian food. They love to bask in the sun on lava rocks, and have an excellent thermo-regulating system; by standing on all fours the are able to reduce their body temperature. At night, *Microlophus* retreats to its cosy nest, made of soil and leaves, in lava cracks.

Lizards are very territorial, but their aggressiveness is shown only to individuals of the same sex. In cases of conflict, males challenge each other by push-ups on their forelegs. They do not face each other, but sideways—displaying their spiny crest—and in opposite directions. They circle one another, sometimes biting each other on the mouth, spilling blood, but that is as far as it goes. Lava lizards have the ability of autotomy (the ability to cast off parts of the body), only once, but the tail will grow up again. This is a self-defense mechanism against predators.

Sexual maturity in the female is from nine months to one and a half years. For the male, it starts at three years. The mating season coincides with the hot season. The male mates with two or three females, after the garua season, in December. The female digs a shallow burrow, where she lays two to six eggs. The hatching will take place two to three months later. Lava lizards can live up to 10 years.

Predators of the lava lizards are snakes, hawks, owls, herons and mockingbirds. Lava lizards are absent on Genovesa, Darwin and Wolf.

MARINE IGUANAS

genus: *Amblyrhynchus*
species: *cristatus*

An endemic genus with one species and seven subspecies. The age of the iguana could be nine million years or more if we consider the fact that it is older than the islands existing today. It is descended from a land iguana from the South American mainland. It most probably reached the Galápagos via vegetation rafts that were drifting on the surface of the ocean. Consequently, it had to adapt to a strictly vegetarian seafood diet.

The only marine iguana in the world, the Galápagos species is found along shore on lava rocks. These creatures of another era gather in herds of a fantastic aspect, individuals packed one on top of another. The length, including the tail, ranges from 60 centimetres for the smallest variety (Genovesa Island) to one metre for the largest (Isabela Island). The tail is half the size of the body. A spiny crest runs along the back, from the top of the head to the tip of the tail (see photo, page 81).

The sooty-black skin—a mimetism with the black lava substrate—is a camouflage against predators and enables the iguana to absorb more heat during its exposure to the sun. Very lazy, even ugly to some people, the marine iguana spends most of its time warming up on the rocks. Flat in the morning, the body, with a prominent abdomen, changes orientation towards the sun as the day progresses. When it is too hot, the iguana raises the front of the body above the ground and allows the breeze to circulate under the stomach.

Like many reptiles, the marine iguana is poikilothermic; ie it may adapt to great temperature variations. It is also ectothermic, ie directly influenced by external heat (mammals, by contrast, are endothermic). Despite an optimal ambient temperature of 35–37° C, these cold-blooded reptiles may have an extreme body temperature 40° C at the hottest hour of the day, helping out in the digestive process, but at night its temperature drops to 24° C.

The iguana feeds on 'Ulva', a chlorophyllian algae, and sometimes on the faeces of sea lions or of its own species. It may easily dive to a depth of 20 metres (over 60 feet) to look for food on the rocks, and spend as much as one hour under water at a time. The compressed tail is well adapted to swimming, above or under water, and while doing so the legs have no use and stick to the sides of the body. The iguana tends to feed at low tide, when the ulva algae are exposed. They frequently eject a salt excess through the nostrils. The spray is thrown 50 centimetres, and may be used to warn off potential predators.

Extremely territorial, iguanas use their tongue and their olfactory sense to recognize their territory. They are sexually mature at around six to eight years, and have a life expectancy of 25 to 30 years. The mating season spreads over November and December, eggs are laid in February and March and will hatch in May or June. Females lay once every two years.

During the mating season, males—always larger than females—take on a red coloration (just like on Española, the southernmost island of the archipelago) and a green colour appears along the back, on the forelegs and hind legs. Males become very aggressive, and defend territories of one to two square metres. After mating, females are in competition to find the right nesting area. Sometimes a female waits for another one to finish a nest, then will try to take it over by force. Head to head fights are spectacular, and the strongest wins. On South Plaza Island, eggs are laid between early February and the end of March; two or three eggs will be left in a burrow of volcanic soil. On Española Island, where soil is scarce, iguanas dig their burrow under the pebbles of the beach. (The operation may be tragic at times, when a rock collapses over the animal and it dies in the nest). After covering the nest with soil, the female will guard it for 10 days.

Eggs have a thin white shell, and weigh from 80 to 100 grams. The gestation lasts about three months (between 84 and 91 days). Predators of the marine iguanas are hawks, herons, snakes and feral dogs.

During the disastrous Niño year 1982-83, the green ulva algae disappeared, leaving only a toxic brown alga. This increased the mortality rate of 60 per cent to the marine iguanas. The population is estimated today at about 200,000 to 300,000 individuals (Ebl-Eibesfeldt).

LAND IGUANAS

genus: *Conolophus*
species: *subcristatus* or *pallidus*

This endemic genus has officially two species, but may have one more if one considers the possibility of an endemic species on Fernandina Island.

Yellow-orange to brown, the land iguana differs from the green iguana, *Iguana iguana*, of South America and the Caribbean, ancestor of the Galápagos iguanas, by a lack of fear towards man. In the Galápagos, two species of land iguanas have been identified:
- *Conolophus subcristatus*: on Santa Cruz, Plaza, Isabela and Fernandina (yellow-orange in colour). Extinct on Santiago Island (see photos, page 85).
- *Conolophus pallidus*: on Santa Fé (whitish to chocolate brown). This is the biggest land iguana; the male weighs six to seven kilograms, the female three kilograms. The eyes are often red, as if injected with blood (see photos, page 87).

Land iguanas do not have a square nose like marine iguanas but a pointed one. Their length is about 1–1.2 metres. *Conolophus* feeds on grass, centipedes and annual plants in season, but its favorite food consists of the pads of the opuntia cactus. Especially the fruits and the yellow flowers, during the hot season. On Fernandina Island, at an elevation of 330 metres, 90 per cent of the food of the iguana is composed of the fruits and flowers of the creeping vine *Ipomea alba* (morning glory). Sometimes land iguanas feed on sea lion's afterbirth, grasshoppers or even dead birds.

Males have an impressive dorsal crest, more conspicuous than the female's, and are larger. Their body temperature ranges from 32.2° C (dry season) to 36° C (wet season). Females are sexually mature at 6 to 10 years. Land iguanas may reach 60 to 70 years old.

Land iguanas form small colonies. They keep to the driest part of the islands and dig burrows in the soil, sometimes under rocks (25 centimetres deep, 15 centimetres long). During the mating season males are territorial, and protect areas of 10 to 20 metres in diameter. Females choose the males. A male may have up to seven females. Each of the females comes back to the same nesting area. After a pair begins courtship the female stays in or around her mate's burrow while he keeps intruders away. After copulation, the female leaves the male for the nesting area, and digs several false nests before laying eggs in the right burrow—females fight over nesting sites. When ready to lay her eggs the female backs into the nest, partially sealing herself into it, and stays there for 24 hours. Thinner after emerging, she leaves the burrow and closes it; for the next week she will defend the nest.

On Fernandina Island, the females nest inside the caldera, near the fumaroles. From the coast, the round-trip takes 32 days. Egg laying peaks during the first two weeks of July. Nests are one to two metres deep. The ground temperature is 32 to 34° C. Clutches consist of 7 to 23 eggs, of a size smaller than those of the marine iguanas (50 grams).

Egg laying occurs during the hot season on Isabela and Plaza islands, and during the dry season on Fernandina, Santa Cruz and Santa Fé. Gestation lasts for three to four months, and the number of eggs ranges from 6 to 20, soft shelled.

Predators of the eggs are beetles; hawks, herons and snakes prey on hatchlings. The survival rate of a young land iguana in the wild is less than ten per cent.

EGG-LAYING OF THE LAND IGUANAS IN THE GALÁPAGOS

	Mating	Hatchings	Clutch	No. of eggs (average)
Isabela	January	May-June	10 to 25	14
Fernandina	June/July	Oct/Nov	8 to 22	10
Santa Cruz	September	January	5 to 17	12
Plaza	Jan/March	May/July	1 to 9	6
Santa Fé	Oct/Nov	Feb/March	7 to 10	8

On South Plaza Island, where marine iguanas are also present, Heidi and Howard Snell think that marine and land iguanas did at one time interbreed, producing hybrid offspring: 'Weirdo' in 1980 and 'Zebra' in 1985. On that particular island, it was common to see land iguanas climbing on shrubs and relaxing on the branches. The last hybrid iguana died of hunger in August 1993.

A symbiotic relationship exists between the small ground finch and land iguanas, in which the birds eat ticks off the iguanas. When the finch comes, the iguana stands on all fours, allowing the bird free access as it hunts for the pests.

Since 1976, and following the attack of wild dogs on the land iguana colonies of Conway Bay (Santa Cruz) and Cartago Bay (Isabela), the Galápagos National Park and the Charles Darwin Research Station have started a programme to protect and conserve the species. Eggs were brought to Puerto Ayora to be incubated, and young to be bred in captivity. Since 1980, more than 250 young iguanas have been returned to Cartago Bay (SPNG, 1988). The repatriation on Conway Bay started in 1987.

In 1991 and 1992, 50 land iguanas were reintroduced onto Baltra Island by the SPNG, after a 40-year absence. The initial source came from North Seymour, through the reproduction centre of the Darwin Station.

MARINE TURTLES

family: Chelonidae
genus: *Chelonia*
species: *agassizi*

There may be eight species of marine turtles in the world, but only four species have been seen in the Galápagos (see drawings, page 101).

- *Dermochelys coriacea*   Leatherback
- *Lepidochelys olivacea*   Olive ridley
- *Eretmochelys imbricata*   Hawksbill
- *Chelonia mydas*   Pacific green turtle

Until now, only one has been common to the islands, the subspecies *Chelonia mydas agassizi*, the Pacific green turtle, which has a circumtropical distribution. Nevertheless, found in the eastern Pacific region from Baja California to the Galápagos, a new species has been recognised by scientists. It is the 'black turtle', *Chelonia agassizi*, which, to some specialists, is a subspecies of the Pacific green turtle. It is precisely this marine turtle that is found in the Galápagos (cf *National Geographic*, February 1994).

The Black Turtle
This turtle feeds on ulva, the chlorophyll alga, on the roots of mangroves, as well as on the leaves of the red mangrove. Males are smaller than the females, with a concave plas-

tron, claws on the bend of the front flippers (to grasp the carapace of the female) and a long tail. The concave plastron facilitates copulation. Females have a convex plastron (see photo, page 91). Sexual maturity is reached at 20 to 25 years. The mating season starts with the hot season, and the peak reproduction and egg laying occur in December-January. Group mating is easily seen in the lagoon of Tortuga Negra (north of Santa Cruz) in November.

Egg laying takes place generally between January and June, but may occur all year-round. The female comes out of the water after dark, and starts digging on the beach (high on the dune) with her hind flippers. After about 20 minutes of digging, she lays 80 to 120 eggs about the size of ping-pong balls at the bottom of the nest. The hardest part is still to come, for she has to work another 30 to 60 minutes covering the nest with sand. Turtle tracks may be observed on the beach the following morning, if the tide has not erased them during the night.

Gestation lasts for about two months (55 days). The hatchlings have a soft black shell, five centimetres long, (the carapace (shell) of the adult is 84 centimetres long, but this measurement will decrease over the years). The temperature of incubation influences the sex of the individual. If it is over 30° C, the egg produces a female; below that temperature, the tendency is towards males. The egg-laying frequency is every two to three years. The main predators of the marine turtles are sharks, orcas and crabs (which feed on hatchlings), and the beetle *Trox suberosus* (which preys on eggs). A few sea birds and shore birds such as herons, frigates and lava gulls also prey on the young as they are crossing the beach towards the sea. This is why the nest usually comes to life after dark, because as soon as the day breaks, the baby turtles are blinded by the sunlight and cannot find their way to the ocean. This is when they become an easy catch for predators.

Between 1975 and 1980, a special programme that marked 7,400 green turtles proved that migrations occur from Costa Rica, Panama, Colombia, Peru and Ecuador.

GIANT TORTOISE OR 'GALÁPAGO'

family: Testudinae
genus: *Geochelone*
species: *elephantopus*

Only two island groups in the world are inhabited by giant tortoises: Aldabra Island in the Seychelles, and the Galápagos Islands. Giant tortoises would have to have reached the Galápagos by floating from South America, which seems unbelievable. The most likely ancestor, *Geochelone chiliensis*, originally came from Argentina, but nothing explains its arrival in the archipelago, which remains a total mystery. No one knows what size these tortoises were in the beginning.

In the Galápagos, female tortoises can weigh up to 50 kilograms and males up to 250

Marine iguana (male), North Seymour 1992

Colony of marine iguanas and crabs (zayapas), Pta. Espinosa, Fernandina 1990

Marine iguanas in the ventilated position, Pta. Espinosa 1989

Marine iguanas of Espanola 1989

Track of a marine iguana, James Bay 1988

Track of a marine iguana, Las Bachas 1990

Marine iguana of Espanola, Punta Suarez 1992

Marine iguana in the mating season, Espanola 1991

Swimming marine iguana, Pta. Espinosa 1990

Land iguana, South Plaza 1993

Land iguana (male), Urvina Bay, Isabela 1986

Iguana iguana, *green iguana of South America, Guayaquil 1989*

Land iguana (male), South Plaza 1993

Land iguana and Opuntia cactus Plaza

Iguana eating a cactus pad, Plaza 1993

Land iguana, Santa Fé 1990

Land iguana, Santa Fé 1991

Land iguana, Santa Fé 1993

Giant tortoise, Volcan Alcedo, Isabela 1985

Giant tortoise digging a burrow against the sun Alcedo 1988

Giant tortoise, Urvina Bay, Isabela 1992

Giant tortoise on the rim of Alcedo volcano 1992

Giant tortoises in the rainy season, Alcedo 1991

Female giant tortoise on a volcano trail, Alcedo 1991

Giant tortoises, Alcedo 1991

Dome-shaped tortoise, Santa Cruz 1993

Saddle-shaped tortoise of Espanola, Station Darwin 1992

The black marine turtle, Chelonia agassizi, *Bartolomé 1993*

Black turtle after laying eggs, Floreana 1993

Marine turtle underwater, Gordon Rocks 1993

Galapagos penguins, Bartolomé 1990

Flightless cormorants in courtship display, Pta. Espinosa, Fernandina 1992

Flightless cormorants, Fernandina 1986

Flightless cormorants, Pta. Albemarle Isabela 1986

Flightless cormorant, Pta. Espinosa 1986

Swallowtail gull, South Plaza 1986

Lava gull, Tortuga Bay 1992

Swallowtail gulls mating, Genovesa 1990

Young swallowtail gull, Genovesa 1993

Albatrosses mating, Espanola 1989

Albatross, Punta Suarez, Espanola 1993

Young albatross, Espanola 1993

kilograms (see photo, page 88). In the past, the population of tortoises was estimated at about 250,000 individuals; In 1980 only 15,000 remained. Before man reached the islands in the time of the pirates, the tortoises had no predators. For the past four centuries, man has been responsible for the destruction of these reptiles. Now the danger comes from other introduced species.

The scientific name of the giant tortoise is *Geochelone elephantopus*. Zoologists have numbered 14 races or subspecies, but only 11 survive today (in fact, the real figure is ten since Lonesome George, the only survivor of Pinta Island, now lives at Darwin Station in Puerta Ayora on Santa Cruz island. The $10,000 reward offered to whoever could provide a female of the same species brought no results, and George will remain an old bachelor.) The giant tortoise is extinct on Fernandina, Floreana, Santa Fé. Contrary to what was once thought, there were never tortoises on Rábida.

Isabela Island, with more than 6,500 individuals, remains the island with the largest giant tortoise population. More than 4,000 Galápagos live in the caldera of Alcedo volcano; 1,000 survive on Wolf volcano, 700 on Cerro Azul, 500 on Darwin, and 400 on Sierra Negra (see map of Isabela). On Santiago Island, the western population was destroyed, and the eastern population numbers 500. There is still a strong population in the east and south of San Cristóbal (despite competition from feral goats), and 250 individuals on Española (compared with 15 in 1960), saved from extinction by the SPNG.

Very independent animals, the giant tortoises live mostly on the summits of the islands. Three groups are distinguishable, based on the shape of the shell:

The Saddleback Type (Española, Pinzón, Pinta and Fernandina)
The carapace is raised in the front, and the neck and legs are very long. By its morphology, this type of tortoise looks for food (cactus pads or leaves) high above the ground, extending its long neck forward like a periscope (see photo, page 90). It is found in the arid zone of the lowlands.

The Dome-shaped Type (Santa Cruz, Isabela)
Heavier and more voluminous than the former type, this tortoise grazes grass directly on the ground. It is found on islands with rich vegetation, in the highlands, around the rim of the volcanoes and in the calderas (see photo, page 89).

The Intermediate Type
This is a variation of the dome shape, including the other races (except those on Wolf volcano and Santa Fé).

Tortoises can survive in dry areas as they are able to conserve water and fat in their internal cavities. This ability first was noticed during their long survival on pirate boats. Nobody knows the maximum age of these land turtles. In the corral of the Darwin Sta-

Population of the giant tortoises

Pinta ⊗

Marchena

Genovesa

Isabela ⊙⌂

Wolf 1000

Darwin 500

Alcedo 4000

Fernandina ⊗

Santiago ⊙⌂

500

Rabida

Pinzon ⊙⌂

Sierra Negra 400

Cerro Azul 700

Santa Cruz ⊙⌂

Santa Fé ⊗

San Cristobal ⊙⌂

Floreana ⊗

Española ⊙⌂

⊙⌂ Still present : 10 races
⊗ Extinct : 4 races

Identification marks on tortoises
here : n° 2054

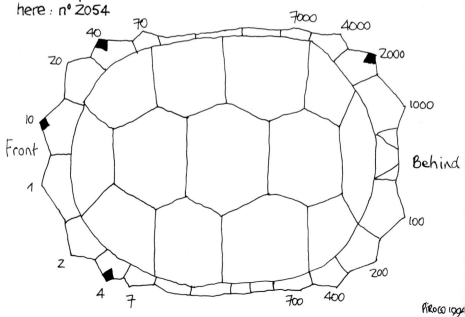

70   7000   4000
40   2000
20
1000
10
Front
1
Behind
100
2
200
4   7   700   400   100

PIROCO 1994

tion, the oldest individual may be as much as 170 years old (and would have known Darwin himself).

Tortoises have a peaceful life. Throughout the year, they eat great quantities of grass, leaves, lower parts of bushes, and the cactus pads of the opuntia. Most of the time they sleep in open spaces, or wade in mudponds during the wet season. At night, they hide under the shrubs. When threatened, their first reaction is to retract head and legs under the shell with a conspicuous hiss. If, by misfortune, one is rolled upon its back, it is difficult for it to get back on its legs. Then it becomes vulnerable.

The mating season coincides with the wet season. Males engage in mock fighting, then look for a female. Later on, between February and May, females start the long journey downhill to the coast, and will look for the right nesting area, in the arid zone, about 20 metres above sea level. Egg laying lasts from June to December. The female digs a nest 30 centimetres deep and 20 centimetres wide, which will be cemented by a lid made of urine and excrement. This jelly is then covered with sand. The construction of the nest takes eight to 12 hours of work on Española, and four to five hours on Santiago Island.

The gestation period lasts from three to eight months, depending on the location of the nest. If it is at low elevation, it will take 120 days; if the elevation is high, then the incubation period may take as long as 200 days. The number of eggs depends on the species: 12 to 15 eggs on Santa Cruz, four to five eggs on Española and Pinzón.

Observation and research carried out by Linda Cayot at the Darwin Station has shown that the temperature of incubation influences the sex of the giant tortoise. If the temperature is higher or equal to 28.5 or 29° C, embryos turn into females. Below that temperature, the eggs produce males. The hatch occurs between mid-January and March. The clutch is of three to eight eggs for the saddleback tortoises and up to 16 eggs or the dome-shaped tortoises. According to some scientists, the sexual maturity of the giant tortoise could be reached at 20 to 30 years.

Predators are numerous. The black rat (*Rattus rattus*), introduced by the pirates, preys on eggs after digging out the nests. Wild pigs do the same. Feral dogs attack small tortoises after hatching (south of Isabela), and dig up the nests (San Cristóbal). As for feral cats, they do not harm tortoises, except in the south of Isabela.

Various means have been adopted by the Galápagos National Park to protect the nest:
- against the rats on Pinzón Island: nothing much can be done but to destroy the rats themselves. This was done in 1989 by the SPNG.
- against feral pigs: by building a stone wall around the nest.
- the incubation of eggs and the breeding of young tortoises at the Darwin Station, helps to develop the existing population.
- feral dogs are the 'plague' of the moment.

Programmes of protection, conservation and breeding of giant tortoises have begun at the Galápagos National Park and at the Darwin Station in 1960. At the time, 13 individuals (11 females and 2 males) from Española Island were the last survivors of a race doomed for extinction. By 1988, 200 saddleback tortoises had been reintroduced on Española, following the successful incubation programme.

Each year, park guards collect tortoise eggs on different islands. These are brought back and incubated at the Darwin Station, where the young will be raised for four years and then returned to their original island. Today, more than 1,000 tortoises have been reintroduced to various islands of the archipelago.

Marine Turtles

Black turtle
(Chelonia agassizi)

Hawksbill turtle
(Eretmochelys imbricata)

Leatherback turtle
(Dermochelys coriacea)

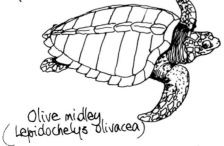

Olive ridley
(Lepidochelys olivacea)

Piroco 89

CHAPTER TWO

SEA BIRDS
SHORE AND LAGOON BIRDS

The bird life of the Galápagos is unique and diversified. In the beginning, migrating sea birds came from Ecuador, Peru, Colombia, and the Caribbean. Trade winds also helped introduced these migrants to the archipelago. Dependent not on the land but on the sea, most probably, sea birds were the first animals to colonize the islands. Half of the resident population of birds is endemic to the archipelago, but only five species of sea birds (of 19) are unique to the Galápagos: the Galápagos penguin, the flightless cormorant, the lava gull, the swallowtail gull and the Galápagos waved albatross. Therefore, 25 per cent of the sea birds are endemic to the islands.

GALÁPAGOS PENGUIN
Spheniscus mendiculus

Endemic. Belongs to the order Sphenisciformes, birds that cannot fly, and in which the wings evolved for use as fins (see photo, page 92).

The Galápagos penguin is related to the Magellan penguin, *Spheniscus magellanicus,* an ancestor thought to be found in southern Chile. It is also related to the penguin of the Falkland Islands and islands near Antarctica. This penguin came to the Galápagos by means of the Humboldt Current. In the islands, its population was 13,000 before the 1982-83 Niño, concentrated around Bartolomé, Rábida, Sombrero Chino, Floreana, the west coast of Isabela and the Bolivar Channel, as well as on the coast of Fernandina, the westernmost island.

The Galápagos penguin swims with its front fins, and its feet help in steering. Swimming slowly at the surface, it moves very fast underwater and sometimes leaps above the water happily; in dolphins, this behavior is known as 'porpoising'. On land the Galápagos penguin walks, hops from rock to rock, and goes 'tobogganing'. Before jumping, it stretches its neck forward as if studying the terrain.

Head and beak movements can be an appeasement response to threatening behavior. They are also a way of greeting without triggering aggression. Crossing beaks is done for the same purpose. During the mating season, Galápagos penguins preen one another's heads, and also slap themselves gently with the front flippers.

Galápagos penguins are opportunistic reproducers. They nest in cavities, where two eggs will be laid three to four days apart. On Fernandina, egg laying occurs in September. Incubation lasts from 38 to 40 days. Very shy animals, penguins nest in groupage They sleep on land and look for food during the day, returning to the shore between 4 and 6:30 pm. In the early morning, they can be seen in the water between 5 and 7 am. They leave a wake behind them, just like ducks.

The disastrous 1982-83 Niño year caused a loss of 77 per cent of the population. By 1985, their number had been slowly recovering and was estimated at 2,000-3,000 individuals. Predators of the Galápagos penguin include red crabs, rice rats, Galápagos snakes, short-eared owls and Galápagos hawks.

FLIGHTLESS CORMORANT   *Nannopetrum harrisi*

Endemic. Belongs to the order of Pelicaniformes. It is a large dark bird with atrophied wings and a strong, long beak with a hooked end. Adults are black above, brown underneath, and have turquoise-blue eyes. The young are black all over, with dull eyes. Males are larger than females (see photo, page 93).

Cormorants are often seen above the tideline, with wings spread out to dry in the wind. This is an ancestral habit which is useless, since the bird cannot fly. A lack of predators has influenced its flightlessness.

Like a penguin, it swims underwater and uses its webbed feet. It feeds on fishes, eels and octopus. This sedentary bird emits a grunt and nests in small colonies on rocks or sheltered beaches. The mating season lasts from November to March, but may be throughout the year since the flightless cormorant is an opportunistic breeder. The male chooses the female. Between March and September, she lays two or three big white eggs in a nest of twigs, algae and marine grass. The incubation time is about 35 days.

Being endemic to the Galápagos, it is one of the rarest bird in the world. Its population is estimated at 800 pairs. It is found on the shore of Fernandina and on the west coast of Isabela, where the nutrient-rich Cromwell current from the central Pacific brings an abundance of fish.

The largest colonies of flightless cormorants are located at Cape Douglas (37 nests), Cape Hammond (28 nests) on Fernandina and at Cape Berkeley (30 nests) on the northwest of Isabela. Visitor sites are Punta Espinosa (Fernandina), Puerta Moreno, Puerta Garcia and Puerta Albermarle (Isabela).

LAVA GULL   *Larus fuliginosus*

Endemic. Belongs to the order Charadriiformes and to the family Laridae (see photo, page 94). The population of this bird was once estimated at 400 pairs, but it is found everywhere in the Galápagos. Adults are sooty grey with a white ring around the eyes. Feet and beak are black. The lava gull has the funny habit of staring between its feet, head bent down. This submissive attitude means 'good intentions' to the protagonist. It also has a loud shriek that can be mistaken for a human laugh.

Frequently encountered in ports, the lava gull feeds on crabs and small marine iguanas, but mainly on dead fish and waste like sea lions' afterbirth. It is a scavenger. Solitary, it nests in rocky overhangs and at the bottom of cliffs near the waterfront. Two olive-green eggs speckled with brown are laid in a nest of twigs. Adults are very protective of the nest, and will scare off any intruder (even bigger than themselves), using their feet to hit the aggressor.

SWALLOWTAIL GULL   *Creagrus furcatus*

Endemic. The only other gull present in the Galápagos. It is differentiated from the lava gull by a black and white spotted swallowtail and a red eyering. The body is pale grey on its back, ventrally white. The beak is black with a white tip, and the feet are red (see photo, page 94). The white marks at the base and tip of the beak help the chick in the nest to see the arrival of its parent at night. Consequently, to obtain food, it will just knock on the beak of the adult. Big black eyes are characteristic of the swallowtail gull, which feeds only at night. Its nocturnal vision is made possible by the red eyering which serves as a sort of sonar. It feeds offshore, looking for fish and squid. This night-feeding habit has developed in response to competition from other sea birds during the daytime, in particular the tropicbird, which feeds during the day on the same food.

The swallowtail gull nests in cliffs and lays only one egg—white speckled with brown—which is easily mistaken with the composition of the nest, which is made of pieces of white coral and black lava gravels. Prosperous couples mate once every nine or ten months.

Swallowtail gulls are often seen at dawn and at dusk when they go or come back from fishing. Their cry is unique and resembles a clanking whose possible function which may be compared to echolocation.

In the Galapagos, other gulls may be seen occasionally migrating such as the Franklin's gull and the laughing gull (Genovesa, March 1995)

WAVED ALBATROSS   *Dimedea irrorata*

There are 13 species of albatross in the world. The albatross belongs to the order Procellariformes, which is recognized by the tube-nose on the top of the beak. This order comprises two families, which feed on plankton: the Diomedeidae (albatross) and the Procellaridae (petrels and puffins).

One of the most majestic birds in the archipelago, the waved albatross is endemic not only to the Galápagos, but also to the island of Española (Hood Island), for this is the only place in the world where it reproduces. Its life expectancy is about 20 years.

This cousin of the petrels and the puffins, has a population of 24,000 individuals. Weighing four kilograms, and with a wingspan of 2.5 metres, this is the largest bird in the Galápagos (see photo, page 96).

The back, wings and tail are light brown, contrasting with the whiteness of the head, neck and belly. Its big yellow beak looks like a tube, hooked at the end.

With sufficient wind, the albatross in flight is a tremendous glider, but in calm weather it has to move its wings harder than other birds. It feeds offshore, on fish, squid and other invertebrates, and may also steal from boobies occasionally. Nevertheless, its feeding habits are nocturnal, and its big black eyes are the proof of it. It feeds on the surface of the water.

The waved albatross is found in the Galápagos only during the dry season, on Española; it arrives around mid-April and leaves around mid-December. It returns to its island to reproduce after six months spent in the open sea of the Pacific Ocean, and as far as Japan. Every year, the ritual is repeated: males arrive first to reconnoitre the terrain and the nesting site; when the females arrive a few days or weeks later, one may see a kind of collective rape. Afterward, serious matters start, and pairs are formed. Albatrosses are faithful to their mate for their whole life (see photo, page 95).

Generally, the courtship of the female by the male does not happen in the same year as nesting, but in two different seasons. The courtship display is remarkable. In their dance, albatrosses cross beaks as two fencers in a duel, then go for a 'sky-pointing display', with the beak opening and loudly snapping shut, and start the love fight again. This display is repeated over and over.

The mating occurs over a period of five days. The single egg, as large as a billiard ball, is laid between mid-April and mid-June. The whole colony reproduces at the same time. The eggs hatch between mid-June and mid-August, after an incubation of 63 days. Curiously, the waved albatross will roll its egg quite a distance between the rocks, pushing it with the beak, as if to give it exercise. Sometimes the egg breaks.

The albatross chick is a big, ugly, brown fluffy thing. It will take 167 days before it flies. The nesting site is abandoned between the end of November and mid-January.

The waved albatross of Española is sexually mature at the age of five or six years. Its lifespan may reach 30 to 40 years. Some albatrosses abandoned at Española have been found as far away as the shores of Japan. There was a massive abandonment of the nests during the Niño year 1982-83.

AUDUBON'S SHEARWATER   *Puffinus lherminieri*

Belongs to the order Procellariformes and to the family Procellaridae. Dorsally dark brown, ventrally white, the Audubon shearwater is originally from the Antilles, but it is also found in the Pacific and Indian oceans (see drawing, page 107). The Audubon shearwater is easily mistaken with the Hawaiian petrel, which is larger and has a white patch on the forehead.

Active during the day, it feeds on plankton and crustaceans. It often fishes in group and flies low above the water. It may dive to a depth of two metres, and uses its wings to swim after small fish.

The Audubon shearwater is an opportunistic breeder. On south Plaza Island, the reproduction cycle is nine months. One white egg is laid with an incubation time of 49 days. The juvenile may fly 75 days later. The population in the Galápagos is estimated at 10,000 pairs. Its predator is the short-eared owl.

HAWAIIAN PETREL   *Pterodroma phaeophygia*

Dorsally black, ventrally white (see drawing, page 107). Two species are found in Hawaii and in the Galápagos. This black bird with a white forehead and white under-wings may be seen in the highlands of Santa Cruz, San Cristóbal, Floreana, James and Isabela, where the vegetation is dense. The Hawaiian petrel nests on the ground, under rocks and in volcanic caves.

The reproduction season differs according to the island:

	Floreana	Santa Cruz	Santiago
Arrival:	end November	May	January
Egg laying:	end December/April	June/September	February/June
Hatch:	end February/June	August/November	April/August
Takeoff:	June/September	December/March	July/November

The reproduction cycle is annual, and only one egg is laid. The incubation time is 51 days, and 120 days are necessary for the juvenile to take off. It feeds on fish and squid, offshore.

The predators of the Hawaiian petrel are rats and cats (which pilfer eggs and chicks), feral dogs and feral pigs. These are a major problem in the Galápagos National Park, which has led a campaign for protection and conservation of the species in Floreana since 1982.

The population of the Hawaiian petrel has been estimated at between 10,000 and 50,000.

Hawaïan Petrel

Audubon
Shearwater

Storm
Petrels

Castro's
storm petrel

Galápagos
storm petrel

Elliot's
storm petrel

PIROCO 89

STORM PETRELS

Belong to the Procellariformes, easily recognized by the tube nose. Three species are found in the Galápagos:
- Castro's storm petrel   (*Oceanodroma castro*)
- Galápagos storm petrel   (*Oceanodroma tethys*)
- Elliot's storm petrel   (*Oceanites gracilis*)

Plankton feeders, these small black petrels skip across the surface of the water, fluttering about like butterflies. They are each differentiated by the white markings at the base of the tail (see drawing, page 107).

CASTRO'S STORM PETREL   *Oceanodroma castro*

Subtropical Atlantic and Pacific distribution. Conspicuous white band on the tail. Nests in cliffs, among rocks and under ledges, on Plaza Island, Daphne Mayor, Guy Fawkes, Cowley's Island, Devil's Crown, Isla Pitt and Genovesa (Tower Island).

This pelagic bird feeds at night, as well as during the day, on small fish and squid. Castro's storm petrel is an annual breeder; two seasons are distinguished: eggs are laid between March and June, or December-January (Plazas). A single white egg is laid. The incubation time is about 42 days.

Its predator is the short-eared owl, mostly during the cold season.

GALÁPAGOS STORM PETREL   *Oceanodroma tethys*

Distinguished by the white cuneiform (wedge-shaped) mark at the base of the tail. Pelagic, its feeding habit is nocturnal, on the surface. Annual reproduction; one single egg is laid between May and June. The population of Galápagos storm petrels is about 200,000 pairs, nesting on Genovesa, Isla Pitt and Rock Redonda.

ELLIOT'S STORM PETREL   *Oceanites gracilis*

Among all petrels, this is the most common. A white lens-shaped mark is conspicuous at the base of the tail. It feeds inshore. One single egg is laid between April and September.

The population of Elliot's storm petrels is several thousand pairs.

BROWN NODDI   *Anous stolidous*

Also known as the noddi tern. Colour is sooty grey to brown, with the top of the head white. The black eye is circled in white (see photo, page 113). A resident tern in the

Galápagos, the noddi builds its nest of twigs in the cliffs. It feeds on the surface of the water, inshore. It may enter the water, but generally hovers low above fish schools. It often associated with Audubon shearwater and brown pelicans; by sitting on the heads of these larger birds it can wait for the small fish they catch.

Known as the 'noddi' because of its courtship display, nodding its head in front of the mate, it is an opportunistic breeder. The noddi tern nests in caves and rocky overhangs. One single egg is laid.

The following terns are present but rare: The royal tern, *Sterna maxima*, is white with the top of the head black and an orange beak. The sooty tern, *Sterna fuscata*, nests only on Darwin Island in the north of the archipelago.

GREAT FRIGATEBIRD   *Fregata minor*

Belongs to the order of Pelicaniformes, which are recognized by reduced or absent external nasal slits.

Frigates, or 'vultures of the sea', are specially designed for life aloft. Their wingspan is as big as that of the albatross. This bird, having lost the waterproofing of its black plumage, never lands on the sea. The uropygial gland, which normally oils the feathers, is atrophied and useless.

Frigates spend time gliding in circles in the sky. When in pursuit of other birds—especially boobies, for example, which they frequently harass for food—they may be very fast. This is called 'cleptoparasitism'. Frigates may also catch small fish on the surface of the water with the mere swipe of the hooked beak.

Males are black with a greenish sheen. Wings are long and pointed, and the tail is scissorlike. During the courtship display, the male inflates a huge leathery red poach under his throat. This seduces and attracts the female to the nest, which the male has already prepared for the purpose of mating. This amazing ritual may be observed in March and April on Frigatebird Hill (San Cristóbal) or on Genovesa Island (Darwin Bay), or throughout the year on North Seymour Island.

Females also have black plumage, but the upper ventral part of the throat is white (see photos, pages 114 and 115). The eyering is conspicuously red on the female, while the male's is bluish green. Frigate chicks are all white at first, then the head and neck turn hazelnut in colour.

The reproduction cycle of the frigate is one and a half to three times longer than that of any other member of the order Pelicaniformes. Ten to 20 days of courtship display are necessary before mating. Frigatebirds reproduce in colony. One single egg is laid in a nest of twigs, always in a tree or a bush. The annual reproduction differs on various islands. Eggs are laid between February and August on Genovesa Island, between April and November on Española Island. The incubation time is 55 days. Maturity takes 130 to 160 days (even 180 days sometimes), before the juvenile can fly. The slow growth of the young, and its ability to fast, are remarkable adaptations to the irregularity of the food supply. The great frigate is therefore a 'tropical breeder', which means that it has a long reproduction cycle. Apparently the frigate reproduces every two years. It always returns to the same nesting site and does not show any sign of territorial aggressivity to other birds of the same species.

The great frigate is an 'offshore feeder', foraging far away from the coast and from the islands, thus avoiding competition with the magnificent frigate, which is an 'inshore feeder' feeding closer to the islands. The great frigate feeds on fish caught on the surface, and also 'hijacks' other sea birds (such as boobies), catching them by the tail and forcing them to regurgitate food in the air. Frigates also prey on turtle eggs and recently hatched young.

Great frigatebirds are found throughout the archipelago on the periphery of the islands. Main colonies are located on Genovesa, Darwin, Wolf, Española, Floreana (Gardner), Tortuga Island, Isla and Punta Pitt. The great frigate is pantropical.

MAGNIFICENT FRIGATE   *Fregata magnificens*

Very similar to the great frigate, but the male has a purple sheen on its black plumage, and the female has a black triangle on the white patch of the throat. The eyering is bluish green on both sexes. Unlike the great frigate, the magnificent frigate is an 'inshore feeder', and feeds near the islands. On North Seymour, where it is easily seen, courtship displays are observed throughout the year. It is also a 'tropical breeder', with long reproduction cycles. Only one egg is laid, with an incubation time of 55 days.

The magnificent frigate nests on the salt bush, *Cryptocarpus pyriformis* (North Seymour) or in the palo santos (San Cristóbal). The main colonies are found on Seymour, Darwin, Wolf, Isabela (Punta Moreno), San Cristóbal (Wreck Bay) and Genovesa.

Magnificent frigates are also found in the Caribbean, on the west coast of Central America and in the north of South America.

TROPICBIRD   *Phaeton aethereus*

Belongs to the order Pelicaniformes and to the family Phaetodontidae, which comprises one genus and three species: the small tropicbird, the great tropicbird and the white tropicbird. The first two are pantropical and the latter is found in the southern Pacific.

This beautiful white bird with short wings has two long and narrow feathers extending from the tail. A black line runs through the eyes, and the bill is coral red in adults. The juvenile lacks the two tail feathers. Its food being pelagic, the tropicbird is an 'offshore feeder'. It feeds on fish and squid by plunge-diving during the daytime.

The tropicbird reproduces in colonies, and lays only one red-brown, spotted egg in a crack of the cliff or between rocks (see photos, page 116). There is a noticeable difference between reproduction cycles of the tropicbirds on South Plaza, Genovesa and Daphné Island:

South Plaza:	annual reproduction, three eggs are laid between August and February
Genovesa:	eggs laid between July and November
Champion, Onslow, Enderby:	egg laying between August and December (islets of Floreana)
Daphné:	eggs are laid any time of the year. Severe intraspecific competition for the nesting sites. Opportunistic breeders, incubation time: 42 days.

Even though three eggs may be laid, only one usually develops into maturity. Chicks are fed until their first flight. They receive fish of an average size (20 centimetres) and squid.

Colonies of tropicbirds are found on Plaza, Seymour, Daphné, Rábida, Sombrero Chino, Tortuga and Floreana (Champion, Enderby, Caldwell, Gardner, Onslow). This bird does not like cold waters, and is therefore rare on Fernandina and Isabela.

BROWN PELICAN   *Pelicanus occidentalis*

One of the largest birds in the archipelago. Adults are grey-brown with the top of the head white. The nape is reddish hazelnut during the mating season. Young do not have these colours and are brown overall. Feet are webbed and grey-black. The beak is very long and hooked at the tipage The lower jaw has a large poach, which inflates with water after plunge-diving.

The pelican fishes along the shore. It will take in a few liters of saltwater, which is ejected later through holes in the beak, before it swallows its fish (see photo, page 117).

In flight, the pelican gives a few strokes of its wings, then glides for a long time. It often flies in formation with other pelicans.

This opportunistic breeder nests in the mangroves, or on the salt bushes. The reproduction cycle of nine months occurs during the hot season. Two or three chalk-white eggs are laid on a platform of twigs. A few juveniles die young after they learned how to fly, usually when they have not mastered the fishing technique.

The brown pelican nests on all central islands, but more easily on Marchena and Española.

BOOBIES   *Sula*

Boobies are very common in the islands. Three species are seen in the Galápagos: the blue-footed, the red-footed and the masked booby. All have an aerodynamic body and a long, pointed bill.

All three live in colonies, but with various habitats. The name 'booby' may derive from the fact that—once they have seen fish while flying—they drop on it like arrows from a height of fifteen metres. Unfortunately, they react in the same way towards fishing lures, plunge- diving on the surface of the ocean behind the boat.

Boobies belong to the family Sulidae, and the order Pelicaniformes (pelicans, frigates, cormorants, tropicbirds). All have webbed feet. The family Sulidae is divided into two groups:
- the genus *Morus* .... three gannets
- the genus *Sula* .... six boobies

The six boobies belong to the genus *Sula*. Three of these are common to the Galápagos. The three others are the Peruvian booby (creator of guano), the brown booby (pantropical) and the Abbott's booby (found in the Christmas Islands, near Java in Indonesia).

Blue-footed boobies are found north to the Gulf of California and south to the coastal islands of northern Peru. The two other boobies of the Galápagos are pantropical. Great concentrations of Sula exist in the regions of cold waters, which are rich in nutrients and organisms. The Humboldt current supports the booby colonies of the archipelago.

Well adapted to extensive flight when looking for food, boobies have the ability to plunge-dive and move underwater, when fishing.

Boobies incubate their eggs with their webbed feet and not with an abdominal pouch.

RED-FOOTED BOOBY   *Sula sula*

This is the lightest booby, with a weight of about one kiogram. Colour is light brown, with a bluish beak. There is also a white variety, called the 'morpho blanco'. The red feet are adapted to gripping branches; thus it is the only booby to nest in trees (eg palo santos or in the bushes) (see photo, pages 118 and 119). The reproduction season depends on the availability of food . The chicks may easily die of hunger during the first weeks of their life. Despite the high mortality rate, only one egg is laid. The time necessary to breed young does not allow an annual cycle of reproduction. Consequently, a period of 14 months elapses before the red-footed booby nests again.

The largest colony of red-footed boobies is on Genovesa Island. The population of the archipelago is 250,000. The red-footed boobies are the largest community of boobies in the Galápagos.

Noddi terns, Pta. Vicente Roca 1992

Great frigate (male), San Cristobal 1981

113

Pair of great frigates, Genovesa, 1990

Female great frigatebird and chick, Genovesa 1992

Young great frigate, Genovesa 1993

Young great frigates in flight 1988

Colony of great frigates in the salt bushes, Genovesa 1993

115

Tropicbird, Punta Suarez, Espanola 1984

Tropicbird in flight, Espanola 1984

Brown pelican (adult), Puerto Ayora 1984

Pelican and young, Pta. Moreno, Isabela 1988

Pelican nesting, Rabida 1989

Pelican feeding its young, Rabida 1990

Red-footed booby, Genovesa 1993

Red-footed booby, Morpho blanco variety, Genovesa 199

Red-footed boobies (young), Genovesa 1990

Blue-footed boobies, Espanola 1980

Blue-footed booby (young), Espanola 1985

Nest of excreta of the blue-footed booby Punta Pitt 1993

Courtship display of the blue-footed boobies, Espanola 1984

Blue-footed booby and chicks, Espanola 1993

Masked booby, Espanola 1992

Pair of masked boobies, Daphné 1993

Masked booby, Espanola 1981

Ventilation posture of a booby, Daphné 1992

Whimbrel, Fernandina 1992

Ruddy turnstone, Fernandina 1992

127

Sanderlings, Seymour 1992

Ruddy turnstones feeding on a sea lion's afterbirth, Seymour 1993

128

BLUE-FOOTED BOOBY   *Sula nebouxii*

This is the most common booby. Its lifespan is about 15 to 20 years. Unlike its red-footed relative, the blue-footed booby fishes inshore. It nests on the coast. The nesting site, on the ground, is marked by sprays of ejecta which draw a radiant white sun on the volcanic sand. Food is usually abundant, and allows two or sometimes three eggs to be laid.

The male is lighter than the female (1.28 kilograms and 1.80 kilograms respectively) and plunge-dives more easily than the female. It is recognized by the black pinpoint pupil of the eye, while the dark iris coloration of the female gives the impression that her pupil is larger. The male whistles, and the female honks (see photo, page 120).

During the mating season, the booby dances with its turquoise-blue feet, spreads out its wings, bring its tail up, point its bill to the sky and whistles loudly. This ceremony is known as 'sky pointing display'. Meanwhile, the female moves about, retracts her beak towards the body, and seems to respond 'no, no'. Sometimes a jealous pretender intrudes on the pair's courtship, trying its luck with the female. But conflict soon erupts, and very noisy beak fighting follows.

The second egg hatches five to seven days after the first, which puts the younger of the two chicks at a great disadvantage. If food is sufficient, the two chicks will be bred together. Otherwise, the stronger firstborn will survive and will kick its sibling out of the nest. Exposed to the fierce equatorial sun, or to the marauding frigates, the abandoned chick will die quickly.

The sexual dimorphism of the blue-footed boobies allows a partial division of activities. The small size and long tail of the male favour its mobility underwater. Consequently, it will be the one fishing while the female sits on the nest. In any case, a parent will always remain with the nest. The feet of the boobies are well irrigated with blood, and their thermo-regulating function insures perfect incubation.

An opportunistic breeder, the blue-footed booby avoids nesting in the hot season, between December and April. It prefers the cold season between May and December, for it needs dry and clear ground which is not covered with vegetation. Once the egg hatches, after one and a half months of incubation, the parent will stay with the chick until it is able to fly, giving it shade and protection. Finally, the juvenile must learn to plunge-dive and to fish. This takes 50 days for the blue-footed booby, and three months for the red-footed booby.

Since their food is abundant, blue-footed boobies may have more than one clutch a year. Nine months' time will be necessary, for the limiting factor is the moult.

The light weight of these birds allows them to build a nest inside a crater (eg Daphné Mayor), from where they may take off easily. Of the three boobies, the blue-footed is the only one to do this.

The population of the blue-footed boobies has been estimated at 10,000, but it may be much more. Large colonies are found on Española (Punta Suarez), Daphné, Tagus Cove and Punta Vicente Roca (west coast of Isabela), Cape Douglas (Fernandina).

MASKED BOOBY *Sula dactylatra*

Heaviest of the three boobies, males weigh 1.63 kilograms, while females are larger at 1.88 kilograms. The plumage is white, wings are fringed with black, and the beak is orange yellow. The conspicuous black mask on the eyes makes it easy to recognize (see photo, page 122).

Like the blue-footed booby, the white or masked booby nests directly on the ground and surrounds its nest with waste. It chooses the site on clifftops, where the air streams allow it to take off easily. The fishing zone is intermediate between those of the other booby species, ie between islands. This adaptation to the environment illustrates the idea of the 'ecological niche'.

In masked boobies, sexual dimorphism is slight. Two eggs are laid five days apart. The incubation time is 43 days, but the clutch is quickly reduced to one chick following an unavoidable fratricide. Food sources are not as abundant as they are for the blue-footed boobies.

The season for reproduction is stable. On Genovesa Island, the masked booby mates from September to November, on Española Island, from November to February.

The population of masked boobies is about 25,000. The largest colonies are found at Punta Suarez (Española Island), where the nests are on the southern cliffs, at Darwin Bay (Genevesa Island), as well as on Wolf and Darwin Island in the north of the archipelago.

SHOREBIRDS AND LAGOON BIRDS

GREAT BLUE HERON   *Ardea herodias*

Greyish blue, with a lighter head and neck, this tall wader nests in the mangrove. Frequently seen at Puerto Ayora (Santa Cruz Island), and around the kitchen of the Hotel Galápagos (an old one with a broken wing). They can be observed at Tortuga bay, strolling down the beach at low tide and looking for small fish. Preys on baby turtles as well (see photo, p 123).

LAVA HERON   *Butoroides sundevalli*

Small grey-black heron, with yellow or red feet, which stalks on the shore and around tide pools. Young may be lighter, with a striated back and yellow legs. On the rocks near the waterline, lava herons look for crabs and small fish, and stands still for long spells, with an amazing stare (see photo, page 123).

NIGHT HERON   *Nyctanassa violacea*

Of intermediate size between the two former species, this heron is streaked grey-brown. It has a black head with yellow and white feathers. Two thin white feathers run behind its head from the top of the skull. This nocturnal wader is found at night under the street lamps of Puerto Ayora (Santa Cruz Island), and can also be frequently seen during the daytime at the entrance of caves or under rock ledges overlooking tide pools, as in Darwin Bay (Genovesa Island) or Puerto Egas (Santiago Island) (see photo, page 124).

CATTLE EGRET   *Bubulcus ibis*

A little white heron, very majestic in flight, with black legs (juveniles) or yellow legs (adults). It is found on the shore at low tide, or even in the arid zone, where it catches lizards and grasshoppers. The nest is made in the mangrove.

It is found in the highlands of Santa Cruz, where it is seen in the company of cows. It also comes near sea lions in search of flies, which is not always to the liking of these mammals! (See photo, page 124).

COMMON OR GREAT EGRET   *Casmerodius alba*

A great white heron with a yellow bill and black legs. It concentrates in the central islands, on the coast, and nests in the mangroves, laying two eggs. The common egret feeds on fish, lizards, grasshoppers and other insects (see photo, page 124).

Shore and lagoon birds (1)

Common stilt

Common Egret

Wandering tattler

Semi-palmated plover

Sanderling

PIROCO 89

Shore and lagoon birds (2)

Northern phalarope

Ruddy turnstone

Common
gallinule

Purple gallinule

Piroo 89

OYSTERCATCHER   *Haematopus ostralaegus*

A brown bird with a white belly, a black head and a red eyering. The bill is long, pencil-like, orange or red. The oystercatcher is the same size as the lava heron. It is found on the littoral (Punta Suarez, Española, Puerto Egas, Santiago Island), but is not common, due to the lack of proper habitat. Feeds on abalone, conical shaped shells fixed on the rocks of the intertidal zone, as well as on pencil sea urchins (see photo, page 125).

FLAMINGO   *Phoenicopterus ruber*

Rare in the Galápagos, it is found in seven saltwater lagoons, behind the mangroves of the littoral. Flamingos may only reside in places where the water is not too deep for wading (less than one metre).

Swinging its neck right and left, it searches for food in the silt, thanks to a sonar in the bill which enables it to detect organisms. These are mainly a small pink shrimp (*Artemia salina*), the water-boatmen (T*richocorixia reticulata*), larvae of coleoptera and diptera, organisms belonging to the ostracidae family and algae. Flamingos feed for seven to 12 hours a day. The tongue sucks the sediment and salt water; everything is filtered through sievelike plates inside the beak, then pumped out the sides.

Mud nests, like small towers, are erected on the border of the lagoon. These are sometime destroyed by floods or by wild pigs.

The flamingo reproduces at the age of five to six years, and mates every three to four years. A single egg is laid with an incubation time of 28 days. Only about 50 per cent of the hatchlings will survive. Of this number, 73 per cent will reach adulthood. Chicks are fluffy white, with big black legs. At the age of two months, they know how to filter food. At four months they become adults. Juveniles are preyed upon by hawks, suffer floods or get lost. A mortality rate of 20 per cent occurs during the first year.

Flamingos have a lifespan of 18 to 24 years. Easily disturbed, they take flight if approached noisily. Common stilts, usually present in the area, always warn flamingos of any potential danger.

The population in the archipelago is estimated at 400 to 600. Flamingos may be observed at Espumilla Beach (Santiago Island), Rocas Bainbridge, and lagoons of Villamil (Isabela Island), Punta Cormorant (Floreana Island) and Rábida Island (see photo, page 125).

COMMON STILT   *Himantopus himantopus*

Another bird of brackish lagoons, which feeds on small animals caught in the silt with its long thin black bill. The common stilt is a slender bird, black dorsally, white ventrally and up to the underparts of neck and head. Legs are long and red. Common stilts share the lagoon with flamingos and white-cheeked pintail ducks (see photo, page 126).

BAHAMA WHITE-CHEEKED PINTAIL   *Anas bahamensis*

Also known as the Bahama duck. This brown duck has white cheeks and a red mark at the base of the beak. It is the only duck to reproduce in the Galápagos. Blown to the islands by the northeast trade winds, this species originated in the Caribbean and is now found in freshwater pools and brackish lagoons (see photo, page 126).

WHIMBREL   *Numenius phaeopus*

This shoreline wader is distinguished by its long curved bill. Brown with white spots, it has a dark streak on the eye and other bands on the top of the head. Found on rocks and on beaches at the border of retreating waves. A very shy bird and easily frightened, it takes off with a conspicuous repetitive shriek (see photo, page 127).

WANDERING TATTLER   *Heteroscelus incanus*

A slate-grey bird with white eyebrows. Ventrally white or speckled, a long thin black bill, and long yellow legs. Usually found on the rocks of the shore at low tide (see photo, page 132).

SEMIPALMATED PLOVER   *Charadrius semipalmatus*

A small bird of the littoral. The back and top of head are brown. Ventrally white, with orange legs. A conspicuous black ring is noticeable around the neck. The bill is short and black, with an orange base. Walks quickly on the beach along the waterline, or on rocks (see drawing, page 132).

SANDERLING   *Calidris alba*

Dorsally grey speckled with white, ventrally white up to the throat. A long, pointed black bill, and black legs. Walks very fast on the beach along the waterline, after the dying wave (see photo, page 128).

Ruddy Turnstone
Arenaria interpes

Dorsally brown, speckled with black and white, ventrally white. A conspicuous black collar under the throat. The legs are orange. The bill is small, sharp and curved upward. Its cry is a deep crackling. When in search of food, it turns over shells and rocks. It has also been observed feeding on sea lions' afterbirth, and sucking blood avidly (Seymour, December 1993). Usually found on the rocks near the water.

Northern Phalarope
Phalaropus lobatus

Dorsally streaked, grey-blue and orange. The head is blue-grey, the throat is white, and a brown-red collar appears during the mating season. Ventrally white with black legs (see drawing, page 133; photo, page 161).

Common Gallinule
Gallinula chloropus

A bird of brackish lagoons. Black to metallic blue, with a yellow-tipped red bill. Big yellow legs. A shy bird, quite rare. When it swims, the head moves back and forth. Feeds on plants and aquatic invertebrates. It may be observed in the lagoons of Puerto Villamil (Isabela Island) (see drawing, page 133).

Purple Gallinule
Porphyrula martinica

Purple-blue on the top of the head and ventrally. Dorsally brownish green. The forehead is turquoise-blue. The bill is red and yellow tipped. Big yellow legs. Found in lagoons with abundant vegetation (see drawing, page 133).

CHAPTER THREE

LAND BIRDS

In the Galápagos, the endemism rate of land birds (76%) is three times higher than the endemism rate of sea birds (35%). This is easily explained by the fact that sea birds are migrants, and land birds are rather sedentary. The latter are also more shy towards man than sea birds.

All land birds in the Galápagos originated in North, Central or South America. They arrived in the islands by chance with the northeast or southeast trade winds. The impossibility of returning to the mainland forced them to adapt to their new environment. Later on, competition and natural selection brought diversification and speciation for some genera. Through evolution, some species became endemic, with no other possible choice (except extinction).

ENDEMIC SPECIES

Nowadays, 29 species of land birds can be identified in the Galápagos, 22 of which are endemic and seven non-endemic.

Among the endemic species: 13 species of Darwin's finches, four species of mockingbird, one dove, one flycatcher, one hawk, one martin, one rail. Among the non-endemic species are: one crake, one cuckoo, two owls, one ani, one warbler, one flycatcher (see Appendix 2, Geographical distribution of the land birds). Since the avifauna come mainly from South America, the distribution of the species is disharmonic. The 1,000 kilometres of the Pacific Ocean between the islands and Ecuador pose an almost impossible barrier to migrations.

EXAMPLES OF DISHARMONY:

	Number of species in world	Number of species in Ecuador	Number of species in Galápagos
Hummingbirds	319	120	0
Parrots	315	44	0
Eagles and Hawks	208	46	
(genus *Buteo*)		12	1
Flycatchers	347	153	2
Mockingbirds	31	6	4 + 7 ssp.
Finches	436	47	13

For some groups, the quality of the environment is the most important. For example, hummingbirds look for big flowers, and parrots look for succulent fruits, all of which are nonexistent in the Galápagos.

All the land birds in the Galápagos breed during the rainy season, at the beginning of the year (January). All, that is, except for one species, the Galápagos rail, which breeds in the cold season, between June and December. The rainy season brings plant growth and thus abundant food for the land birds. This immediate response to the presence of food is called 'opportunistic breeding'.

No land bird species has gone extinct throughout the islands, whereas in Hawaii the islandwide extinction rate is 40%. In the Galápagos, extinctions are localized. Three species have disappeared on Floreana: the mockingbird, the large-bill ground finch, and the barn owl (killed by man). The Galápagos hawk is also extinct on San Cristóbal (because of man), but a few pairs are left on Santa Cruz.

GALÁPAGOS MOCKINGBIRD   *Nesomimus*

The ancestor of the Galápagos mockingbird is the longtail mockingbird, *Mimus longicaudatus*, from Ecuador. In the Galápagos, the four species and six subspecies of mockingbirds are all endemic:
- Galápagos mockingbird (on all islands except Pinzón)
- Hood mockingbird (endemic to Española and Gardner)
- Cristobal mockingbird (endemic to San Cristóbal Island)
- Floreana mockingbird (only found on the satellite islands of Floreana: Champion and Gardner).

These noisy birds, very curious by nature, are greyish brown dorsally and cream-coloured ventrally. The beak is black and curved downward.

Predatory birds, they feed on small finches, lava lizards, centipedes and insects. They also crave the eggs of sea birds, such as boobies and albatrosses. Very social birds, they have no fear of man, and are quite common to the archipelago.

Out of the breeding season, mockingbirds establish communities, with up to nine individuals on Genovesa Island and up to 40 individuals on Española Island. All associate for the defense of the territory and for the search of food. Serious fights may occur at the border of two territories. Two rows of antagonists face one another, and the fighting is fierce between the opposing parties (see photo, page 161).

GALÁPAGOS DOVE   *Zenaida galapagoensis*

Endemic. This little dove, dorsally reddish brown, ventrally beige to pink, has a conspicuous turquoise-blue ring around the eye. Very tame towards man, as the pirate William

Dampier related in 1684: 'One could easily kill a few dozen with a stick, during the morning.' Obviously, this would not be possible nowadays.

The Galápagos dove feeds on the ground, on seeds, usually of the opuntia cactus and of the croton shrub (of which fruits are also eaten), and on caterpillars.

The optimal time of breeding is during the wet season. The Galápagos dove nests on the ground of the arid zone, sometimes under lava rocks. It uses also old nests of mockingbirds. During the breeding season, ritual fights and nodding ceremonies occur. Two eggs are laid.

The Galápagos dove is found on Genovesa, Española, Santiago, Rábida, but it became rare on the inhabited islands of Santa Cruz, Floreana and Cristobal (see photo, page 162).

VERMILLION FLYCATCHER   *Pyrocephalus rubinus*

A very colorful bird, red on the head and on the belly, dorsally black. It has a conspicuous black mask on the eyes. Vermillion flycatchers are found in the humid (scalesia) forest of the highlands, mostly in the central islands. Absent on Genovesa and Española.

The female is yellow ventrally, black dorsally, as is the juvenile male, which turns to red in a later phase.

Originally from South America, it is now found up as far as Mexico and southern California. Known locally as 'brujo' or sorcerer (see photo, page 162).

LARGE-BILLED FLYCATCHER   *Myiarchus magnirostris*

Endemic. May be observed in the highlands, and also in the transition and arid zones. Larger than the former species, it has a yellow belly and a grey throat. Dorsally brown, the top of the head may have a slight crest at times.

Inquisitive by nature, it has the habit of collecting human hair for the construction of its nest (see photo, page 163).

YELLOW WARBLER   *Dendroica petechia*

Originally from the North American mainland, and found from Alaska to southern Peru. This small, insect-eating bird is entirely yellow; the male has a reddish brown patch on the top of the head. The bill is sharp and pointed. Yellow warblers often enter houses to search for flies against the windowpanes.

Common to all these islands, it is found in mangroves, in arid zones and humid zones with dense vegetation. Confined to the Galápagos and Cocos Island (see photo, page 164).

GALÁPAGOS MARTIN   *Progue modesta*

Endemic. Distributed in small groups on central islands. Resembles a big dark swallow. The male is bluish black; the female is light grey. Although rare, it may be observed circling in the sky. Its flight alternates between quick wing flapping and periods of gliding.

The Galápagos martin nests in the holes of cliffs, in calderas and on the rim of volcanoes (Sugar Loaf, on Santiago Island and Daphné Island).

DARK-BILLED CUCKOO   *Coccyzus melacoryphus*

This is a rare bird. Twice as big as the yellow warbler, it is mainly speckled grey, with the top of the head black, and a long tail. Dorsally dark brown, ventrally pale. Widely distributed in South America, it arrived in the Galápagos recently, where it can be observed mainly in the highlands. Very frequent in the lowlands during the Niño year 1982/83. Related to the black-billed cuckoo of North America (see drawing, page 141).

SMOOTH-BILLED ANI   *Crotophaga ani*

Reached the Galápagos recently from Ecuador. It was probably introduced by settlers in 1962 to protect cattle from ticks. This black bird has a feathery black tail, and a smooth broad black bill humped on the topage Poorly adapted to long-distance flight, it was discovered on Genovesa Island, 90 kilometres away from Santa Cruz.

Anis are gregarious. They are found in the humid highlands, where they are company to cattle, from which they eat ticks and other parasites. The smooth-billed ani belongs to the Cuculidae family (cuckoos and anis). (See drawing, page 141.)

GALÁPAGOS RAIL   *Laterallus spilonotus*

Endemic. About 15 centimetres long, dark colour with hazelnut markings and white spots on the wings. Feeds on insects and other invertebrates on the ground, and on dead leaves. Omnivorous, it lost its ability to fly, due to its feeding habits. Nevertheless, it may fly ten to 15 metres. The rail lives in the highlands between 350 and 600 metres (San Cristóbal, Santa Cruz, Santiago, Isabela, Floreana, Pinta and Fernandina).

It is the only land bird to breed in the cold season between June and December. The incubation period of the egg is 23 to 25 days.

PAINT-BILLED RAIL   *Neocrex erythrops*

Slightly larger than the Galápagos rail, it is distinguished by dark plumage with no markings, a yellow and red bill, and red legs.

Land birds

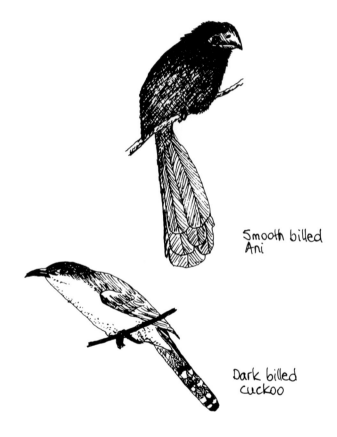

Smooth billed
Ani

Dark billed
cuckoo

Galápagos
rail

Paint-billed
Crake

Piroco 89

A poor flier, it was discovered in 1953 in the agricultural zone of Santa Cruz and Floreana Island (see drawing, page 141).

GALÁPAGOS HAWK   *Buteo galapagoensis*

Endemic. This magnificent predator was for a time extinct on Santa Cruz. But recently (Gemelos, November1993) the author observed the return of the hawks to the highlands of that island. Practically extinct on Floreana and San Cristóbal, due to hunting by the settlers. The hawk is common to Pinzón Island (for a long time infested with black rats), and to Santiago and Isabela islands.

The adult has dark brown plumage, a tail striped with white, and yellow legs. Juveniles are lighter and speckled with white. This bird of prey is unique, having no predators itself, and is therefore on the top of the 'food chain'. With its sharp eyesight, the hawk may detect prey—mainly lizards, iguanas, snakes, finches, boobies, flycatchers and young goats—from a great distance. It will also eat dead animals, such as sea lions, sea birds, marine iguanas, goats and fishes.

The Galápagos hawk builds its nest in trees and on rocks. Two or three eggs are laid, and the chicks may be bred simultaneously. The reproduction system, known as 'cooperative polyandry', is unusual. A female hawk will mate with up to four males and make four different nests. Each male will take care of a nest. The female is larger than the male. The reason for this polyandry may be due to the difficulty in finding an appropriate territory, or to the limited number of available territories (see photo, page 165).

SHORT-EARED OWL   *Asio flammeus*

Endemic subspecies. Present on all islands except Wolf. This diurnal hunter is seen in the highlands and close to the sea bird colonies. Short-eared owls feed on rats, land birds and sea birds such as storm petrels. It has no fear of man whatsoever, provided it is not approached too closely.

On Santa Cruz, it hunts early morning from 5 to 10 am, then in the evening from 4 to 10 pm. It nests on the ground, among high grasses. When hawks and barn owls inhabit the same island, the short-eared owl is rare (see photo, page 166).

BARN OWL   *Tyto alba*

Endemic subspecies. Unlike the short-eared owl, the barn owl is a nocturnal predator, feeding on rats and mice only. It is found on the big central islands: Fernandina, Isabela, Santiago, Santa Cruz and San Cristóbal. The barn owl is not afraid of man.

It nests in rock caves, holes in trees and in abandoned houses. The population is about 8,500 pairs (see photo, page 166).

Darwin's Finches

The theory of evolution brought fame to Darwin's finches. The dark-coloured birds are about the size of a sparrow and are distributed on all the islands. They are often very noisy birds and have no fear of man.

Although they belong to the finch family, they make a subfamily called Geospizae, which is found only in the Galápagos and on Cocos Island to the northeast. Thirteen species are endemic to the archipelago; all originated from an original species, *Melanospiza richardsonii*, found on Sainte Lucie Island in the Caribbean.

All the finches are strikingly alike, and it takes the trained eye of a specialist to distinguish them perfectly. The diversity of structure apparent in this little group of birds aroused Darwin's interest in 1835. He came to understand, long after his journey, that a mother species had modified to different ends and for specific functions (1845).

Finches may be classified in different genera, following the characteristic shape of their beak and feeding habits. Four main groups and six genera are distinguished, with the Cocos finch:

- Ground finches   (Geospiza, 6 species)
- Vegetarian finch   (Platyspiza, 1 species)
- Tree finches   (Camarynchus, 3 species; Cactospiza, 2 species)
- Warbler finch   (Certhidea, 1 species)

CLASSIFICATION OF THE 14 DARWIN'S FINCHES

Cocos finch	*Pinaroloxias inornata*
Cactus finch	*Geospiza scandens*
Large cactus finch	*Geospiza conirostris*
Small ground finch	*Geospiza fuliginosa*
Medium ground finch	*Geospiza fortis*
Large ground finch	*Geospiza magnirostris*
Sharpbill ground finch	*Geospiza difficilis*
Small tree finch	*Camarynchus parvulus*
Medium tree finch	*Camarynchus pauper*
Large tree finch	*Camarynchus psittacula*
Carpenter finch	*Cactospiza pallidus*
Mangrove finch	*Cactospiza heliobates*
Vegetarian finch	*Platyspiza cassirostris*
Warbler finch	*Certhidea olivacea*

Lack and Bowan, two scientists who studied finches after Darwin, each have their own views on their evolution. Lack thinks that isolation and competition were important factors in the evolution of the finches. Bowan thinks that only differences in food brought about a particular adaptation. Therefore, there was no competition between species. Ground finches are distributed in the dry arid zone, and look for seeds on the ground. Tree finches are more often in the humid zone. The medium tree finch is only found on Isabela Island. The sharpbill ground finch, also known as the 'blood-sucking' finch or 'vampire' finch (on Wolf Island), draws blood from the base of the feathers of masked and red-footed boobies. The cactus finch appears in the coastal and transition zones. The large cactus finch is only found on Genovesa and Española islands. The carpenter finch, which uses a stick as a tool, is found from the arid zone to the highlands. The mangrove finch is found in the elevated mangroves of Isabela and Fernandina islands.

Finches lay four eggs after the mating season. The incubation time is 14 days (see photo, page 167–69). See Appendix 2: Distribution of land birds according to vegetation zones.

Darwin's finches

" Pinson de Darwin. "

1	Large billed ground Finch	7	Small tree Finch
2	Medium ground Finch	8	Medium tree Finch
3	Small ground Finch	9	Large tree Finch
4	Sharpbilled ground Finch	10	Carpenter Finch
5	Cactus Finch	11	Mangrove Finch
6	Large cactus Finch	12	Vegetarian Finch
		13	Warbler Finch

CHAPTER FOUR

MAMMALS

Like most oceanic islands, the archipelago is poor in native mammals: two species of bats, a few species of rats and, of course, sea lions.

The paucity of native mammals in the islands is explained by the fact that the islands were never connected to the mainland. Today only mammals introduced by man can be considered the only existing mammals. Before the arrival of man the only mammals were rice rats. Later man brought goats, dogs, donkeys, horses and the black rat.

BATS   *Lasiurus*

Two species are present. They inhabit the mangroves, the crowns of opuntia cactus,and the hollow tree trunks introduced by man, such as the guayabillo (*Psidium galapageium*).

One of these bats, *Lasiurus brachyotis,* is endemic, related to the red bat of South America, but smaller and with short ears. The other species is the hoary bat (*Lasiurus cinereus*), with whitish grey hair and light brown fur. Feeding on insects, these bats are found on Santa Cruz (coast and highlands), on San Cristóbal, Floreana and West Isabela (mangroves).

GALÁPAGOS RICE RATS   *Oryzomis*

Endemic to the Galápagos Islands, these rodents belong to the genus *Oryzomis,* distributed on the American mainland. This small brown rat with big bulging black eyes has no fear of man. It digs nests under the rocks of the arid zone, as well as in the highlands. The rice rats are omnivorous. Seven species have been identified.

The Galápagos rice rats have been studied by Brosset (1963), a Frenchman, who divided them into two categories:

    1) genus *Oryzomis*: two endemic species, found on San Cristóbal.

    Oryzomis galapagoensis and on Santa Fé, and *Oryzomis bauri*. The latter, mainly vegetarian, feeds on seeds and vegetation.

    2) genus *Nesoryzomis:* four species, found on Fernandina and Santiago Island. Extinct on Baltra, Santa Cruz and Isabela.

A third genus, now extinct, was found in the highlands of Santa Cruz and Isabela. It is known as *Megaoryzomys*, the giant rice rat. The endemic rice rat of the Galápagos has been disappearing since the introduction of the black rat (*Rattus rattus*) during the time of the pirates. Three factors speed its extinction: competition and disease. The natural predators of the rice rat are the short-eared owl, the barn owl and the Galápagos hawk.

SEA LION   *Zalophus californianus*

Belonging to the family Otaridae the Galápagos sea lion is related to the California sea lion, but is smaller, and is different from the Peruvian sea lion (*Otaria flavescens*), which is from a more southern distribution.

Abundant in the archipelago, sea lions gather in colonies on sand or on the rocks. The male is polygamous, but there is no such thing as a 'harem' in the strict sense of the word, for the female is free to come and go as she pleases, in and out of the groupage. The male is distinguished from the female by its huge size and by a conspicuous hump on the forehead, while the female has a smooth forehead.

The male becomes adult at the age of 10 years and weighs up to 250 kilograms. The female matures at around six to eight years and weighs up to 120 kilograms.

The male is very territorial, especially at the beginning of the mating season, and patrols on the beach or in the water constantly to chase occasional intruders. He keeps an eye on the young, which may wander off too far from the safety of the beach, and may be attacked by sharks.

The mating season occurs between May and January, more or less the time of the garua. It stretches over a period of six to eight months, with a peak from September to November. The male defends a territory of 40 to 100 square metres with a group of up to 30 females. Those which do not have territories gather in 'bachelor clubs'. This is often a voluntary retreat, following a tiring period of holding a territory. A territorial male has very little time to feed, and he keeps his territory for about 14 to 29 days before it is taken over by another male.

Mating occurs in the water. The female gives birth on land—after retiring to a chosen site—and walks away from the afterbirth, with the pup in her mouth. Frigates, gulls, hawks, mockingbirds and ruddy turnstones have been seen feeding on the afterbirth. The newborn sea lion pup weighs about five to six kilograms; one year later it will weigh 20 to 30 kilograms.

Mother and pup recognize one another by cry and smell. The female stays five to six days with the young and teaches it to suck from her four teats. Then the mother goes back to the sea. The pup will lose its first fur five months later, and will have its adult pelt. It will suckle the female for one to two years maximum, before it is left on its own.

Four weeks after giving birth, the female mates again, but the fertilization of the new egg will be effective only two months later. This is known as the 'delayed implantation'. The next birth will occur after a gestation of nine months.

The Annual Cycle of the Galápagos Sea Lion

| Jan | Feb | March | April | May | June | July | Aug | Sept | Oct | Nov | Dec |

```
———————— + ——— + ———————— + ——————————————————————
————————→ B ——— M ———————— I ———————— 9 months ——————————→
```

B: birth
M: mating
I: implantation

Seventy per cent of the sea lion's diet is composed of sardines. The sea lion may dive to a depth of 30 to 60 metres, and dives down to 100 metres have been recorded. It feeds during the day, as opposed to the fur sea lion, which feeds at night.

One of the sea lion's favourite games is surfing a big wave as it is about to crash on the shore (eg on North Seymour Island). Another game is 'water polo', using a marine iguana instead of a ball. The unfortunate reptile is caught by the tail and gleefully thrown up in the air.

The lifespan of sea lions is 18 to 20 years. Females are sexually active after three years. Males become sexually active at about six or seven years, when they can defend a territory against other males or challenge a dominant male.

Sea lion colonies are found on South Plaza, Santa Fé, Rábida, James Bay (Santiago Island), Española, San Cristóbal, Isabela. The global population is estimated at 20,000 to 50,000 individuals.

Since 1970, a viral disease, the 'seal pox', has affected sea lions, contributing to a loss of 50 per cent of the population. The disease is evidenced by an infection of the eyes and purulent warts all over the body. The natural predators of the sea lions are sharks and orcas (see photo, page 170–72).

Fur Sea Lion   *Arctocephalus galapagoensis*

Whatever people may tell you, there are no fur seals in the Galápagos, but only fur sea lions. This species originated in the Southern Hemisphere, and reached the islands via the Humboldt current. The mother species is *Arctocephalus australis*, and the existing Galápagos subspecies, *Arctocephalus galapagoensis*, is endemic. Another branch of the genus *Arctocephalus* is found in South Africa and on the west coast of Namibia, *Arctocephalus capensis*, the Cape sea lion, which enjoys the cold Benguella current—the equivalent of the Humboldt current in the eastern Atlantic.

The fur sea lion of the Galápagos was near extinction at the beginning of the 20th century, following the plundering of their numbers by whalers and other skin hunters. It is the only tropical species of the genus, which was at first subantarctic. It is also the smallest (see photo, page 172).

Differences between seals and sea lions include the following:
- seals do not have external ears, sea lions do.
- seals cannot support themselves on their front flippers, and creep on the ground.
- seals swim with their posterior flippers, sea lions with the front flippers. Sea lions possess strong front flippers, on which they stand and which they use to swim.

The fur sea lion may be easily distinguished from the sea lion by its smaller size, its pointed nose, big round sad eyes with a glossy glare and apparent ears. Most of the time it lies under rocks or in lava cracks, hiding from the sun. Males weigh up to 75 kilograms and females up to 35 kilograms.

Fur sea lions feed at night on squid and schools of small fish. They may dive to depths of 40 to 100 metres. Mating occurs on land during the garua season, between mid-August and mid-November. Many pups are born in early October. The female is sexually mature at the age of three years, and takes care of the young for two or three years. The pup changes skin and fur at the age of six months.

As in the California sea lion, there is a delayed implantation, three months after the birth of the first pup, making for an annual breeding cycle. Males hold territories for between 27 and 51 days. Since they do not have time to feed, they lose up to 25 per cent of their original weight. For males defending a territory, the mortality rate is 30 per cent the first year. After the birth of the pups, the territorial structure disappears, and the males leave, exhausted.

These *lobos de dos pelos* ('double-fur sea wolves'), as they are known locally, are found in Puerto Egas (Santiago Island), on Fernandina Island and on the northern islands of Marchena, Pinta, Isabela, Fernandina, Wolf and Darwin.

At present, the global population is stable, with 30,000 to 40,000 individuals. The two species of sea lions suffer shark attacks, especially on full-moon nights. Therefore, these marine mammals avoid going out on these nights!

CHAPTER FIVE

MARINE LIFE

The Galápagos are bathed by three currents—the cold Humboldt and Cromwell currents, and the warm Panama flow (or El Niño)—providing the islands with a rich, diverse and unique underwater fauna. Organisms originated from three main regions or oceanic provinces:
- the southeastern Pacific, on the Peru-Chile coast
- the eastern Pacific, stretching from Panama to Baja California
- the western Pacific, or Indo-Pacific region, for the tropical species of warm waters.

In 1978, the number of species of fish was estimated at 306 (McCosker, Taylor and Warner). Of this number:

51 species,	or 17%,	are endemic to the Galápagos
177 species,	or 58%,	belong to the Panamic region
43 species,	or 14%,	belong to the Indo-Pacific province
21 species,	or 7%,	belong to the Peru-Chile province
7 species,	or 2%,	are insular endemic: Galápagos, Cocos, Revillagigedos, Malpelo
4 species,	or 1%,	belong to the Atlantic province

The number of fish above is far from exhaustive. According to the most recent research (1992) of Jack Grove and Dr. Lavenberg, of the Los Angeles County Museum in California, the number could easily go beyond 400 species, and the rate of endemism would be reduced to 7 per cent.

Among the numerous fish found in the archipelago, there are 18 species of morays, five species of rays (stingrays, golden ray, marbled ray, spotted eagle ray and manta rays). There are also about 12 species of sharks, which so far have not been harmful to man. No serious incidents have occurred, although some shark attacks have been reported from Pinzón Island. The dangerous great white shark is not an inhabitant of the archipelago; it is found farther north and away from the islands. The most common sharks are the white-tip reef shark, the black-tip reef shark, two species of hammerheads, the Galápagos shark, the grey reef shark, the tiger shark, the hornshark and the whale shark (Gordon Rock, 1984; Darwin Island).

Among the cetaceans, at least 16 species of whales and seven species of dolphins have been identified. Of the latter, the most common are the bottle-nosed dolphin (*Tursiops truncatus*) and the common dolphin. Whales include the sperm whale, the humpback whale, the pilot whale, the orca and the false killer whale, Sei whale, Minke whale, Bryde's whale, Cuvier's beaked whale and other beaked whales. All these whales are distributed throughout the archipelago and are easily observed in the west of Isabela and Fernandina due to the 'upwelling' of the Cromwell current, rich in organisms and plankton. Another species of whale was added to the list in 1993; a few sightings of blue whales were reported by the research sailboat *Odyssey* to the north of Isabela and Fernandina (David Day).

The littoral is also rich in various organisms such as sea stars and cushion stars, sea urchins, sea cucumbers and red crabs ('*zayapas*') with turquoise blue colorations. A few coral reefs—hermatypic hexacorallians and octacorallians—are present to the west of Santiago, south of Genovesa and Santa Cruz (Tortuga bay), north of Floreana. Ahermatypic solitary corals are also found. Corals need particular conditions for their development: clear water with a minimal temperature of 18° C to 20° C, and an optimal depth of 20 metres (see map and drawing, pages 186–87).

Among shells we may mention: cones (*Conidae*), mitre shells (*Mitridae*), cowries (*Cypraeidae*), nerites (*Neritidae*), periwinkles (*Littorinidae*), creepers (*Cerithiidae*), strombs (*Strombidae*), helmet shells (*Cassidae*), murex shells (*Muricidae*), horse conches.

CLASSIFICATION OF THE CETACEANS IN GALÁPAGOS   *Order of marine mammals*

Size		
	SUBORDER OF MYSTICETI (Baleen whales)	
	Rorquals (Family Balaenopteridae)	
19 metres	Sei whale	*Balaenoptera borealis*
15 metres	Bryde's whale	*Balaenoptera edeni*
10 metres	Minke whale	*Balaenoptera acutorostrata*
19 metres	Humpback whale	*Megaptera novaeangliae*
30 metres	Blue whale	*Balaenoptera musculus*
	SUBORDER OF THE ODONTOCETI (Toothed whales)	
	Sperm whales (Family Physeteridae)	
21 metres	Sperm whale	*Physeter catodon*
3.7 metres	Pygmy sperm whale	*Kogia breviceps*
2.7 metres	Dwarf sperm whale	*Kogia simus*

CLASSIFICATION OF THE CETACEANS IN GALÁPAGOS   *Order of Marine Mammals*

SIZE	**Beaked whales** (Family Ziphiidae)	
7 metres	Cuvier's beaked whale	*Ziphius cavirostris*
5 metres	Beaked whales	*Mesoplodon* sp.
	Marine dolphins (Family Delphinidae)	
10 metres	Orca, killer whale	*Orcinus orca*
2.7 metres	Pygmy killer whale	*Feresa attenuata*
6 metres	False killer whale	*Pseudorca crassidens*
7 metres	Shortfin pilot whale	*Globycephala macrorhynchus*
2.8 metres	Melon-headed whale	*Peponocephala electra*
2.4 metres	Fraser's dolphin	*Lagenodelphis hosei*
4.5 metres	Risso's dolphin or Grey grampus	*Grampus griseus*
2.6 metres	Common dolphin or White-bellied dolphin	*Delphinus delphis*
4 metres	Bottle-nosed dolphin	*Tursiops truncatus*
2 metres	Spotted dolphin	*Stenella attenuata*
2.7 metres	Striped dolphin	*Stenella coeruleoalba*
2 metres	Spinner dolphin	*Stenella longirostris*

(List of Cetaceans, after David Day, Noticias de Galápagos, April 1994).

**List of the fishes, whales, dolphins and other marine animals
of the Galápagos (368 species)**   (E) = Endemic

1/ **Cornetfishes, trumpetfishes, pipefishes:**
   Reef cornet fish   *Fistularia commersonii*
   Trumpetfish   *Aulostomus chinensis*
   Fantail pipefish   *Doryrhampus melanopleura*
    Pacific seahorse   *Hippocampus ingens*
2/ **Needlefishes, halfbeaks, flying fishes:**
   Pike needlefish   *Strongylura exilis*
   Silverstripe halfbeak   *Hyporhampus unifasciatus*
   Ribbon halfbeak   *Euleptorhamphus longirostris*
   Longfin halfbeak   *Hemirhampus saltator*
   Sharpchin flying fish   *Fodiator acutus*
   Flying fish   *Cheilopogon dorsomaculata*
   Flying fish   *Exocoetus monocirrhus*
   Flying fish   *Prognichthys seali*

Baleen whales

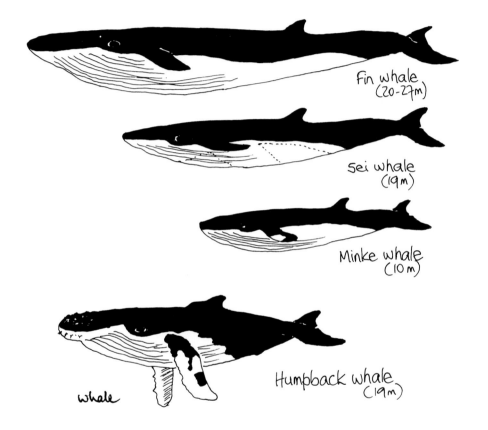

Fin whale
(20-27m)

Sei whale
(19m)

Minke whale
(10m)

Humpback whale
(19m)

whale

Bryde's whale
(15m)

Piroco 89

Toothed whales

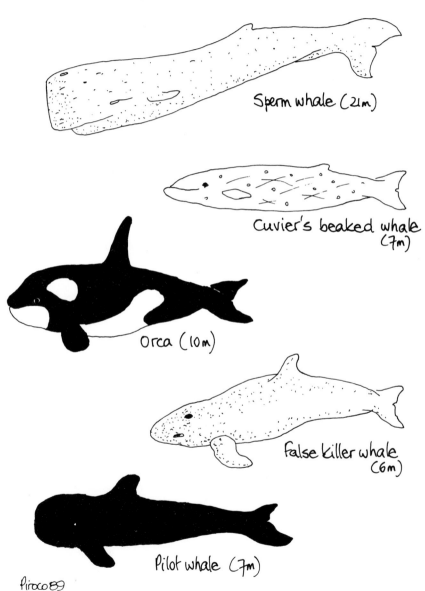

Sperm whale (21m)

Cuvier's beaked whale (7m)

Orca (10m)

False killer whale (6m)

Pilot whale (7m)

Piroco89

3/ **Parrotfishes, wrasses:**

Bluechin parrotfish	*Scarus ghobban*
Bumphead parrotfish	*Scarus perrico*
Bicolor parrotfish	*Scarus rubroviolaceus*
Azure parrotfish	*Scarus compressus*
Loosetooth parrotfish	*Nicholsina denticulata*
Mexican hogfish	*Bodianus diplotaenia*
Harlequin wrasse	*Bodianus eclancheri*
Cortez rainbow wrasse	*Thalassoma lucasanum*
Sunset wrasse	*Thalassoma lutescens*
Chameleon wrasse	*Halichoeres dispilus*
Spinster wrasse (or goldspot wrasse)	*Halichoeres nicholsi*
Dragon wrasse	*Novaculichthys taeniourus*
Surge wrasse	*Thalassoma purpureum*
Galápagos sheephead	*Semicossyphus darwini*
Pacific beakfish, Tigris	*Oplegnathus insigne*

4/ **Surgeonfishes, angelfishes, damselfishes, butterflyfishes:**

Yellowtail surgeonfish	*Prionurus laticlavius*
Gold-rimmed surgeonfish	*Acanthurus glaucopareius*
Yellowfin surgeonfish	*Acanthurus xanthopterus*
Convict tang	*Acanthurus triostegus*
Spotted unicorn	*Naso brevirostris*
Vlaminck unicorn	*Naso vlamingii*
Moorish Idol	*Zanclus canescens*
King angelfish	*Holocanthus passer*
Barberfish	*Heniochus nigrirostris*
Scythe butterflyfish	*Chaetodon falcifer*
Three-banded butterflyfish	*Chaetodon humeralis*
Meyer's butterflyfish	*Chaetodon meyeri*
Raccoon butterflyfish	*Chaetodon lunula*
Threadfin butterflyfish	*Chaetodon auriga*
Duskybarred butterflyfish	*Chaetodon kleinii*
Longnose butterflyfish	*Foreipiger flavissimus*
Panama sergeant major	*Abudefduf troschelli*
Night sergeant	*Nexilarius concolor*
Rusty damselfish	*Nexilosus latifrons*
Yellowtail damselfish	*Eupomacentrus arcifrons*
Acapulco damselfish	*Eupomacentrus acapulcoensis*
Galápagos whitetail damsel	*Stegastes leucorus beebei*
Giant damselfish	*Microspathodon dorsalis*
Bumphead damselfish	*Microspathodon bairdii*
Whitespot chromis	*Chromis atrilobata*
Blackspot chromis	*Azurina eupalama*
White striped chromis	*Chromis alta*

5/ **Puffers, porcupinefishes, boxfishes:**

Galápagos pufferfish	*Spherodes angusticeps*
Concentric pufferfish	*Spherodes annulatus*
Guineafowl puffer	*Arothron meleagris*
White-spotted puffer	*Arothron hispidus*
Spotted sharpnosed pufferfish	*Canthigaster punctatissima*
Balloonfish	*Diodon holocanthus*
Porcupinefish	*Diodon hystrix*
Galápagos blue porcupinefish	*Chilomycterus affinis galapagoensis*
Yellow spotted burrfish	*Cyclichthys spilostylus*
Pacific boxfish	*Ostracion meleagris*

6/ **Triggerfishes, filefishes:**

Yellow bellied triggerfish	*Sufflamen verres*
Black triggerfish	*Melichthys niger*
Pink tail triggerfish	*Melichthys vidua*
Blunthead triggerfish	*Pseudobalistes naufragium*
Finescale triggerfish	*Balistes polyepsis*
Red tail triggerfish	*Xanthichthys mento*
Blue-striped triggerfish	*Xanthichthys caeruleolineatus*
Scrawled filefish	*Aluterus scriptus*
Vagabond filefish	*Cantherines dumerlii*

7/ **Blennies, clinid blennies (klipfishes), combtooth blennies, gobies:**

Large-banded blenny	*Ophioblennius steindachneri*	
Sabretooth blenny	*Plagiotremus azaleus*	
Castro's blenny	*Acanthemblemaria castroii*	(E)
Red-spotted barnacle blenny	*Hypsoblennius brevipinnis*	
Galápagos four-eyed blenny	*Dialommus fuscus*	(E)
Bravo clinid	*Labrisomus dentriticus*	(E)
Large mouth blenny	*Labrisomus xanti*	
Jenkins clinid	*Labrisomus jenkinsi*	(E)
Porehead blenny	*Labrisomus multiporosus*	
Galápagos triplefin blenny	*Enneapterygius corallicola*	(E)
?	*Malacoctenus afuerae*	
?	*Malacoctenus zonogaster*	(E)
Throatspotted blenny	*Malacoctenus tetranemus*	
?	*Starksia galapagensis*	(E)
Ophidiid	*Caecogilbia galapagoensis*	
De Roy's ophidiid	*Caecogilbia deroyi*	
Tagus goby	*Chriolepis tagus*	(E)
Blackeye goby	*Coryphopterus urospilus*	
Goby species	*Eleotrica cableae*	(E)
Galápagos blue-banded goby	*Lythrypnus gilberti*	(E)
Goby species	*Lythryphus rizophora*	

Banded cleaner goby	*Elacatinus nesiotes*
?	*Gobisoma* species

8/ Groupers, seabasses, grunts, mojarras, snappers, seachubs:

Flag cabrilla	*Epinephelus labriformis*	
Spotted cabrilla grouper	*Epinephelus analogus*	
Panama graysby	*Epinephelus panamensis*	
Mutton hamlet	*Epinephelus afer*	
Leather bass	*Epinephelus dermatolepis*	
Misty grouper, mero	*Epinephelus mystacinus*	(E)
Rainbow basslet	*Liopropoma fasciatum*	
Bacalao, yellow grouper	*Mycteroperca olfax*	
Camotillo, white spotted seabass	*Paralabrax albomaculatus*	(E)
Barred serrano	*Serranus fasciatus*	
Creolefish	*Paranthias colonus*	
Gray threadfin seabass, plumero	*Cratinus agassizi*	
Galápagos grunt	*Orthopristis forbesi*	
Grey grunt, Golden-eye grunt	*Haemulon scudderi*	
Graybar grunt	*Haemulon sexfasciatum*	
Burrito grunt, yellowtail grunt	*Anisotremus interruptus*	
Peruvian grunt	*Anisotremus scapularis*	
Black-striped salema	*Xenocys jessiae*	
White salema	*Xenichthys agassizi*	
Pacific flagfin mojarra	*Eucinostomus californiensis*	
Spotfin mojarra	*Eucinostomus argenteus*	
Yellowfin mojarra	*Gerres cinereus*	
Stripe-tail aholehole	*Kuhila taeniura*	
Machete	*Elops affinis*	
Blue and gold snapper	*Lutjanus viridis*	
Yellowtail snapper	*Lutjanus argiventris*	
Mullet snapper	*Lutjanus aratus*	
Pacific dog snapper	*Lutjanus novemfasciatus*	
Barred pargo	*Hoplopagrus guentheri*	
Jordan's snapper	*Lutjanus jordani*	
Dusky chub	*Girella fremenvillei*	
Cortez sea chub	*Kyphosus elegans*	
Blue bronze chub	*Kyphosus analogus*	
Rainbow chub	*Sector ocyurus*	
Shiner perch	*Cymatogaster aggregata*	

9/ Squirrelfishes, bigeyes, cardinalfishes:

Crimson soldierfish	*Myripristis leiognathos*	
Big eyed soldierfish	*Myripristis murdjan*	
Whitetip soldierfish	*Myripristis* species	(E)

Sun squirrelfish	*Sargocentron suborbitalis*	
Glasseye	*Priacanthus cruentatus*	
Popeye catalufa	*Pseudopriacanthus serrula*	
Tail spot cardinalfish	*Apogon dovii*	
Pacific cardinalfish	*Apogon pacificus*	
Blacktip cardinalfish	*Apogon atradorsatus*	(E)
Percelle	*Cheilodipterus species*	

10/ Scorpionfishes, hawkfishes:

Spotted scorpionfish	*Scorpaena plumieri mystes*	
Rainbow scorpionfish	*Scorpaenodes xyris*	
Scorpionfish	*Scorpaena histrio*	
Red scorpionfish	*Pontinus species*	
Hieroglyphic hawkfish	*Cirrhitus rivulatus*	
Coral hawkfish	*Cirrhitichthys oxycephalus*	
Longnosed hawkfish	*Oxycirrhites typus*	

11/ Goatfishes, searobins, lizardfishes:

Mexican goatfish	*Mullodichthys dentatus*	
Galápagos searobin	*Prionotus miles*	(E)
White margin searobin	*Prionotus albirostris*	
Sauro lizardfish	*Synodus lacertinus*	
California lizardfish	*Synodus lucioceps*	
Spotted lizardfish	*Synodus scituliceps*	
Lizardfish	*Synodus jenkinsii*	
Marchena lizardfish	*Synodus marchenae*	(E)
Galápagos clingfish	*Arcos poecilophtalmus*	(E)

12/ Anchovies, herrings, remoras, silversides:

Anchovy	*Anchoa naso*	
Galápagos thread herring	*Opisthonema berlangai*	(E)
Peruvian Pacific sardine	*Sardinops sadax sadax*	
Remora, sharksucker	*Remora remora*	
Silverside	*Eurystole eriarcha*	
Silverside	*Nectarges nesiotes*	(E)

13/ Porgies, bonefishes, tilefishes, dolphins, sunfishes:

Pacific porgy	*Calamus brachysomus*	
Galápagos porgy	*Calamus taurinus*	
Galápagos seabrim	*Archosargus pourtalesi*	
Bonefish	*Albula vulpes*	
Ocean whitefish	*Caulolatilus princeps*	
Dolphinfish	*Coryphaena hippurus*	
Ocean sunfish	*Mola mola*	
Pacific spadefish	*Chaetodipterus zonatus*	

14/ **Jacks, pompanos:**

Gafftopsail pompano	*Trachinotus rhodopus*
Paloma pompano	*Trachinotus païtensis*
Steel pompano	*Trachinotus stilbe*
African pompano	*Alectis ciliaris*
Green jack	*Caranx caballus*
Pacific crevalle jack	*Caranx caninus*
Black jack	*Caranx lugubris*
Gold-spotted jack	*Carangodes orthogrammus*
Bigeye jack	*Caranx sexfasciatus*
Horse eye jack	*Caranx latus*
Blue fin jack	*Caranx melampygus*
Rainbow runner	*Elagatis bipinnulatus*
Mackerel jack	*Decapterus pinnulatus*
Bigeye scad, Chinchard	*Selar crumenophtalmus*
Pacific amberjack	*Seriola colburni*
= Almaco amberjack	*Seriola rivoliana*
Yellowtail	*Seriola lalandei*
Pilot fish	*Naucrates ductor*

15/ **Barracudas, mackerels, tunas, marlins:**

Pelican barracuda	*Sphyraena idiastes*
Wahoo	*Acanthocybium solanderi*
Sierra mackerel	*Scomberomorus sierra*
Pacific bonito	*Sarda chilensis*
Skipjack tuna	*Euthynnus pelamis*
Yellowfin tuna	*Thunnus albacares*
Chub mackerel	*Scomber japonicus*
Striped marlin	*Makaira mitsukurii*
Black marlin	*Makaira marlina*

16/ **Croakers, drums, mullets, snooks:**

Gungo drum, rock croaker	*Pareques viola*
Yelloweye croaker	*Odontoscion xanthops*
Bronze croaker	*Odontoscion eurymesops*
Galápagos croaker	*Umbrina galapagorum*
Striped mullet	*Mugil cephalus*
Yellowtail mullet, lisa	*Mugil cephalus rammelsbergii*
Orange-eyed mullet	*Xenomugil thoburni*
Galápagos mullet	*Mugil galapagensis*
Snook	*Centropomus nigrescens*

17/ **Batfishes, frogfishes:**

Galápagos redlips batfish	*Ogcocephalus darwinii*

160

Sanguine frogfish   *Antennarius sanguineus*
Bandtail frogfish   *Antennarius strigatus*
18/ **Flounders, soles, tonguefishes:**
Pacific sanddab   *Citharichthys sordidus*
Speckled sanddab   *Citharichthys stigmaeus*
Blue-eyed flounder   *Bothus mancus*
Striped sole   *Achirus fonsecensis*
Galápagos Sole   *Asergodes herrei*
Rainbow tonguefish   *Symphurus atramentatus*
19/ **Morays, snake eels, conger eels:**
Hardtail moray   *Anarchias galapagensis*
Black-spot moray   *Muraena clepsydra*
Panamic green moray   *Muraena castaneus*
Magnificent moray   *Muraena argus*
Lentil moray   *Muraena lentiginosa*
Zebra moray   *Echidna zebra*
Night moray   *Echidna nocturna*
Yellowmargin moray   *Gymnothorax flavimarginatus*
Whitish speckled moray   *Gymnothorax pictus*
Black moray   *Gymnothorax buroensis*
Masked moray   *Gymnothorax panamensis*
Fine-spotted moray   *Gymnothorax dovii*
?   *Gymnothorax funebris*
Whitemouth moray   *Gymnothorax meleagris*
Slenderjaw moray   *Enchelycore octaviana*
Mosac moray   *Enchelycore lichenosa*
Peppered moray   *Uropterygius polysticus*
Rusty moray   *Uropterygius necturus*
?   *Uropterygius species*
Burrowing Galápagossnake eel   *Callechelys galapagensis*   (E)
Snake eel   *Paraletharchus opercularis*   (E)
Snake eel   *Caecula equatorialis*   (E)
Tiger snake eel   *Myrichthys tigrinus (M.maculosus)*
Pacific snake eel   *Ophichthus triserialis*
Galápagos cusk eel   *Ophidion species*
Panama conger eel   *Anosoma gilberti*
Galápagos garden eel   *Tanioconger klausewitzi*
20/ **Stingrays, golden rays, eagle rays, mantas:**
Whiptail stingray   *Dasyatis brevis*
Longtail stingray   *Dasyatis longus*
Round stingray   *Urotrygon species*
Marbled ray   *Taeniura meyeri*
Pacific cownose ray   *Rhinoptera steindachneri*

Northern phalarope in winter plumage, Rabida 1993

Espanola mockingbird, Gardner Bay 1984

Galapagos dove, Sullivan Bay 1990

Vermillion flycatcher (male), Los Gemelos, Santa Cruz 1993

Vermillion flycatcher (female), Santa Cruz 1993

Large-billed flycatcher, Floreana 1990

Yellow warbler, James Bay 1990

Smooth-billed anis, Santa Cruz 1992

Galapagos hawk feeding on a marine iguana, Fernandina 1992

Galapagos hawk (young), Alcedo 1991

Hawk and mockingbird, Espumilla, Santiago 1990

Short-eared owl, Santa Cruz 1986

Barn owl, Santa Cruz 1982

Small-billed ground finch 1989

Large-billed ground finch, Darwin Station 1988

Cactus finch (male), Santa Cruz 1991

Large cactus finch, Espanola 1991

168

Small-billed tree finch, Gemelos 1988

Small-billed tree finch (young), Gemelos 1993

169

Sealions colony, Gardner Bay, Espanola 1992

Female sea lions, Cristobal 1989

Sea lion pups, Espanola 1993

Sea lion (male), Gardner Bay, Espanola 1992

Fur sea lion, James Bay, Santiago 1990

Fur sea lion, Santiago 1985

Slipper lobster, Tagus Cove, Isabela 1992

Red spiny lobster and slipper lobsters, Sombrero Chino 1986

Blue lobster, Elizabeth Bay, Isabela 1986

173

Sea cucumber or pepino, Isostichopus fuscus, *Santa Fé 1991*

Spotted eagle ray, Bartolomé 1992

Golden cownose rays, Tortuga Negra 1984

Marine turtles mating, Tortuga Negra 1990

Stingrays, Floreana 1990

False killer whales surfacing, Darwin 1993

Common dolphin, Banks Bay, Isabela 1992

Spotted eagle ray	*Aetobatus narinari*
Pacific manta	*Manta hamiltoni*

21/ Sharks:

Whitetip reef shark	*Triaenodon obesus*
Galápagos requiem shark	*Carcharhinus galapagensis*
Blacktip shark	*Carcharhinus limbatus*
Silvertip shark	*Carcharhinus albimarginatus*
Grey reef shark	*Carcharhinus amblyrhynchos*
Silky shark	*Carcharhinus falciformis*
Tiger shark	*Galeocerdo cuvieri*
Smooth hammerhead	*Sphyrna zygaena*
Scalloped hammerhead	*Sphyrna lewini*
Spotted houndshark	*Triakis maculata*
Galápagos hornshark	*Heterodontus quoyi*
Whale shark	*Rhincodon typus*
Shortfin mako	*Isurus oxyrinchus*
Great white shark	*Carcharodon carcharias*

22/ Baleen whales: rorquals:

Sei whale	*Balaenoptera borealis*
Bryde's whale	*Balaenoptera edeni*
Minke whale	*Balaenoptera acutorostrata*
Blue whale	*Balaenoptera musculus*
Humpback whale	*Megaptera novaeangliae*

23/ Toothed whales, ocean dolphins:

Sperm whale, cachalot	*Physeter catodon*
Pygmy sperm whale	*Kogia breviceps*
Dwarf sperm whale	*Kogia simus*
Cuvier's beaked whale	*Ziphius cavirostris*
Beaked whales species	*Mesoplodon species*
Melon-headed whale	*Peponocephala electra*
Pygmy killer whale	*Feresa attenuata*
Killer whale, orca	*Orcinus orca*
False killer whale	*Pseudorca crassidens*
Short-finned pilot whale	*Globicephala macrorhynchus*
Fraser's dolphin	*Lagenodelphis hosei*
Risso's dolphin, grey grampus	*Grampus griseus*
Common dolphin, white bellied	*Delphinus delphis*
Bottle nosed dolphin	*Tursiops truncatus*
Spotted dolphin	*Stenella attenuata*
Spinner dolphin	*Stenella longirostris*
Striped dolphin	*Stenella coeruleoalba*

(List of Cetaceans after David Day, *Noticias de Galápagos*, April 1994)

Total = 292 species

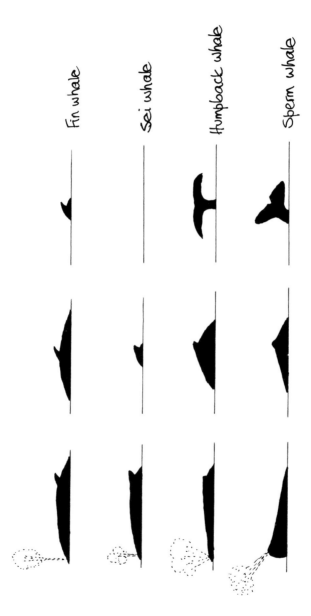

Diving sequence of a few whales
[after Gordon C. Pike, 1956].

Fin whale

Sei whale

Humpback whale

Sperm whale

True Dolphins

Risso's dolphin (4,5m)

Bottlenose dolphin (4m)

Common dolphin (2,6m)

Spotted dolphin (2m)

Spinner dolphin (2m)

Striped dolphin (2,7m)

Piroco 89

Sharks (1)

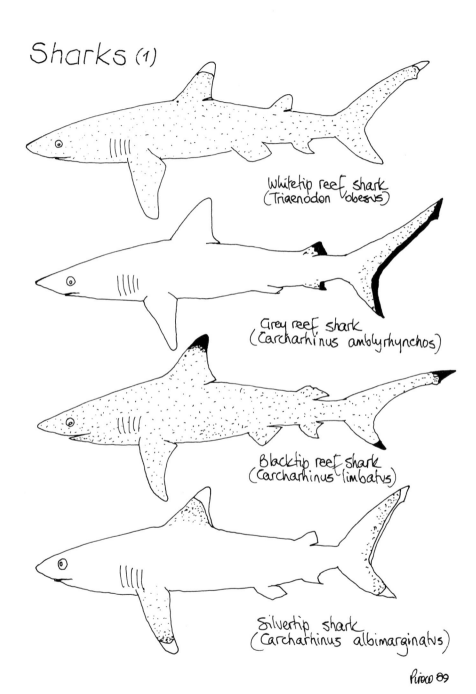

Whitetip reef shark
(Triaenodon obesus)

Grey reef shark
(Carcharhinus amblyrhynchos)

Blacktip reef shark
(Carcharhinus limbatus)

Silvertip shark
(Carcharhinus albimarginatus)

Piroco 89

Sharks (2)

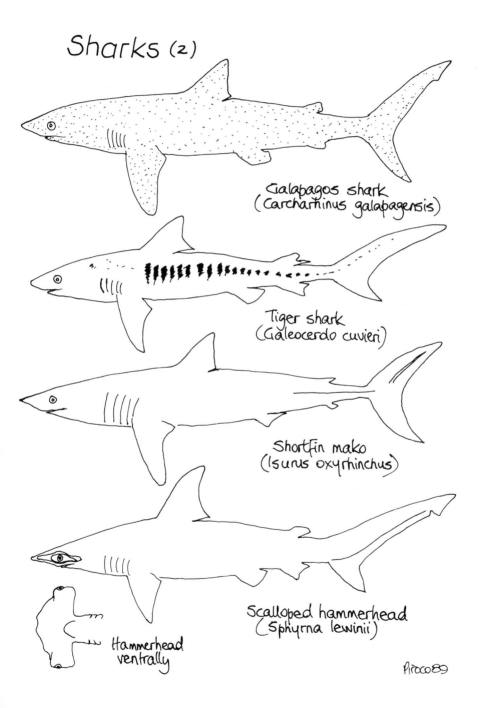

Galapagos shark
(Carcharhinus galapagensis)

Tiger shark
(Galeocerdo cuvieri)

Shortfin mako
(Isurus oxyrhinchus)

Scalloped hammerhead
(Sphyrna lewinii)

Hammerhead
ventrally

Piroco89

Sharks (3)

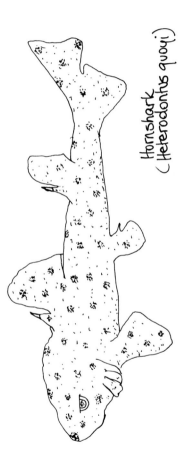

Hornshark
(Heterodontus quoyi)

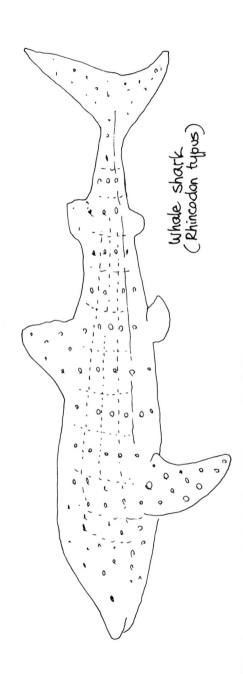

Whale shark
(Rhincodon typus)

OTHER MARINE ANIMALS

PHYLUM CNIDARIA

1/ Class Anthozoa: anemones, corals, gorgonians:

Pacific tube anemone	Pachycerianthus fimbriatus
Anemone	Bunodactis mexicana
Anemone	Bunodosoma species
Leopard spotted anemone	Antiparactis species
Anemone	Anthopleura species
Zoanthid	Palythoa species
Zoanthid	Zoanthus species
Golden sea fan	Muricea species
Orange cup coral	Tubastrea coccinea
Tagus cup coral	Tubastrea tagusensis
Pink cup coral	Tubastrea species
Yellow polyp black coral	Antipathes galapagensis
Panama black coral	Antipathes panamensis
	Cycloseris elegans
Pebble coral	Cycloseris mexicana
	Gardineroseris planulata
	Psammocora stellata
	Psammocora brighami
	Pocillopora damicornis
	Pocillopora elegans
Corals	Pocillopora capitata
	Agaricella species
	Porites lobata
	Pavona clavus
	Pavona gigantea
	Pavona varians

PHYLUM ANNELIDA

2/ Class Polychaeta: segmented worms:

Common fireworm	Eurythoe complanata
Ornate fireworm	Chloeia viridis

PHYLUM MOLLUSCA

3/ Class Polyplacophora: chitons

Rippled chiton	Chiton sulcatus	(E)
Chiton	Chiton goodallii	(E)

4/ Class Gastropoda: snails, sea slugs, sea hares, nudibranchs:

Panamic horse conch	Pleuroploca princeps
Galápagos black sea slug	Onchidella steindachneri (E)
Blue-striped sea slug	Tambja mullineri
Starry night nudibranch	Hypselodoris lapizlazuli
Carnivorous nudibranch	?
Sea hare	Dolabrifera dolabrifera
Purple sea hare	Aplysia sp

PHYLUM ARTHROPODA

5/ Class Crustacea: crabs, shrimps, lobsters:

Galápagos pebblestone crab	Mithrax sp
Giant hermit crab	Petrochirus californiensis
Hairy hermit crab	Aniculus elegans
Bar-eyed hermit crab	Dardanus fucosus
Swimming crab	Cronius ruber
Red crab	Cancer sp
Sally lightfoot crab	Grapsus grapsus
Princely fiddler crab	Uca princeps
Panamic arrowhead crab	Stenorhynchus debilis
Shamed face box crab	Calappa convexa
Ghost crab	Ocypode sp
Sea star shrimp	Periclimenes soror
Banded coral shrimp	Stenopus hispidus
Giant khaki shrimp	Penaeus californiensis
Yellowsnout red shrimp	Rhynchocinetes sp
Red spiny lobster	Panulirus penicillatus
Blue lobster	Panulirus gracilis
Slipper lobster	Scyllarides astori

PHYLUM ECHINODERMATA

6/ Class Asteroidea: seastars:

Armored sand star	Astropecten armatus
Panamic cushion star	Pentaceraster cummingi
(or Gulf star)	Oreaster occidentalis
Chocolate chipstar	Nidorellia armata
Pyramid sea star	Pharia pyramidata
Tan sea star	Phataria unifascialis
Troschel's sea star	Evasterias troschelii
Pacific comet star	Linckia columbiae
Sunstar	Heliaster multiradiata
Bradley sea star	Mithrodia bradleyi

7/ Class Ophiuroidea: brittle stars:

Alexander's spiny brittle star	Ophiocma alexandri
Multicolored brittle star	Ophioderma variegatum

8/ Class Echinoidea: sea urchins:

Pencil sea urchin	Eucidaris thouarsii
Crowned sea urchin	Centrostephanus coronatus
Galápagos green sea urchin	Lytechinus semituberculatus (E)
Flower sea urchin	Toxopneustes roseus
Giant sand dollar	Clypeaster europacificus
Heart urchin, sea porcupine	Lovenia cordiformis
Grooved heart urchin	Agassizia scobiculata

9/ Class Holothuroidea: sea cucumbers:

Brown spotted sea cucumber	Holothuria impatiens
Sulfur sea cucumber	Holothuria lubrica
Giant sea cucumber	Isostichopus fuscus

Reptiles

Sea snake	Pelamis platurus
Marine iguana	Amblyrhynchus cristatus
Pacific green sea turtle	Chelonia mydas agassizi

Other Mammals

Sea lion	Zalophus californianus
Fur sea lion	Arctocephalus galapagoensis

Total: 80 species

COMMERCIAL FISHING

Commercial fishing includes: artisanal fishing, industrial fishing and sport fishing.

Of the 30 species which are fished in the Galápagos, 90 per cent belong to the family Serranidae (groupers and seabasses). In the 1950s, mainly *bacalao* (yellow grouper), *lisa* (yellowtail mullet) and lobster were caught. Between the 1930s and 1950s, bacalao were caught on a line (*pinchagua*), then cut in half, salted, dried on the rocks, and exported to the mainland. In the 1980s, bacalao accounted for 50 per cent of industrial fishing, followed by *camotillo* and *mero* (two other groupers). Tuna fishing lagged far behind.

In 1986, annual fishing brought in 150 to 250 tons. Bacalao fishing occurs six months out of the year between October and March, mainly around Isabela Island (until the Marine Reserve was created).

The *norteno* fishing, during the first three months of the year, occurs in the northern islands of Marchena, Darwin and Wolf. The last three months of the year are the season for *camotillo* fishing.

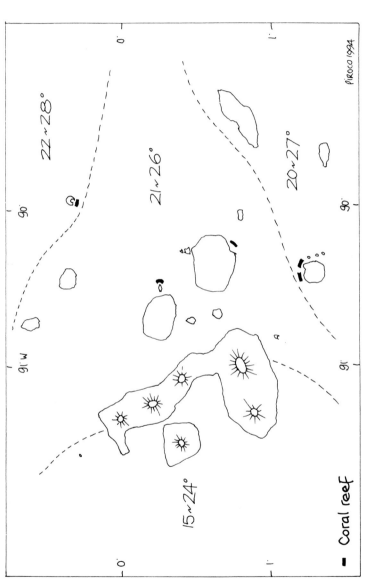

Sea Temperature

22~28°

21~26°

20~27°

15~24°

90

90

90

16'W

■ — Coral reef

PIROCO 1994

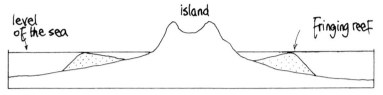

level
of the sea

island

Fringing reef

1- Volcanic island. Construction of a coral reef around it.

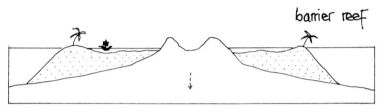

barrier reef

2- The island sinks and is eroded. The reef builds up
vertically. e.g. Bora Bora (Society islands).

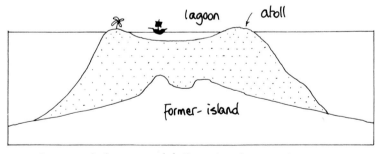

lagoon   atoll

Former- island

3- The island disappears totally, with the reef building up.
The circular reef leaves an atoll.

Evolution of a coral reef
after Darwin

Piraco 1994

List of the fishes exploited by the fishing industry in the Galápagos

Family		Scientific name	Local name	English
Serranidae	(E)	*Mycteroperca olfax*	Bacalao	Yellow grouper
	(E)	*Paralabrax albomaculatus*	Camotillo	White-spotted rock grouper
	(E)	*Epinephelus mystacinus*	Mero	Misty grouper
	(E)	*Epinephelus sp*	Norteno	Norteno
		Epinephelus labriformis	Cabrilla	Flag cabrilla
		Epinephelus dermatolepis	Cagaleche	Leather bass
		Cratinus agassizi	Plumero, gallo	Threadfin seabass
Labridae		*Semicossyphus darwinii*	Vieja	Sheephead
Lutjanidae		*Lutjanus novemfasciatus*	Pargo	Pacific dog snapper
		Lutjanus argiventris	Pargo	Yellowtail snapper
Carangidae		*Seriola rivoliana*	Palometa	Pacific amberjack
Scorpaenidae		*Scorpaena sp*	Brujo	Scorpionfish
Scombridae		*Euthynnus lineatus*	Atun negro	Skipjack tuna
		Sarda chilensis	Atun blanco	Pacific bonito
		Scomberomorus sierra	Sierra	Sierra mackerel
		Acanthocybium solanderi	Guajo	Wahoo

Fishes for bait

Family		Scientific name	Local name	English
Clupeidae		*Opisthonema berlangai*	Sardina	Thread herring
Engraulidae		*Anchoa nasus*	Plástico	Anchovy
Haemulidae		*Xenocys jessiae*	Ojon	Black-striped salema
Mugilidae	(E)	*Mugil galapagensis*	Lisa	Yellowtail mullet

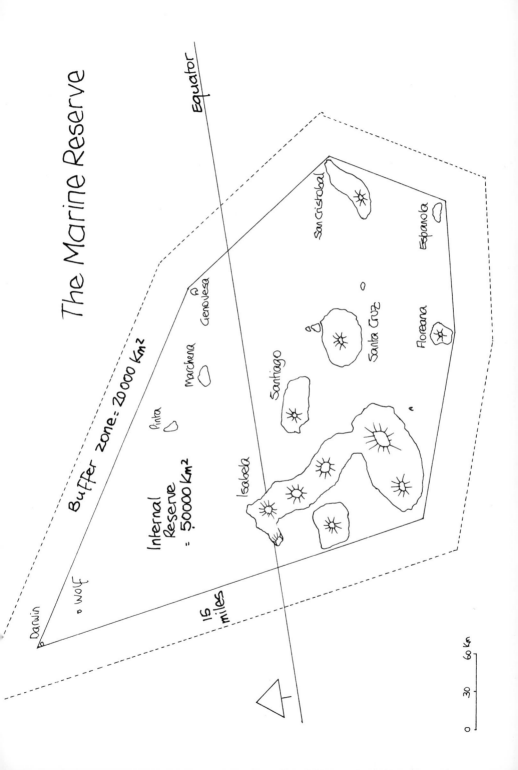

The Marine Reserve

Equator

Buffer zone: 20000 Km²

Darwin

o Wolf

Pinta

Marchena

Genovesa

Internal Reserve = 50000 Km²

Isabela

Santiago

Santa Cruz

San Cristobal

Española

Floreana

15 miles

0   30   60 Km

Lobster and Black Coral

Three species of lobster are present in the Galápagos, which are commercially exploited:

Common name	Scientific name	Local name
Red lobster	*Panulirus penicillatus*	Langosta roja
Blue lobster	*Panulirus gracilis*	Langosta azul
Slipper lobster	*Scyllarides astori*	Langostino

The red lobster, found in the central and northern islands, and northeast of Isabela Island, once made up 60 per cent of the catch. The blue lobster, once 40 per cent of the catch, is larger, and is distributed mostly on the west coast of Isabela (Urvina and Elizabeth Bay) and around the southern coast, as far as Cartago Bay to the east of Isabela Island.

The minimum legal size is 25 centimetres from head to tail. In 1960, the production was 180 tons; in 1965, 65 tons, and in 1983, 94 tons (of which 33 tons consisted of tails). To allow annual reproduction and the survival of the species, a ban on lobster fishing was enforced each year January-February and June—July. Nevertheless, the abusive catch of recent years has brought a dramatic reduction of the resource and, as a result, the Ecuadorian government imposed a total ban for seven years—from January 1, 1993, until the year 2000—in order to restock the lobster species.

Nevertheless, after strikes and protests led by fishermen in 1993-94, the government reopened lobster fishing for three months per year, from July 15 to October15.

Another problem for the Park is the exploitation of the black coral, Antipathes panamensis, which is not endemic to the Galápagos, unlike Antipathes galapagensis which is endemic.

Black coral is sought by the craftsmen of Puerta Ayora (Santa Cruz) and Puerto Baquerizo Moreno (San Cristóbal). The coral is carved and polished to make jewellery and other fancy gifts which are then sold in shops as Galápagos souvenirs. At present the Galápagos National Park does not have the power to ban sales or stop this exploitation.

The Marine Reserve

On May 13, 1986, the Ecuadorian government, by presidential decree of Leon Febrès Cordero, established the Reserve of the Galápagos Marine Resources. The 50,000 square kilometres of ocean surface comprises the internal waters of the archipelago. A strip of 15 nautical miles (28 kilometres), extending from the outlying points of the islands, was added. This 'buffer zone' represents another 20,000 square kilometres, bringing the total surface of the Marine Reserve to 70,000 square kilometres.

A committee was created to supervise and control the reserve. Its members are representative of the following departments: agriculture, foreign affairs, defense, industry and commercial fisheries, energy and mining, planning and the INGALA (Instituto Nacional Galápagos).

This biological reserve aims to protect and preserve a number of ecological aspects of the islands, as well as the interaction of the National Park with the Marine Reserve. Industrial fishing is not allowed, but local or artisanal fishing go on as before (see drawing of the Marine Reserve, page 189).

ILLEGAL FISHING AND THE 'PEPINOS' AFFAIR

As expected, abuses were not long in surfacing. Striking fishermen came to knock at the government's door to show their anger in 1993. At issue are illegal shark fishing and shark finning (which has caused a furor for some years now), as well as pepino (sea cucumber) fishing. All are pirate fisheries, conducted by sophisticated Japanese fishing boats. The 'pepino war' has gained considerable press attention since 1992.

The shark fishing, stimulated by the Japanese fishing industry, began to cause a stir as far back as 1983. In violation of Ecuadorian law, Japanese boats were penetrating Galápagos waters in the northern islands and around Isabela Island. They were seen on a number of occasions, then escorted away, after paying dubious fines'. The Japanese then conceived the following stratagem: They used Ecuadorian boats from Manta (Ecuador), which could be sent into Galápagos waters to fish, while the Japanese mother-ship would safely wait for the catch in international waters. The Japanese ship Choki Maru was nevertheless hailed in 1991, with a shipment of 5,000 shark fins, six kilometres from Cartago Bay, on the east coast of Isabela Island. In 1992, a patrol boat of the Ecuadorian navy captured the Donai, a fishing boat from Manta, near Pinta Island, with a load of 50 hammerhead sharks on board.

The scandal of the sea cucumbers or pepinos blew up in 1992, when pirate camps were discovered on the basaltic coast of Fernandina Island. Local fishermen had settled with their families and were collecting 130,000 to 150,000 pepinos per day. These sea cucumbers, of the species *Isostichopus fuscus,* are marine invertebrates of commercial value in eastern Asian countries. The larvae are an important part of the plankton, which is food for a great number of fish. The sea cucumbers live on rocky bottoms, at a depth of two to 20 metres, and are important for the purification of sea water. The exploitation of the pepinos is a worldwide business which lays waste to an area of the globe for two to four years; the fishermen plunder the resources, then start somewhere else. It started on the coast of Ecuador in 1988, before it spread out to the Galápagos (see photo, page 174).

PART THREE

DESCRIPTION OF THE ISLANDS

"Marine iguanas"

DESCRIPTION OF THE ISLANDS

Baltra - North Seymour
Santa Cruz
South Plaza
Santa Fé   CENTRAL ISLANDS
Daphné
Rábida
Pinzon

Floreana
Española   SOUTHERN ISLANDS
San Cristobal

Genovesa
Marchena
Pinta   NORTHERN ISLANDS
Wolf
Darwin

Santiago
Bartolomé
Sombrero
Chino   WESTERN ISLANDS
Isabela
Fernandina

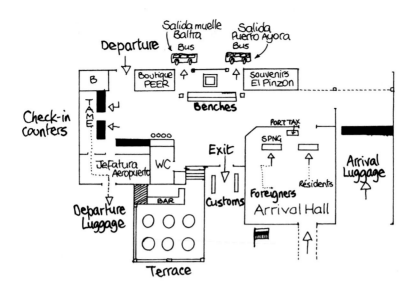

Baltra airport

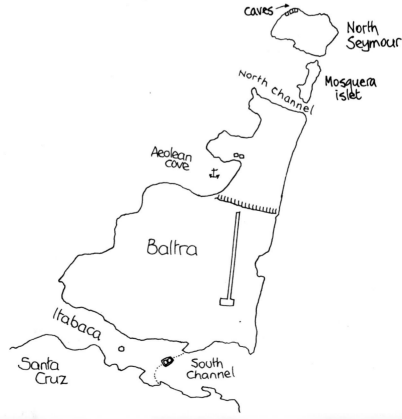

PIROCO 199

CHAPTER ONE

CENTRAL ISLANDS

BALTRA

The plane leaves Quito at 9:30 am and stops over at Guayaquil. It takes off again at around 11 am. After an hour and a quarter of cloudless flight, you'll be in sight of San Cristobal Island, which will appear on the port side, bedecked with a layer of cotton-shaped clouds. The black-indented shoreline is fringed with waves of white foam. A few minutes later, you may view the Gordon Rocks, then the Plaza Islands in the distant haze. Finally, you will fly over the luminous sandbar of Mosquera Island. The plane will tilt to port before landing on the island of Baltra. The B-747 of TAME airlines, inaugurated on October 22, 1980, stops in the heart of the arid zone, a land covered with cacti.

At Baltra Island, the Galápagos National Park customs will ask you to pay an entry fee of US$80 (since 1993), and you will be given a leaflet of visitor's rules. You are also expected to pay US$11 for port fees.

A small island north of Santa Cruz, Baltra is a basaltic plateau—which belongs geologically to Santa Cruz—faulted in an east-west direction. In the distant past, the island was once connected to Santa Cruz and North Seymour. Some fossiliferous tuff beds, between lava flows, are the proof of an ancient tectonic uplift. Sheer cliffs rise to the north, to the east and south. The entire island leans towards the west.

On the west coast, Aeolean Cove offers smooth sand beaches. This port is used by the Ecuadorian navy and is also the site of an air force base. Departures and arrivals of numerous tourist boats are made from there. A few cargo ships which visit the archipelago also call in. Baltra Airport was built by the Americans during World War II. The army base was intended to defend the Panama Canal against Japanese air raids, but the attack never came. Rumour has it that the Americans were partly responsible for the eradication of land iguanas on the island, aided by the presence of feral goats, which ate all the vegetation edible to iguanas. The Ecuadorian air force received the base at the end of the war; today it's a civil and military airport, as well as a naval base.

After a 40-year absence, land iguanas were reintroduced to Baltra by the Galápagos National Park. On June 19, 1991, 35 iguanas (five years old) from the breeding centre in Santa Cruz were freed on the island. The following year, in April 1992, 12 land iguanas (8 to 10 years old) were released. The first year of the project showed a survival rate of at least 40 per cent.

Baltra is connected to the island of Santa Cruz by a ferry that crosses daily the Itabaca Channel. From the landing site it is 40 kilometres to the town of Puerto Ayora, or one and a half hours by the minibus of CITTEG, the local transport company (see map of Baltra, page 194).

NORTH SEYMOUR

North of Baltra, Seymour is a small flat island with a land surface of two square kilometres, very similar to Baltra and typical of the arid zone. Palo santos are endemic to the island. Opuntia, the local prickly pear cactus, is the food of the land iguanas.
A trail, about two kilometres long, makes a loop to the southwest, inland and along the rocky coast, crossing the colony of blue-footed boobies then the colony of magnificent frigates. The nesting area of the frigatebirds mixes with that of the boobies. Two species of frigates share the same habitat in harmony. Their nests of twigs are made on the palo santos, as well as on the salt bushes bordering the beach. A few marine iguanas walk across the white coral sand, leaving tracks of their tail and claws. Sea lions bask on the black lava rocks, and the surf crashes on the rocky shore of the west coast at sunset. In the background, the eroded tuff cones of Daphné Mayor and Daphné Minor rise above the ocean surface.
   At Seymour, the dry landing on rocks is sometimes difficult, depending on the tide and the season. Rocks may be slippery, and shoes should be worn. A short distance away, Mosquera Islet is an ideal place for a walk when the sun goes down. White sands host a colony of sea lions. Beware of the territorial males, which are known to be aggressive, even in the water. A cautious swim is highly recommended (see map, page 197).

SANTA CRUZ

land surface: 986 square km
elevation: 864 m
main town: Puerto Ayora

The most populous of the islands, Santa Cruz possesses a radio which emits at 1410 KHz (since 1974). Of the five inhabited islands of the Galápagos, Santa Cruz and particularly Puerto Ayora, the touristic capital, have for the last 15 years had the highest immigration rate in the archipelago. The population of the Galápagos is estimated at about 20,000 people—four times the number in 1980.
   All the vegetation zones are represented on Santa Cruz, stretching from the littoral zone up to the fern zone at the top of Mount Crocker. The windward side is more humid and diversified than the leeward side, which is very dry. This is especially understandable when one considers that the dominant winds are the southeast tradewinds, and that the precipitation of garua falls on that side of the island.

North Seymour

Frigates

Palo santos and Opuntia

Frigates

marine iguanas

Palos santos

Blue Footed boobies

S.T. gulls

Sea lions

Basalt cliff

Surf and sealions

0   100 m

Mosquera

Seymour

sea lions

10 m

beach

13 m

Sea lions

rocks

Baltra

Santa Cruz

Baltra

Tortuga negra

Venezia   las Bachas

Conway Bay

Caleta Tiburon

Eden

Whale Bay

Cerro Iguana   Cerro Ventana

Los Gemelos

Scalesia Forest

Cerro Colorado

Gordon rocks

Plaza islands

Cerro Ballena

Salasaca

Cerro Crocker
864m
Media Luna

Camote

Cascajo

Pta. Roca Fuerte

Reserve SPNG

Santa Rosa

Mutiny

rancho Mariposa

Tunnels

Bellavista

Caseta

Tunnel

Puerto Ayora
Darwin Station

Puerto Nuñez

Punta Nuñez

Punta Tamayo

Tortuga Bay

Pta. Estrada

isla Caamaño

0 2 4 6 Km

Pizoco 1994

Puerto Ayora ~ Santa Cruz

Legend:

1. Main jetty
2. Peninsular supermarket
3. Correo - Post Office
4. Catholic church
5. CITTEG - Minibus to Baltra
6. Hospital
7. INGALA
8. IMETEL
9. School
10. Hotel Palmeras
11. "Black Lady" boutique
12. Boutique PEZ + minimarket "Ajay"
13. Five Fingers - Bar, Restaurant, disco
14. "Rincon del Alma" restaurant
15. Capitania del Puerto
16. Hotel Salinas
17. Hotel Vilmita
18. "mas y mas" restaurant
19. Municipio
20. Hotel Lobo de Mar
21. Police / Immigration
22. TAME
23. "La Garrapata" restaurant
24. "La Panga" disco + "El Reciclado" boutique
25. D'Todo
26. Hotel Sol y Mar
27. Banco del Pacifico
28. Drugstore
29. Movie hall
30. "4 Linternas" restaurant
31. Galápagos Suboaqua
32. Quasar Nautica
33. Pension Gloria
34. New Residencial Angermeyer
35. Gimnasio Formas
36. BAMBU artesanias
37. Mistral - Galeria Johanna
38. Tea shirt shop
39. "Iguanas-bananas" shop
40. Hotel Galápagos
41. Scuba Iguana
42. Galápagos Nat. Park
43. Kiosco Parque Nacional
44. M/N Iguana wreck (1968)
45. ETICA
46. Hotel Delfin
47. Red Mangrove Inn

Baltra - 42 Km.

to Tortuga Bay

Laguna Las Ninfas

Pelican Bay

Academy Bay

Cliff + Opuntia cacti

El Otro lado

Cimetière

Práco 1994

The Galapagos National Park and Darwin Station

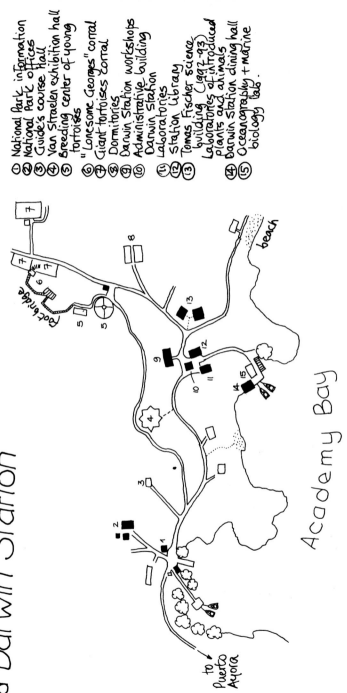

PIRACO 1995

① National Park information
② National Park offices
③ Guide's course hall
④ Van Straelen exhibition hall
⑤ Breeding center of young tortoises
⑥ "Lonesome George's" corral
⑦ Giant tortoises Corral
⑧ Dormitories
⑨ Darwin Station workshops
⑩ Administrative building
⑪ Darwin Station Laboratories
⑫ Station Library
⑬ Tomas Fischer science building (1992-93)
    Laboratories of introduced plants and animals
⑭ Darwin Station dining hall
⑮ Oceanography + marine biology lab.

Academy Bay

beach

Footbridge

to Puerto Ayora

Geologically, Santa Cruz is well eroded, and the oldest formations are found to the northeast. Facing the Plazas Islands is Cerro Colorado (the Red Rock), a tectonically uplifted hill in which basaltic lava and fossiliferous tuff are layered with volcanic tuffs of Miocene geological times. The human history started in the 20th century, when European and American settlers arrived between the two world wars. The soil being fertile, the villages of Bellavista and Santa Rosa were founded in the tropical humid zone of the highlands. A great number of exotic plants were introduced: sugarcane, coffee, bananas, oranges, lemon trees and avocado trees. Domestic animals were also introduced. Most of them turned feral, creating a serious and disastrous impact on the native species of the island. But this will be explained later.

A colony of land iguanas may be observed at Conway Bay, on the northwest coast. Facing the bay, on Eden Island, is a small colony of sea lions. Marine iguanas are well represented on the shores all around Santa Cruz, but a colony is established on Isla Coamaño (facing Puerto Ayora), as well as in Punta Nunez, on the southern coast. Eight species of finch are found on the island, and the Hawaiian petrel nests in the highlands. Almost all the species of birds found in the Galápagos have been observed on Santa Cruz.

Punta Ayora is the commercial and tourist centre of the archipelago. From here, cattle and coffee are exported to the mainland. The southwestern part of the port is inhabited by a small colony of European immigrants, who arrived in the 1920s and 30s (see Appendix 3, Population of the Galápagos).

From Puerto Ayora, it is possible to make day trips or tours around the islands by chartering a small boat (with cook, captain and guide) among five to eight people. The cost involved is about $35–50 per person per day. The cruise usually lasts up to one week, and the itinerary is decided by the passengers.

HOTELS (PRICES IN US$)

Hotel Galápagos (on the way to Darwin Station), luxury bungalows facing Academy bay, single: $72; double: $120.
Hotel Sol y mar (Pelican Bay), on the waterfront, single: $24, double: $108.
Hotel Fernandina: $12 to $15, clean rooms and a little garden.
New Angermeyer (exotic), used to be the Garden of Eden pension of Lucrecia Angermeyer before she sold it to a German (in 1993), who reconstructed the whole place. Rooms at $50.
Residencial Las Ninfas (near port).
Hotel Salinas, $3 to $5.
Pension Gloria, ideal for backpackers, $3 to $5. There is also an abandoned camping ground behind the cemetery on the way to the Darwin Station.

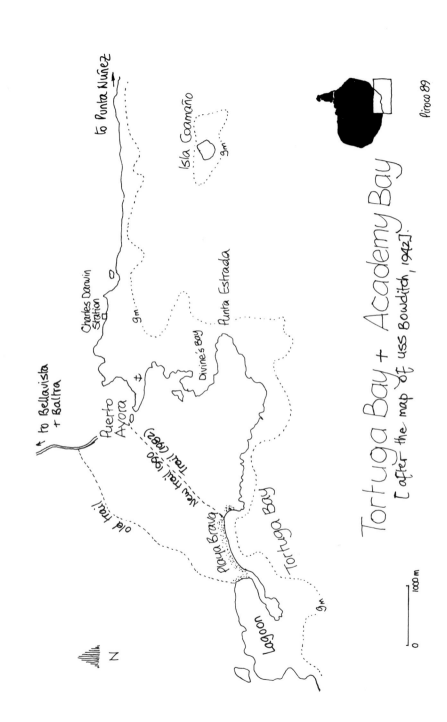

Tortuga Bay + Academy Bay
[after the map of USS Bowditch, 1942]

N

to Bellavista + Baltra

to Punta Núñez

Charles Darwin Station

Isla Caamaño

9m

Punta Estrada

Divine's Bay

Puerto Ayora

9m

New Trail (1980)

Old Trail

Playa Brava

Tortuga Bay

Lagoon

9m

1000 m

0

Piroca 89

RESTAURANTS

4 Linternas (Pelican Bay), run by an Italian woman called Sylvana. Good atmosphere.
La Trattoria de Pipo (Italian), Pelican Bay.
Five fingers, bar-restaurant with terrace and disco on the second floor, facing the Capitania del Puerto (naval base).
La Garrapata, near the disco-bar La Panga.
El Rincón del Alma, facing the naval base where there are more local restaurants and foodstalls.
Salvavidas Bar and Restaurant, on the harbour (since 1994).
Kathy's Kitchen, downtown, on the main place, road to Baltra.

OTHER

Banco del Pacifico (Pelican Bay), bank, near Hotel Sol y Mar.
Scuba Iguana, dive club operated at Hotel Galápagos by Matthias Espinosa and Jack Nelson, starting at US$78/2 dives.
Nautidiving, PADI dive school and club, run by Vicente and Polo Navarro, at the 'Red Mangrove Inn', near Hotel Galápagos, from US$75 to US$110/2 dives.
EMETEL, telephone office. Connections with the mainland since 1993, international calls available since 1994.
Port Captain (Capitania del Puerto), for visiting sailboats, the right to drop anchor is for 48 hours in Puerto Ayora (72 hours in San Cristobal). Port fees: the arrival tax (*arribo*) or departure tax (*salida*) are 2,400 sucres or slightly more than a dollar. Mooring fees (*Faros y boyas*): $3 per ton, mooring: $0.1/ton/day. The Galápagos National Park tax is not required, but if the crew plans to visit the islands of the National Park, that would be on a local boat only. For foreign vessels a longer anchoring time in port will only be allowed in case of damage to the boat, which has rendered it unsailable.

SIGHTSEEING

The Charles Darwin Research Station, open from 7 am to 5 pm, Monday to Friday, and Saturday 8 am to 12 pm.
Van Straelen Exhibition Hall (museum on Galápagos Natural History).
Breeding centre for young tortoises, with elevated walkways and tortoise corrals, including that of Lonesome George, the survivor of Pinta Island.
A few **sandy beaches** can be found beyond the Darwin Station, when you head towards the cliff of Punta Nunez. The dirt road leading to the Darwin Station is 1.5 kilometres long, bordered with red, black and white mangroves; giant cacti (Opuntia and Jasminocereus); spiny shrubs such as *Scutia pauciflora,* and other shrubs such as *Maytenus octogona.* The administrative building of the Galápagos National Park is on the way to the Darwin Station, at the first road crossing to the left (see maps of Puerto Ayora and of the Darwin Station, page 198–99).

EXCURSIONS FROM PUERTO AYORA

TORTUGA BAY (TURTLE BAY)
To reach this white sand beach, less than one hour away from Puerto Ayora, first take the road to Baltra, in town, then turn left about 150 metres after leaving the main square on the port. A volcanic gravel road climbs to the top of the *barranco* (canyon) along a stairway before changing to a decent trail. An easy graveled way, opened in 1982, replaces the old track on the lava rocks, crossing the arid zone of the palo santos and cacti (sport shoes are advised). Don't forget your hat, sun protection and drinking water, for the equatorial sun is fierce.

In Tortuga Bay, you may see nesting pelicans in the mangroves (warm season), and maybe flamingos in the lagoon. If you go for a swim, do not venture beyond the last wave, for the currents are dangerous at low tide, and sharks could be waiting. Return before sunset (6 pm). The excursion is worth it (see map, page 200).

LOS GEMELOS (THE TWINS)
On the road to Baltra, beyond the village of Santa Rosa, in the humid tropical zone of the scalesia (*Scalesia pedunculata*) forest. The Gemelos are two pit-craters over 30 metres deep located on either side of the road. They may be explosion craters, or they may have been created by the collapse of the roof of some magma chamber, following circumferencial fissures. A few trails wander around the craters. Many land birds may be seen, such as the vermillion flycatcher, the large bill flycatcher, the short-eared owl, the Galápagos dove, and a great number of Darwin's finches, including the carpenter finch, which uses a stick as a tool to help extract larvae from old stumps.

It is advisable to go to Los Gemelos in the early morning, around 8 am, with the minibus of CITTEG heading to Baltra. (There is no chance of finding a bus during the daytime; transport is by hire only.) The village of Santa Rosa is about two kilometres downhill.

THE TORTOISE RESERVE (CASETA AND EL CHATO)
In the humid zone, this is the ideal place to observe giant tortoises in the wild. From Santa Rosa, a trail—five kilometres long and sometimes very muddy—leads to Caseta and to El Chato. It takes two to three hours on foot. The vegetation is composed of high scalesia, guayabillo (*Psidium galapageium*) and pega pega (*Pisonia floribunda*) grasses. Darwin's finches are plentiful, as are flycatchers. There is a camping site at Caseta, and it is possible to hire horses at Santa Rosa (see map of Santa Cruz, page 197).

Alternatively, one may see tortoises in private farms, such as Poza Pamela or, even better, at Rancho Mariposa, run by Steve and Jenny Divine, who have a cozy little country

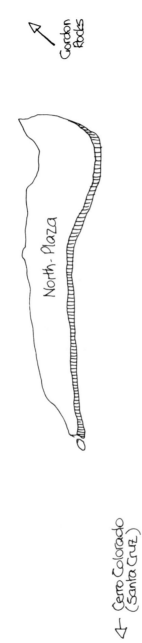

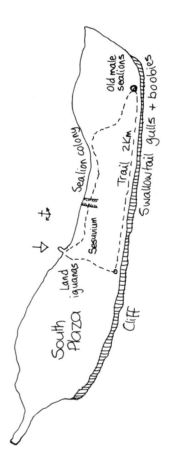

restaurant (expect to pay about US$10 for a meal) with great scenery, and a pond where tortoises come to drink freely. An entry fee is charged.

LOS TUNNELES (THE LAVA TUNNELS)

Lava tubes, a few hundred metres to a few kilometres long, are one of the curiosities of Santa Cruz. There is a small one, three kilometres away from Puerto Ayora on the left side of the road. With a diameter of about 10 metres, it is large enough for a subway train to go through. Another tunnel, two kilometres long, is found east of Bellavista on a private land. There is another in Salasaca, west of Santa Rosa, and a third on the land of Furio—an Italian man who has a ranch and a restaurant named Mutiny ($12 per meal)—facing the access road to Steve Divine, not far from Santa Rosa.

MEDIA LUNA AND MOUNT CROCKER

The trail which leads to the *zona alta* or highlands starts from Bellavista and crosses the agricultural zone (with coffee and avocado plantations) before it gets to the pampa of the miconias (see chapter on flora). It takes an hour to and hour and a half to see Media Luna, a half-moon volcanic cone covered with miconia bushes. In this garua-swept area, the trail is muddy and slippery so expect to get your feet wet. The garua may be so thick that nothing can be seen once the miconia zone is reached. Do not venture further or you may get lost. This walk is very good for observing the vegetation zones and the trees introduced by the settlers, including *Psidium guayaba*, with yellow fruit, or *goyava*, bordering the trail. Cows graze in the fields, in the company of cattle egrets (*Bubulcus ibis*), often sitting on their backs.

On a clear day you may walk farther up to Puntudo, a small volcano at the top of the island, with a conspicuous conical shape. Mount Crocker, the highest summit of Santa Cruz, culminates at 864 metres (two hours from Bellavista and three kilometres beyond Media luna). The site is extraordinary, with a 360-degree panorama, taking in Baltra and Seymour to the north and the two Daphnés to the northwest. This lunar landscape is utterly spectacular, with a chain of tuff cones, broken lava tubes (where volcanic water holes are numerous) and the scalesia forest sliding up the slopes like a wave up the beach (see map of Santa Cruz, page 197).

SOUTH PLAZA

land surface: 13 square km
elevation: 25 m

The Plazas Islands (North and South) are east of Santa Cruz, a few hundred metres from the coast. There, Cerro Colorado (the Red Rock) rises up with its fossiliferous tuff beds. The two islands were uplifted by tectonic action at the same time as Cerro Colorado, and are both tilted towards the north.

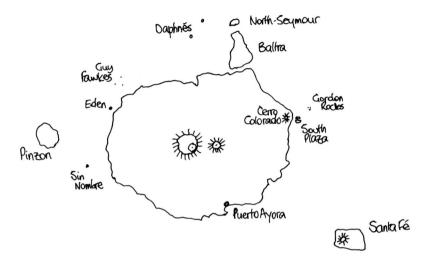

Daphnés

North-Seymour

Baltra

Guy Fawkes

Gordon Rocks

Eden

Cerro Colorado

South Plaza

Pinzon

Sin Nombre

Puerto Ayora

Santa Fé

Santa Fe ~ north east bay

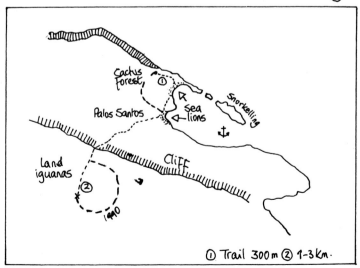

Cactus Forest

①

Snorkelling

Palos Santos

Sea lions

Land iguanas

②

Cliff

① Trail 300 m ② 1-3 Km.

Only South Plaza Island is open to visitors, the other island being closed and reserved for scientific research (see drawing, page 204).

The vegetation belongs to the arid zone and is represented by annual plants such as sesuvium, and by opuntia cacti. *Sesuvium edmonstonei* (endemic) is a plant of the succulent family, with red or green almond-shaped leaves, depending on the dry or the wet season. The island wears a red carpet during the months of May to December.

A colony of about 1,000 sea lions inhabits the island. A great number of these marine mammals gather around the disembarking site, playing or porpoising out of the water like dolphins. Do not get close to the male named Charlie, who is known to be aggressive and even bites on occasion.

South Plaza is a good place for observing yellow-brown land iguanas. It is prohibited to feed the reptiles. Years back, when the rules of the Galápagos National Park were not so strict, visitors used to bring oranges and hand them over to the iguanas, who loved the fruit. They became conditioned to such an extent that when a group of tourists arrived at the landing site, land iguanas would run to meet the newcomers, and climb on the visitors' knees to eat the precious fruit. The food balance of the reptiles was seriously affected, and the Galápagos National Park had to bring an end to these illicit practices.

A dangerous cliff borders the south of the island, where many sea lions rest. You may observe swallowtail gulls, tropicbirds, frigates, blue-footed boobies, and masked boobies, Audubon shearwaters, pelicans gliding in the sky. From the top of the cliff (watch out: two guides fell over and ended up at the hospital or died), you may see turtles, rays, yellowtail mullets and sharks. The feral goats were eradicated from the island in 1961. South Plaza is an easy day trip from Puerto Ayora. Gordon Rocks, a short distance away, is a good diving site.

SANTA FÉ

land surface: 24 square km
elevation: 259 m

Another island uplifted by tectonic action, where some of the oldest basaltic rocks of the archipelago have been dated at 2.7 million years. Santa Fé is to the southeast of Santa Cruz, and can be easily seen from Puerto Ayora (see map, page 206).

In the middle of a sunny day, the lagoon of Santa Fé turns into an eye-catching turquoise blue. The white sandy bottom is only a few metres below the surface. On the beach, sea lions bask lazily in the sun. A trail leads inland to the top of a cliff, from where the view is breathtaking. Two species of land iguanas inhabit the archipelago, but one of these, the endemic *Conolophus pallidus*, dwells only on Santa Fé; it is bigger, with a whitish colour, sometimes chocolate brown when moulting. It sports a prominent dorsal crest, and the eyes are often blood shot.

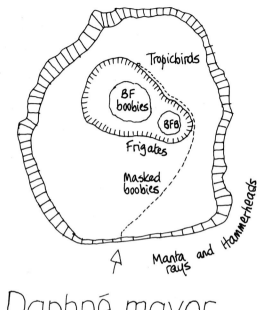

Daphné mayor

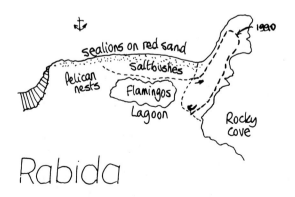

Rabida

Bottlenose dolphins, Banks Bay, Isabela 1988

Surfing sealions, Seymour 1991

Mexican goatfishes, Marchena 1993

Yellowtail surgeonfishes, Marchena 1992

Sea lion in the black coral, Cousin's rock 1990

Cushion star, Tagus cove, Isabela 1991

Orange cup coral, 1990

Bluechin parrotfish (female), Bartolomé 1992

Whitetip reef shark, Devil's Crown 1989

Scalloped hammerhead shark, Darwin 1993

Barracudas, Roca Redonda 1990

School of hammerhead sharks, Darwin 1993

Rainbow scorpionfish, Isabela 1990

Pacific amberjacks, Devil's Crown 1990

Redtail triggerfish, Wolf 1992

Longnose hawkfish in black coral, Cousin's Rock 1991

Cerianthid anemone and red crab, Tagus Cove, Isabela 1990

Bigeye jacks, Darwin 1993

Yellowtail grunts and blue and gold snappers, Marchena 1993

Fine spotted moray, Gymnothorax dovii *Marchena 1993*

The vegetation is of the arid type. The forest of the giant prickly pear cacti, *Opuntia echios* var. *barringtonensis,* is striking for the size of the trunks.

The Galápagos hawk often overlooks the beach from the top of a salt bush or a palo santo. A species of endemic rice rat is also known to inhabit the island.

Sea lions, sea turtles, small white-tip reef sharks, spotted eagle rays and round stingrays are common to the small bay. Feral goats were eradicated in 1971. Watch out for stingrays in shallow water.

DAPHNÉ

land surface: 32 ha
elevation: 120 m

North of Santa Island and west of Baltra Island, Daphné is a tuff cone above the surface of the ocean, which can be observed from the airport. In fact there are two islands: Daphné Mayor and Daphné Minor. The latter is the older, and erosion has reduced the original cone to a cylinder-shaped island with sheer cliffs. Daphné Mayor has kept its full cone, with a main crater and a second lateral crater, on the south rim.

Vegetation is poor and mainly represented by croton, palo santos, opuntia cacti and sesuvium. The curiosity of Daphné is the colony of blue-footed boobies, dwelling on the floor of the crater, where the birds nest between April and December.

Magnificent frigatebirds are found on the slopes and on the rim, as well as masked boobies, finches and short-eared owls. Tropicbirds nest in the cliff of Daphné Minor, but fly over Daphné Mayor, too. The landscape is splendid in the early morning after sunrise. The palo santo of Daphné is endemic (see map, page 208).

RÁBIDA (JERVIS)

land surface: 5 square km
elevation: 367 m

Jervis, the English name of Rábida Island, is located near the geographic centre of the archipelago. The island is made of eroded hills and lava ejected from spatter cones. Rábida is more volcanically diversified than any other island of the Galápagos.

Vegetation is composed of palo santos, opuntias and spiny shrubs. Behind the red sand beach at the north of the island, a brackish lagoon shelters a population of flamingos, Bahama pintail ducks and common stilts. Pelicans nest by the beach in the salt bushes (*Cryptocarpus pyriformis*), locally known as *monte salado*. Blue-footed boobies and masked boobies are found in the cliffs.

A new trail leads to the top of a small hill, on the left of the beach. Downhill, on the the right side, portions of the purple-red cliff frequently crumble into the sea. Feral goats were exterminated in 1970 and 1975. (see map, page 208).

PINZÓN

land surface: 12 squarekm
max. elevation: 450 m

West of Santa Cruz, Pinzón is a small island of no apparent interest except, like Rábida, for its geological diversity. The west and southwest parts of the volcano collapsed due to marine erosion and volcanic fractures. On the west coast, the cliffs rise up to 150 metres. Disembarking on the island is therefore difficult.

The vegetation is represented by croton and by spiny shrubs. Inland, near the old crater, lives a population of giant tortoises. Finches are tame, and Galápagos hawks are plentiful. Lava lizards and snakes are also present. One of the great problems of Pinzón was until recently the proliferation of *Rattus rattus*, the black rat, which feeds on eggs and young reptiles. The SPNG, the Galápagos National Park Service, eradicated the rats by traps and poison in September-November 1989.

"Blue footed boobies"

CHAPTER TWO

THE SOUTHERN ISLANDS

FLOREANA

land surface: 24 square km
elevation: 864 m

The southernmost island of the archipelago, along with Española, Floreana is of volcanic origin, very old, and its numerous volcanoes have reached an advanced stage of erosion. No volcanic activity was reported for a long time. South of Post Office Bay, Cerro Paja, the summit of the island, seems to be lost in its eternal sleep. Puerto Velasco Ibarra, the capital, is a mere village under the sun, and its population was just 65 inhabitants in 1986.

In the highlands, the vegetation is diversified and luxurious. Since Floreana was the first colonized island in the 19th century, it contains many species of plants introduced by the settlers. The visitor sites are Punta Cormorant, Corona del Diablo (or Devil's Crown), Post Office Bay and Black Beach on the west coast.

PUNTA CORMORANT

North of Floreana, this is a beautiful green sand beach. The colour is due to the abundance of green olivine crystals in the volcanic tuff. The beach is fringed by white and black mangroves, behind which is a flamingo lagoon. These waders are easily frightened; be as quiet as possible when observing. Adults are pink and juveniles whitish. Flamingos feed on an aquatic insect, *Trichocorixia*, and a small lagoon shrimp *Artemia*. The site is also favorable for observing common stilts, Bahama pintails, whimbrels and ruddy turnstones.

A great number of plants are endemic to Punta Cormorant, such as *Lecocarpus pinnatifidus* and *Scalesia villosa,* with arrow-shaped leaves covered with white hair. On the top of the dune of the white sand beach grows *Nolana galapageia,* a dense shrub with fat yellow almond-shaped leaves (see photo, page 220).

CORONA DEL DIABLO

Also known as Onslow or Devil's Crown, the marine site is a short distance from Punta Cormorant, 250 metres offshore. It used to be good for skin or scuba diving.

The submarine life—Pocillopora, Pavona and Porites corals, pencil sea urchins, parrotfish, wrasses, king angelfishes, yellowtail surgeonfish, Mexican hogfish—is the main attraction here, but it was much visited in the last 10 years. Other creatures to be seen include amberjacks, blue and gold snappers, white-tip sharks, hammerhead sharks (sometimes), rays and turtles (see drawing, page 220). On the outside of the crown (to the north), the current is strong from east to west.

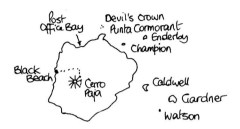

Floreana

Post Office Bay
Devil's Crown
Punta Cormorant
Enderby
Champion
Black Beach
Cerro Paja
Caldwell
Gardner
Watson

Post office barrel
Cave

Post Office Bay

Devil's Crown
(Snorkelling)

Green sand
Mangrove
Flamingos
(stingrays)
Lagoon
Palos Santos

Punta Cormorant + Devil's crown

POST OFFICE BAY

At this historic site a man named Hathaway erected a wooden barrel in 1793. It was used as a post office for passing ships, first by whalers and later by visiting yachts and tourists. A trail behind the barrel leads to a cave (lava tube) not far inland (see map, page 220).

In 1926, Norwegians settled on Floreana to start a fish-canning factory. Unfortunately, the experience ended two years later. Loberia Islet, near Post Office Bay, has a colony of sea lions.

BLACK BEACH AND PUERTO VELASCO IBARRA

In the early 20th century, Floreana was the theatre where tragic and mysterious events were played out which drew the attention of Europe to this faraway island in the eastern Pacific. One day in 1929, Dr. Friedrich Ritter, a German dentist by profession and a philosopher by nature, arrived on the deserted island with his assistant and mistress Dore Strauch, and asked to disembark at Black Beach, as if it were the most natural thing to do. Both of them lived as Robinson Crusoes for the next three years, before the arrival of the Wittmers in 1932, a German family of farmers from Bayern, with a poliomyelitic son.

This little world managed on its own until the arrival later that year of Baroness von Wagner de Bousquet, a German diva, with her two lovers, Lorenz and Philipson. She had it in mind to construct a hotel for 'millionaires', but built nothing more than a shack of planks and corrugated iron, which she proudly named Hacienda Paraíso. Soon, she claimed the island for her own and declared herself 'Empress of Floreana', intending to impose her rule by the whip and the revolver. Things rapidly turned bitter.

To make a long story short, the baroness and Philipson disappeared without a trace in 1935. Lorenz escaped with a Norwegian fisherman from San Cristobal and a few months later was found dead and mummified on a deserted beach of Marchena Island, after having capsized. Four days later, on November 21, Dr Ritter, learning about the drama, died on Floreana. It is suspected that he was poisoned by Dore Strauch with a rotten chicken, though he was known to be a strict vegetarian. The woman returned to Germany, where she published a book entitled *Satan Came to Eden*. Nobody knows the truth of the story, nor will ever know. But in the end, it seems that Lorenz killed the baroness and Philipson, with the help of Wittmer and Dr. Ritter. Margret Wittmer denies the fact, claiming that the cursed couple left the island for Tahiti on a private yacht (see *The Galapagos Affair*, by John Treherne, London 1983).

Margret Wittmer, the only survivor, celebrated her 90th birthday in 1994, and she certainly knows more than she wants to say. She lives at Black Beach with her daughters, where she owns a small hotel, a restaurant and a souvenir shop, and runs the local *correos*, the Ecuadorian post office. She does not make orange wine anymore, as in the

isla Gardner

Punta Suarez

Punta Cevallos

Española (Hood)

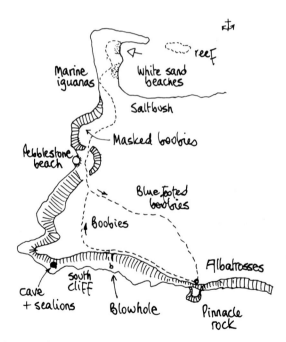

reef

Marine iguanas

White sand beaches

Saltbush

Masked boobies

Pebblestone beach

Blue footed boobies

Boobies

Albatrosses

cave + sealions

South cliff

Blowhole

Pinnacle rock

Punta Suarez

N

past, but has recently opened an eight-room hotel with toilets and showers ($30 per day, full board).

It is possible to hire a pickup for $16 round-trip to visit the highlands of Floreana, as well as the freshwater spring used by pirates in the 17th century and the caves carved in the volcanic tuff where they found a refuge well before the arrival of the Wittmers.

ESPANOLA

land surface: 61 square km
max. elevation: 206 m

Known in English as Hood, this volcanic island has a central volcano. Another island was discovered recently, east of Española, submerged a few metres under the ocean surface. This proves that the archipelago is older than once thought, and that it has long been in subduction under the South American mainland.

Bordered by steep cliffs, the southern coast is washed by surf and spray. The vegetation is typical of the arid and transition zones, with a number of spiny shrubs. Feral goats were eradicated from Española in 1978. Under the programme started in 1970, the SPNG has reintroduced 369 small giant tortoises on Española over the course of 20 years.

The richness of the fauna is not only evidenced in the colonies of seabirds, such as the blue-footed and masked boobies, but also in the presence of the endemic albatross, *Diomedea irrorata*. Despite its inhospitable look, Punta Suarez hosts a great variety of seabirds and land birds. Albatrosses nest on the island between mid-March and mid-December. Boobies are inland or on the cliffs all year-round. swallowtail gulls, oyster-catchers, lava herons, night herons, Galápagos doves, the small ground finches, warbler finches, large cactus finches, Española mockingbirds (endemic to Española), Galápagos hawks, marine iguanas, lava lizards the Galápagos snakes are also found on Hood, as well as the saddleback turtle (which you will not see!).

There is a blowhole on the basaltic shore, at the end of the trail in Punta Suarez. The seawater rushes violently under the lava bedrock, then is ejected upward through cracks in a vaporous plume to a height of 25 metres.

To the northeast of Española, Gardner Bay has a very long sandy beach facing an island of the same name. Sea lions bask lazily in the sun and the Española mockingbirds swarm on the beach, eminently curious about all visitors (see drawing, page 222).

SAN CRISTOBAL

land surface: 558 square km
elevation: 730 m

The administrative centre of the archipelago, with Puerto Baquerizo Moreno as capital, San Cristobal is also the islands' second Ecuadorian naval base. The population was nearly 8,000 people in 1993 (versus 2,752 in 1986). The radio 'Voz de Galápagos' has broadcast since 1969.

The geography of the island is composed of two distinct parts. The west part has a central volcano culminating at about 700 metres (San Joaquin), with a few parasitic cones. The eastern part of the island, made of spatter cones and lava flows, does not rise above 160 metres. It was once thought that San Cristobal was the oldest island because it is the easternmost of the Galápagos, but there is no proof of this. The slopes exposed to the north are arid and desolated, while those oriented to the south are more humid, being exposed to the southeast tradewinds.

Wreck Bay, the southwest tip of San Cristobal, shelters the village of Puerto Baquerizo Moreno. The old wooden houses that faced the sea in the past, separated by lava flows and yellow sand beaches, has given way gradually to concrete buildings and houses made of volcanic rocks. Over the last 15 years the provincial town has gained some kind of charm and is definitely attached to its image of progress.

In the highlands, eight kilometres away, the village of Progreso was once the site of the penal colony founded by Manuel Cobos in 1888. Cobos created a sugarcane factory, where the convicts were put to hard labour. A notorious tyrant, Manuel Cobos abused the women of his men, and he was eventually killed by a Colombian convict with a machete in 1904.

The humid zone of San Cristobal does not produce sugarcane any longer, but bananas, oranges, grapefruits, lemons, guavas, avocados and coffee are grown. The settlers introduced animals such as goats, rats, cats, dogs, and a species of salamander.

The visitor's sites are Cerro de Las Tijeretas (Frigatebird Hill), the freshwater lake of El Junco. Kicker Rock (Leon Dormido) and Stephens Bay, the Loberia and Isla Lobos.

HOTELS *(see map of Puerto Baquerizo Moreno, opposite)*
Gran Hotel San Cristobal (Playa Mann), single $31, double $42, triple $54, with terrace and restaurant.
Hotel Northia, single $13, double $20.
Hotel Mar Azul
Hostal Galápagos
Cabanas Don Jorge (towards Playa Mann), friendly bungalows at $9.
Residencial San Francisco (on the waterfront). Rooms for $3.50.

RESTAURANTS
Hotel San Cristobal
Restaurant Rosita
Cevicheria Langostino
Soda-bar Nathaly and other small *comedores* in port.

Puerto Baquerizo Moreno · Cristobal

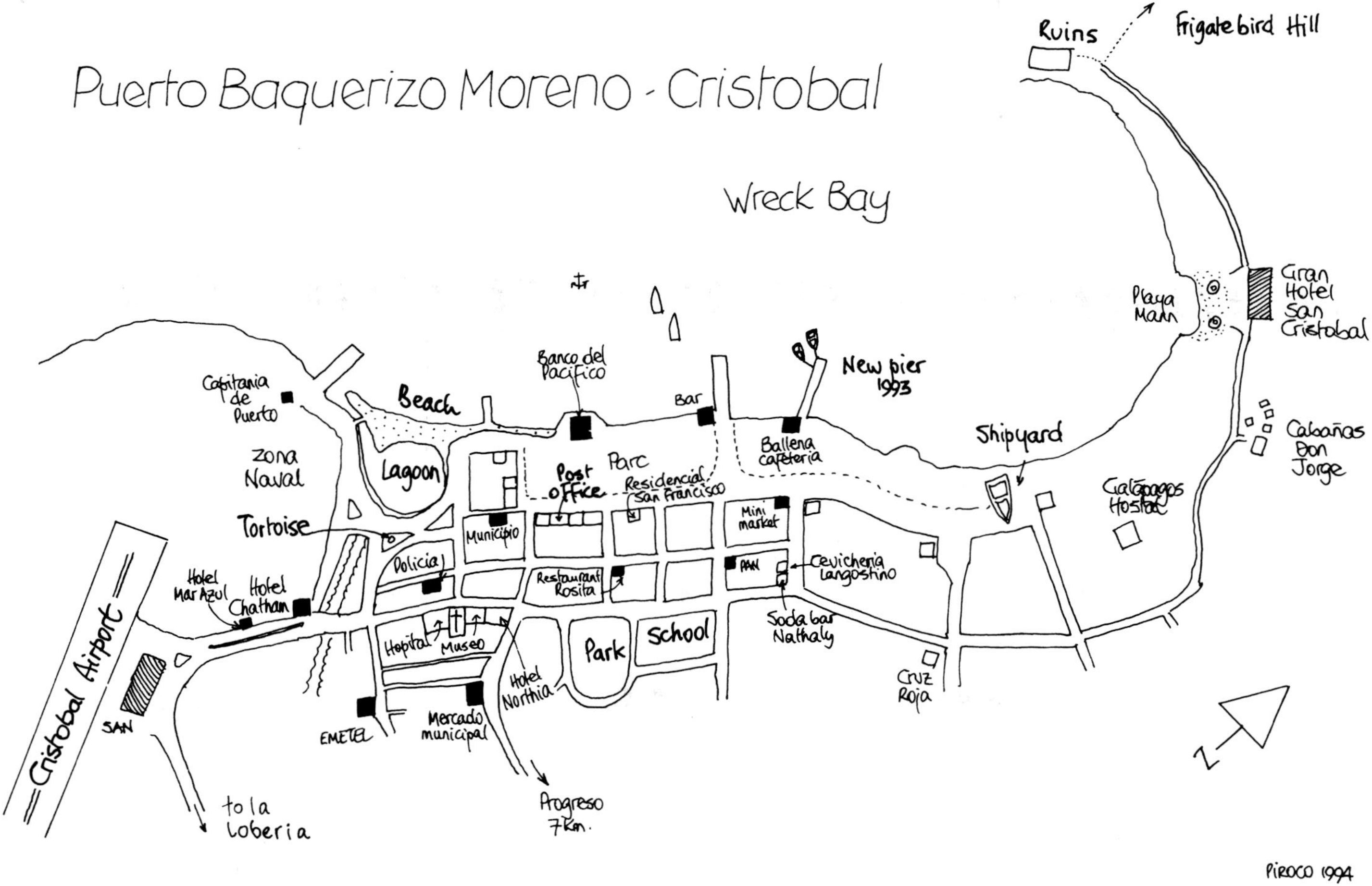

Frigate bird Hill

Ruins

Wreck Bay

Gran Hotel San Cristobal

Cabañas Don Jorge

Playa Mann

Galapagos Hostal

Shipyard

New pier 1993

Ballena Cafeteria

Cevicheria Langoshino

Soda bar Nathaly

Min. market

PAX

Cruz Roja

Bar

Barco del Pacifico

Parc

Residencial San Francisco

Post Office

Restaurant Rosita

Municipio

Hotel Northia

Park

School

Progreso 7 km.

Beach

Lagoon

Policia

Hospital Museo

Mercado municipal

EMETEL

Zona Naval

Capitania de Puerto

Tortoise

Hotel Mar Azul

Hotel Chatham

to la Loberia

Cristobal Airport

Piecco 1994

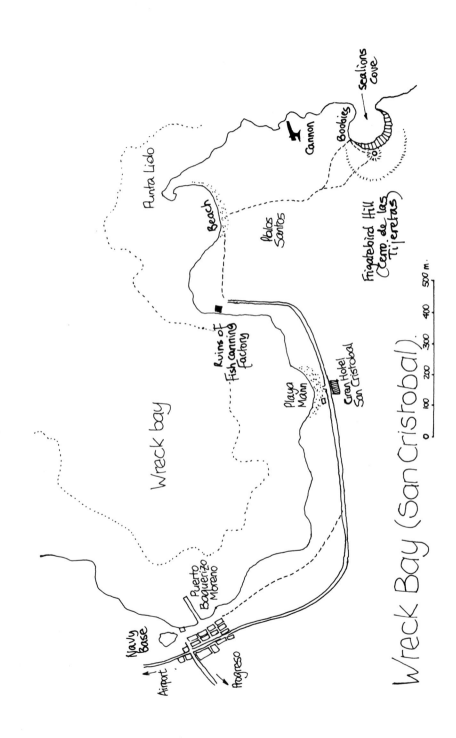

Wreck Bay (San Cristobal)

Puerto Baquerizo has developed a lot since the opening of the new airport in 1986 and the influx of tourism. SAN Airlines has a daily flight to San Cristobal from Quito or Guayaquil (12 pm), except on Sundays. The return flight costs $375 from Quito, or $330 from Guayaquil. Foreign students younger than 26, with a bona fide student card, get a 25 per cent discount on the cost of the ticket ($328). To make you feel any better, nationals pay 396,000 sucres, or $203, roundtrip from Quito, and Galápagos residents pay 144,000 sucres, or $74, from Guayaquil. Hard to believe.

To SEE
Museo de San Cristobal (opened in 1990), open Monday-Saturday 8:30–12:00 pm, and 3:30–5:30 pm. Little museum of natural history.
La Loberia, half an hour's walk beyond the airport, has a small colony of sea lions, on a white sand beach.

EXCURSIONS AROUND SAN CRISTOBAL

CERRO DE LAS TIJERETAS (FRIGATEBIRD HILL)
A short distance from the port of San Cristobal, beyond Playa Mann, is a hill covered with palo santos, overlooking an almost circular cove. The trail passes by an abandoned fish-canning factory and goes on to another beach. From there, turn right uphill. The track may be covered by vegetation in the hot season. Nevertheless, you may observe frigates having their courtship display in March-April. Birds are few, however, in the dry season. There's a beautiful panoramic view of the surrounding coastline, heading to the northeast.

LAGUNA EL JUNCO
This natural lagoon is located in the highlands at an elevation of 700 metres, 19 kilometres from Puerto Baquerizo Moreno. The only freshwater pool on the island. This crater lake has a diameter of 270 metres, a surface of 360,000 square metres and a depth of 6 metres. It is supplied by rain water only.

The sedimentary deposits of this lagoon were studied by the American geologist Paul Colinvaux (1966), who concluded that the age of El Junco was 48,000 years. The name 'Junco' comes from the sedges that invade the banks of the lake. In 1978, the lake even overflowed after the hard rains, and a small creek occasionally flows towards the south of the island. The best period to visit El Junco is from December to May during the hot season. A daily local bus links Pto. Baquerizo and Progreso, from where it is a two-hour walk to the lake. On a clear day, the view from the summit is excellent. A few resident birds live at the lake, including the Bahama pintail, the moorhen, the whimbrel and the semipalmated plover.

LEON DORMIDO

Also known as Kicker's Rock, this cathedral of tuff rises in the middle of the ocean, off Stephens Bay, to the northeast of Puerto Baquerizo. It is a three-hour trip by local boat. The 'Sleeping Lion' has vertiginous cliffs and hosts a number of seabirds, such as masked boobies, blue-footed boobies, great frigates and tropicbirds. Some sea lions rest on the rocks at the base of the cliff. A narrow channel allows a panga to go through Leon Dormido, between the sheer tuff walls, cutting through from east to west. Sharks are present in the troubled waters.

Facing Kicker's Rock on the coast, Cerro Brujo (the 'Sorcerer's Mountain') stands at the end of a long white sand beach. A sea lion colony, shorebirds, pelicans and boobies are seen. A beautiful place for a swim or for a stroll at sunset.

ISLA LOBOS

One hour by boat on the way to Leon Dormido. This insignificant island of basaltic rocks is separated from San Cristobal by a narrow arm of seawater. Sea lions inhabit the site, and blue-footed boobies nest on the white sand. A relaxing atmosphere in a landscape of primitive beauty. A 300-metre trail crosses the island from east to west.

PUNTA PITT

This site was opened by the Galápagos National Park in the beginning of 1989. It is the eastern tip of the Galápagos archipelago. The mountainous landscape is carved from the tuff formations of an ancient eroded volcano. The green sand cove where one disembarks is guarded by two tuff cones, furrowed by erosion. Behind the beach, where a few old sea lion males lie at times, the vegetation of saltbushes and spiny shrubs (*Scutia pauciflora*) gives way to a mini-canyon which climbs up a hill. The panorama from the viewpoint is magnificent. The trail draws a half moon around the site, goes over a pass, and climbs downhill and south to a vegetation of palo santos (where some frigates nest). *Muyuyos* (or *Cordea lutea*) trees and big yellow-green shrubs (*Nolana galapageia*) are often nesting sites for red-footed boobies. One may observe the 'morpho blanco' variety of red-footed boobies. Blue-footed boobies nest on the ground in the middle of the trail, marking their nesting site with a corona of their excrement. The trail climbs slightly, with good views on the sea, where at times dolphins porpoise along the coast. All around you the succulent plant sesuvium covers the ground with a red carpet in the dry season. The track makes a loop before returning to the starting point (see drawing, page 229).

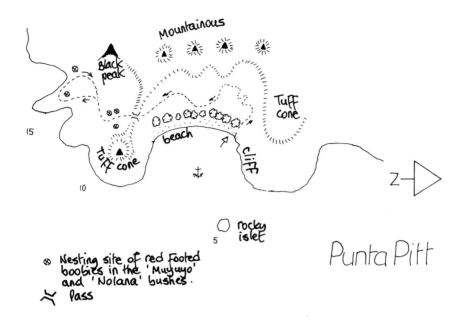

Mountainous

Black peak

Tuff cone

15

Tuff cone

beach

cliff

10

N→▷

○ rocky islet

5

Punta Pitt

⊗ Nesting site of red footed boobies in the 'Muyuyo' and 'Nolana' bushes.

⋊ Pass

San Cristobal

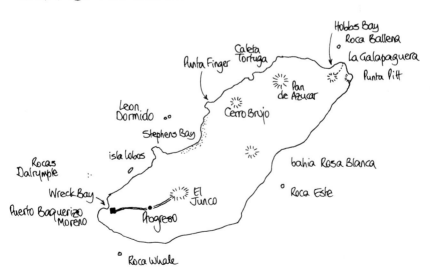

Hobbs Bay
Roca Ballena
La Galapaguera
Punta Pitt

Caleta Tortuga

Punta Finger

Pan de Azucar

Leon Dormido

Cerro Brujo

Stephens Bay

isla Lobos

Rocas Dalrymple

bahia Rosa Blanca

Roca Este

Wreck Bay

El Junco

Puerto Baquerizo Moreno

Progreso

Roca Whale

0   6 Km

Piroco 1994

A small rocky islet facing Punta Pitt is a fine spot for skin diving. The water is often crystal clear, but also chilly.

LA GALAPAGUERA

Not far from Punta Pitt and to the west, la Galapaguera is a site where you may meet giant tortoises. But one may walk a lot and get lost, since the trail is not clear and is covered with vegetation in the hot season. Not all guides know about the site, and many dare not venture there.

CHAPTER THREE

The Northern Islands

Genovesa

land surface: 14 square km
elevation: 75 m

This rather flat island to the northwest of the archipelago looks like a huge parrot beak, opened towards the rest of the Galápagos. The central volcano is now a big caldera filled with seawater to a depth of 65 metres. Darwin Bay, open to the ocean, is also a huge collapsed caldera submerged by seawater, 180 metres deep in the centre. A narrow and shallow passage allows sailboats and other ships to enter the bay by following an alignment of beacons. Cliffs rise up to 20 or 30 metres all around the bay.

Darwin Bay

One disembarks on a small white coral beach, under the indifferent eye of the swallowtail gulls. Salt bushes (*Cryptocarpus pyriformis*) border the beach, where red-footed boobies, masked boobies and great frigates nest throughout the year. The species do not always get along too well; frigates tend to steal the nests of the boobies, while boobies destroy the eggs of the frigates.

Some tide pools are hidden behind a lava ridge bordering the bay. Night and lava herons, looking for small fry, are common. Sea lions come to have a swim there at times. The trail climbs onto the cliff. Swallowtail gulls make a nest of white coral pieces and black volcanic gravel, where they lay a big white egg speckled brownish black (camouflaging it against the background). Opuntia cacti and *Croton scouleri* shrubs are everywhere. Red-footed boobies (juveniles), gulls and frigates hover above the cliff overlooking the bay, taking advantage of the rising winds.

Prince Philip's steps

The name was given after the visit of Prince Philip of the United Kingdom some years ago. The site, south of Darwin Bay is on the top of a cliff. After a dry landing on rocks, one climbs up 25 metres through a *barranco* and reaches the arid zone of palo santos, where great frigates nest in the trees and masked boobies on the ground. The trail heads inland to the east coast, an old *pahoehoe* lava flow, reddish brown because of oxidation and erosion. One will notice a big crack, which was created when the lava was still hot and fluid and flowed back into the fracture, like icing on a chocolate cake. Storm petrels swarm the sky by hundreds. A colony of hundreds of thousands is believed to inhabit the area. Short-eared owls hide in the crack of the lava flow (see drawing, page 232) and prey on the storm petrels.

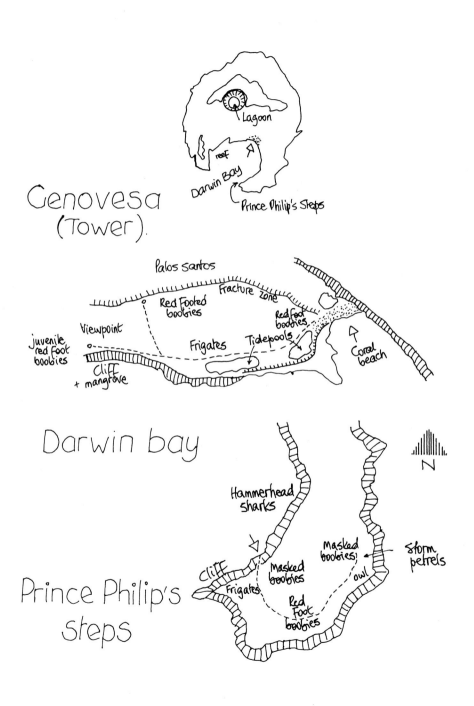

Genovesa
(Tower).

Lagoon

reef

Darwin Bay

Prince Philip's Steps

Palos santos

Red Footed boobies

Fracture zone

Viewpoint

Red Foot boobies

juvenile red foot boobies

Frigates

Tidepools

Coral beach

Cliff + mangrove

Darwin bay

N

Hammerhead sharks

Cliff

Frigates

Masked boobies

Masked boobies

owl

Storm petrels

Red Foot boobies

Prince Philip's Steps

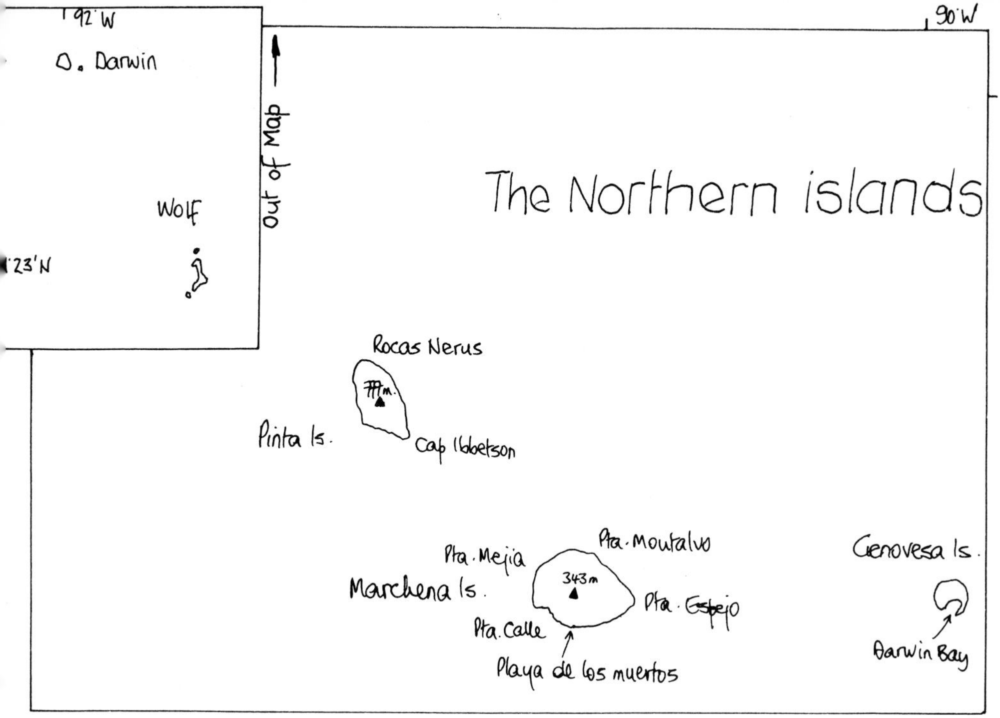

92 W

O. Darwin

Wolf

23'N

Out of Map

90 W

1'N

The Northern islands

Rocas Nerus
777 m.
Cap Ibbetson

Pinta Is.

Pta. Montalvo
Pta. Mejia
Marchena Is. 343 m
Pta. Calle Pta. Espejo
Playa de los muertos

Genovesa Is.

Darwin Bay

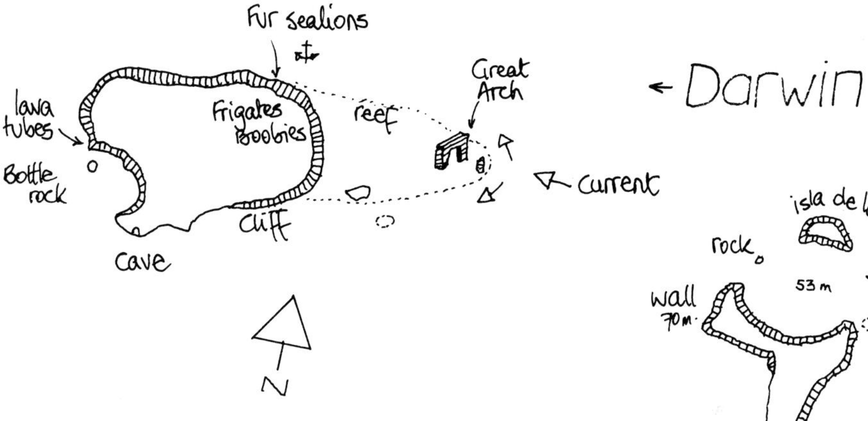

Fur sealions

Great Arch

← Darwin

lava tubes
Frigates Boobies reef
Bottle rock
Cliff
Cave

current

current

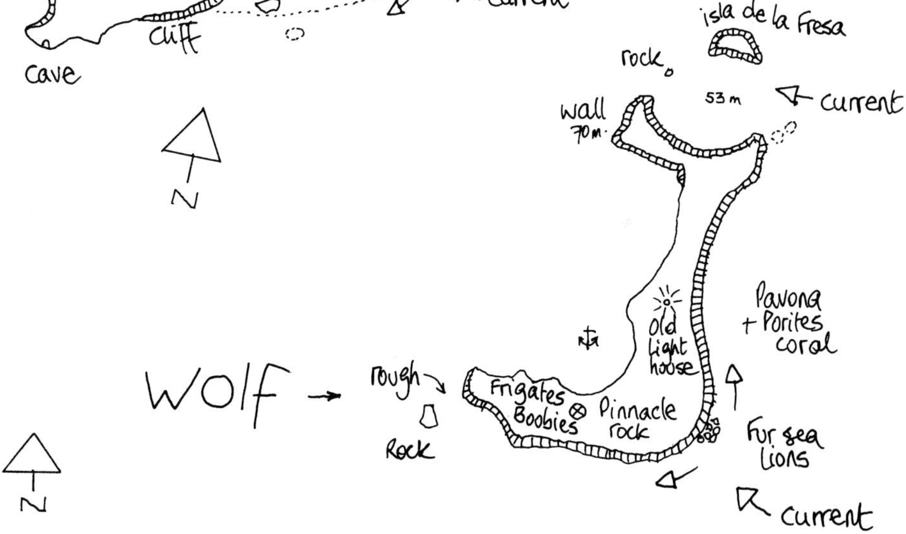

isla de la Fresa
rock
wall 70 m 53 m
current

N

N

WOLF → rough Rock

Frigates Boobies Pinnacle rock
old light house
Pavona + Porites coral

Fur sea lions

current

PIROCO 1994

MARCHENA

land surface: 115 square km
elevation: 343 m

Desolated by its external aspect, Marchena is located 50 kilometres west of Genovesa. The island is the top of a large shield volcano, with numerous small volcanic cones in the caldera and on the slopes of the volcano. The first recorded eruption occurred on September 25, 1991, with incandescent clouds during the night and lava flows to the southwest.

Marchena is not officially open to visitors, even though it is possible to disembark on the black sand beach on the southwest of the island. The Playa de los Muertos is the place where Lorenz was found dead in 1934, after being shipwrecked with a Norwegian fisherman.

PINTA

Northwest of Marchena, Pinta rises to an elevation of 750 metres. Two geological areas are distinguished. The oldest is a narrow band on the west coast, the remains of an old volcano that collapsed into the ocean. Cliffs rise up to 90 metres. A crack separates this old cliff from a younger volcano (765 metres in elevation). No eruption has been recorded on Pinta.

It is possible to drop anchor at Cape Ibbetson, to the south of the island. The vegetation is dry on the coast, humid in the highlands. For a long time, Pinta was the home of Lonesome George, last survivor of the giant tortoises. He is now a resident of the Darwin Station.

DARWIN AND WOLF

Isolated like two black sheep to the northwest of the archipelago, Darwin and Wolf, also known as Culpepper and Wenman, seem to be outcasts. These islands are the eroded summits of two large calderas, which rise 1,800 metres from the bottom of the ocean (see drawings, page 233).

DARWIN

A flat island, 165 metres in elevation, surrounded on all sides by vertical cliffs, where the surf breaks. A helicopter landed on the high plateau of Darwin in 1964. Two hundred metres off the eastern shore of the island, a monumental arch is erected on a shallow platform. Like an Arc de Triomphe facing east, this symbolic gate reminds people of the first navigators, who came from that direction. Masked boobies and red-footed boobies dwell on Darwin Arch, while hammerhead sharks and whale sharks silently roam in the blue depths. False killer whales have been seen surfacing along the northeast coast of Darwin (author's own observation, December 1993). Royal terns and sooty terns are also frequent residents on Darwin.

WOLF

Very similar to its neighbour, Wolf rises up to 250 metres, with high cliffs, 225 metres in elevation. Even though it is not a visitor's site, it is possible to disembark on the island, but climbing to the top is risky. An old abandoned lighthouse has stood there for years.

Like Darwin, Wolf is a haven for seabirds, such as great frigatebirds, red-footed boobies, masked boobies, tropicbirds and swallowtail gulls, which nest in the cliff. Fur sea lions have a small colony in the north of the island, and also on a pile of rocks on the east coast. Hammerhead sharks cruise back and forth offshore. Dolphins often accompany boats approaching Wolf as far as the anchorage on the west coast.

The common vegetation is the croton shrub and the opuntia cactus. The sharpbill ground finch, known as the 'vampire finch', lives on Wolf and drinks the blood of masked boobies from the base of the wing feathers.

Both Darwin and Wolf are excellent diving sites.

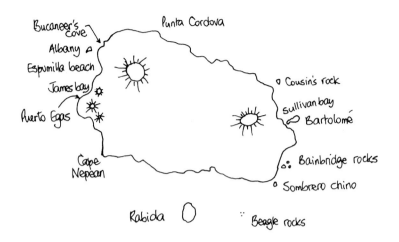

Bucaneer's Cove
Albany
Espumilla beach
James bay
Puerto Egas
Cape Nepean

Punta Cordova

Cousin's rock
Sullivan bay
Bartolomé
Bainbridge rocks
Sombrero chino
Beagle rocks

Rabida

Santiago (James).

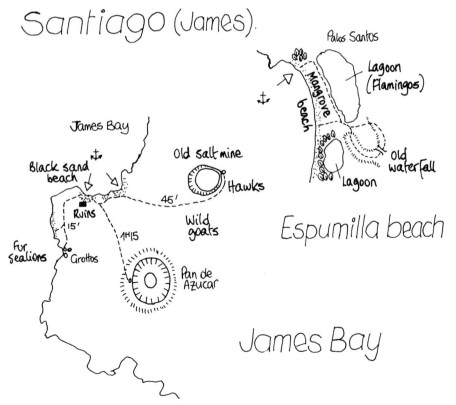

Palos Santos

Mangrove beach

Lagoon (Flamingos)

Old waterfall

Lagoon

James Bay

Black sand beach

Old salt mine

Hawks

45'

Ruins

15'

1H15

Fur sealions

Grottos

Wild goats

Pan de Azucar

Espumilla beach

James Bay

CHAPTER FOUR

THE WESTERN ISLANDS

SANTIAGO

Also known as James or San Salvador, the island, located west of Santa Cruz, is composed of a number of tuff cones and a central volcano bedecked with vegetation. Many volcanic eruptions were recorded in the last century. The vegetation is dense in the highlands, and a scalesia forest covers the northwest side of the central volcano. The southern coast, and a five-kilometres band inland, are only lava flows with arid vegetation.

Many animals were introduced by man in the time of the pirates, such as goats, pigs, donkeys and rats. The visitor's sites are James Bay (Puerto Egas), Espumilla Beach, Buccaneer's Cove and Sullivan Bay. James Bay Puerto Egas, on the west coast of Santiago, with a black sand beach and small cliffs of tuff formations, was once upon a time colonized by man. In the 1920s and again in the 1960s, salt was extracted from the crater of a tuff cone, a 45-minute walk away (three kilometres). The remains of some buildings still stand on the cliff. The vegetation around is poor and was destroyed by the population of feral goats that inhabit the area, except for the shrub *Castela galapageia*—with little oval-shaped leaves and round red fruits—which are poisonous to the goats.

A 'Sugar Loaf' rises above James Bay. It's hard to climb, but you'll be rewarded with a spectacular view of two craters of tuff cones and the panorama of the bay. An easier walk would be to 'the grottos', basaltic marine caves with open roof, on the littoral. These natural pools are an enchanting place, where sea lions and fur sea lions come to play.

Shorebirds are numerous, and include as lava herons, oystercatchers, whimbrels, semipalmated plovers and wandering tattlers. *Zayapas*, red and turquoise blue crabs, are everywhere. Galápagos doves and Galápagos hawks are also common in the area (see map, page 236).

PLAYA ESPUMILLA

North of James Bay, Espumilla (which means 'Foam' in Spanish) is a beautiful golden sand beach, fringed with mangroves. Two brackish lagoons lie behind, with a few resident birds: flamingos, common stilts, Bahama pintail ducks, semipalmated plovers. Many turtle nests may be found in the sand dunes under the mangrove trees. Sometimes turtles get lost in the lagoon, and die if they cannot find their way back to the sea. A trail to the right climbs over the hill, where land birds such as vermillion flycatchers and large-bill flycatchers can be seen.

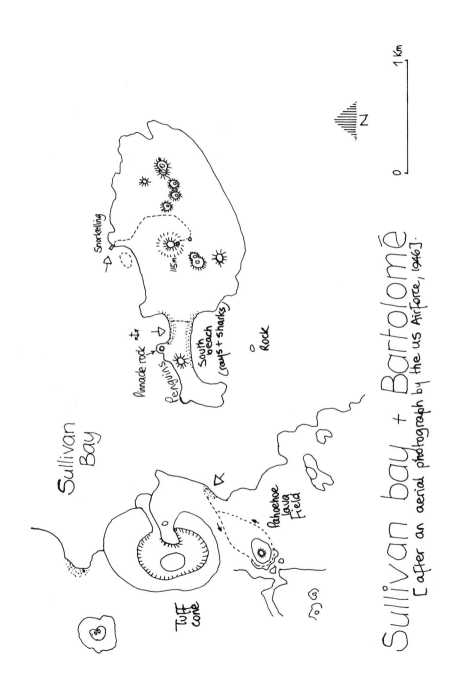

Sullivan bay + Bartolomé
[after an aerial photograph by the US Airforce, 1946].

N

0 _____ 1 Km

Sullivan Bay

Tuff cone

Pahoehoe Lava Field

Snorkelling

115m

Pinnacle rock

Penguins

South beach (rays + sharks)

Rock

BUCCANEER'S COVE

Farther north is beautiful Buccaneer's Cove, with red-purple sand. Pirates used to come here to refit their boats and search for water and tortoises. Ceramic jars were found at the bottom of the bay; some had wine, others marmalade.

Sea lions bask on the beach. One should be aware of the dangerous surf that crashes on the beach when disembarking or embarking. Cliffs of tuff formations surround the cove, the natural statue of 'the Monk' guarding this magic site, and the small islet in the centre of the bay are all part of the fabulous landscape that is created in the warm light of sunset (see map of Santiago, page 236).

SULLIVAN BAY

Facing Bartolomé Island, on the east coast of Santiago. Two imposing tuff cones rise in the middle of an enormous lava field, of a *pahoehoe* surface type. The landscape of ropey lava, the intestinal figures created by the lava flow and the *hornitos* (pockets of gas and water trapped under a crust of lava, and later exploded) are among the curiosities of Sullivan Bay. The loop trail, marked with small black and white posts, can be walked in an hour and 15 minutes. Oystercatchers often wander along the shoreline.

BARTOLOMÉ

land surface: 1.2 squarekm
max. elevation: 114 m

A very impressive little island in front of Sullivan Bay, with a landscape of real volcanic desolation: tuff cones, spatter cones, scoria formations and black volcanic sand. A trail leads to the summit of the central volcano; a stairway made of *cedrela* wood was constructed by the Galápagos National Park to stop the island's quick erosion caused by daily visitors. From the top of the volcano, the view is extraordinary. Towards the east, a field of spatter cones punctuates the island. Towards the west, one is amazed by the isthmus of Bartolomé, covered by mangroves and bordered by two small coves of golden sand in the shape of half moons. On the north beach, the Pinnacle Rock stands like a finger pointed to the sky. This volcanic needle is the last remaining piece of a tuff cone, eroded and partially bombed by American pilots during the World War II. Today it is the most photographed part of the island (see drawing, page 238).

The only vegetation on the slopes of the volcano is Ti*quilia*, a little white plant which grows in the volcanic sand, and *Chamaesycae* (an Euphorbiacae), which forms a small tuft of green or red with tiny white flowers. The lava cactus, *Brachycereus*, an endemic genus, grows on the old lava flow uphill of the first stairway. One may notice some broken lava tubes which climb down the slope of the volcano. It is possible to swim and skin dive at the north cove, under Pinnacle Rock, where the underwater life is attractive. Maybe you will be lucky enough to meet some Galápagos penguins swimming

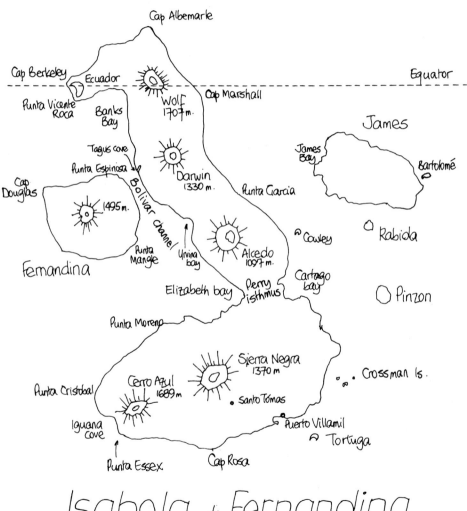

Roca Redonda

Cap Albemarle

Cap Berkeley · Ecuador · Equator

Punta Vicente Roca · Banks Bay · Cap Marshall

Wolf 1707 m.

James

Tagus cove · James Bay · Bartolomé

Punta Espinosa

Cap Douglas · 1495 m. · Darwin 1330 m. · Punta Garcia

Bolivar channel

Cowley · Rabida

Fernandina · Punta Mangle · Urvina bay · Alcedo 1097 m.

Cartago bay · Pinzon

Elizabeth bay · Perry isthmus

Punta Moreno

Sierra Negra 1370 m

Crossman Is.

Punta Cristobal · Cerro Azul 1689 m

Santo Tómas

Iguana Cove · Puerto Villamil · Tortuga

Punta Essex · Cap Rosa

Isabela + Fernandina

about, porpoising at the surface, or speeding like torpedoes behind a school of fish. There is a small colony in a sheltered cove behind Pinnacle Rock.

The south beach is unsuitable for swimming due to stingrays, small whitetip and blacktip sharks. Spotted eagle rays can be observed at the surface, and black turtles are plentiful during the months of November and December, when they come to lay eggs on the beach. Herons prey on baby turtles running down the beach after they hatch.

Sombrero Chino

Only a hundred metres from the southeastern coast of Santiago island, Sombrero Chino ('Chinese Hat') is separated from the big island by a marvellous turquoise-blue lagoon. The island is made of a few adjacent craters and very old, fragile *pahoehoe* lava flows. The vegetation is meager, but some very colourful sesuvium plants are scattered around.

The trail, 350 metres long, runs from the northern white sand beach, where sea lions and penguins are common, to the western part of the island. There, the lava bedrock hosts a colony of marine iguanas, which often wallow in tide pools. The waves crash against the nearby cliffs, spraying the whole area with mist. Some Galápagos hawks overlook their kingdom from the top of the island.

Sombrero Chino is an ideal place for snorkelling or skin diving in the lagoon.

Isabela

land surface: 4,588 square km
elevation: 1,707 m

By far the biggest island of the archipelago, Isabela's land surface accounts for half of the archipelago's total. It measures 132 kilometres from north to south and 84 kilometres at its greatest width. The island is composed of six main volcanoes, five of which evolved in calderas, the old stage of a shield volcano. The largest caldera is 10 kilometres in diameter. From the oldest to the youngest these volcanoes are: Sierra Negra, Alcedo, Darwin, Wolf, Cerro Azul. The sixth is Ecuador volcano, at the northwestern tip of the island (the seahorse nose of Isabela), has been destroyed by erosion and wave action. It is estimated that more than 2,500 cones are present on Isabela. Wolf Volcano is the highest summit, culminating at 1,707 metres. The equator passes through both Ecuador and Wolf volcanoes. All these volcanoes are considered very active. The most recent eruptions occurred on Cerro Azul and Sierra Negra in 1979, on Wolf in 1982. Some earthquakes shook Alcedo in March 1991.

Alcedo Volcano

max. elevation: 1,150 m

The trail to Alcedo starts from the small black cove of Alcedo Beach (volcanic gravel), on the east coast of the island. It follows an *aa* lava flow and a canyon dug by rain water.

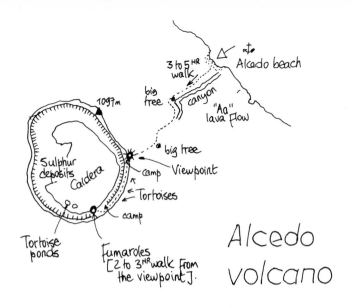

3 to 5 HR walk

big tree

canyon

"Aa" lava Flow

Alcedo beach

1097m

Sulphur deposits

Caldera

camp

big tree

Viewpoint

Tortoises

camp

Tortoise ponds

Fumaroles [2 to 3 HR walk from the viewpoint].

Alcedo volcano

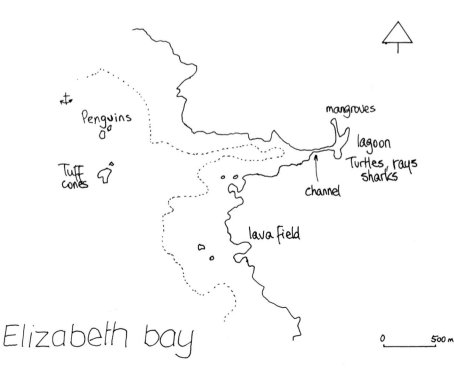

Penguins

Tuff cones

mangroves

lagoon

Turtles, rays sharks

channel

lava field

Elizabeth bay

0   500 m

The track crosses the arid zone of palo santos and croton. The climb should be made early, before sunrise, because the heat becomes torrid during the day. Fortunately, some big trees provide shade along the way at two possible stops. Expect it to take three to five hours to reach the rim of the crater, depending on the individual. After a slow ascent for most of the hike, the last climb is very strenuous before you get to the top, and volcanic gravel slips under your feet. You may meet some female tortoises on the trail in the hot season, as they walk down to the lowlands to nest in June.

The caldera of Alcedo is seven kilometres wide; the crater floor, 200 metres below the rim, is an immense lava field bedecked with palo santos and spiny shrubs. The rim is covered with shrubs and small trees, such as cat's claws, *Zanthoxylum fagara* (local name *una de gato*), and *Tournefortia pubescens*. There are also some endemic tree ferns of the species *Cyathea weatherbyana*.

Fumaroles can be observed on the southern slope of the caldera (another two or three hours' walk). The 'geyser' is no more than a hot waterhole spewing vaporous fumes. Sulphur deposits are also seen farther away. On the rim and inside the caldera, thousands of tortoises gather during the wet season to wallow happily in muddy rain pools, which rehydrates them and protects them from ticks. With a population estimated at 5,000 individuals, the Alcedo tortoise is the most flourishing in the Galápagos. In the dry season, tortoises hide in the bushes, on the rim of the crater, or dig a sort of burrow to hide from the fierce sun.

The Galápagos hawk is very common in the hot season, and the inquisitive juveniles often hover over your head. Goats, donkeys and cats live on the slopes of the volcano, causing minor damage to the vegetation and to land birds.

It is possible to camp on Alcedo, but fires are prohibited. Bring your stove, enough water (two litres per day) and a flashlight if you spend the night (see map, page 242).

PUNTA GARCIA

This site used to be accessible by *panga* only. The aa landscape was once a breeding site of flightless cormorants, just above the waterline, but the birds seem to have deserted the place. This rare seabird of the Galápagos breeds from March to September. Brown pelicans are sometimes present. The lagoon is not very safe for swimming, due to troubled water and sharks.

PUNTA ALBEMARLE

At the northern tip of Isabela Island, this site was an American radar base during World War II. Disembarking is not easy because of the surf. The largest species of marine iguana in the Galápagos is found at Punta Albemarle. There are quite a few nests of flightless cormorants, and a little colony of fur sea lions.

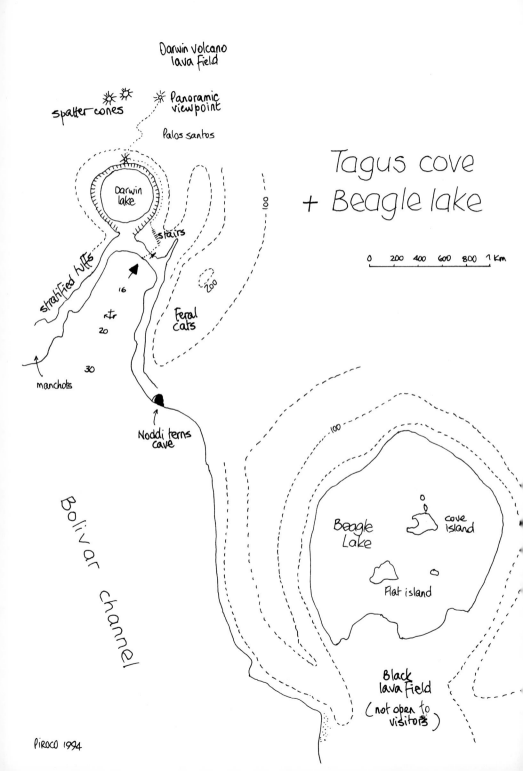

Darwin volcano lava Field

☀ ☀ spatter cones ☀ Panoramic viewpoint

Palos santos

Tagus cove
+ Beagle lake

☀ Darwin lake

stratified tuffs

stairs

100

0   200 400 600 800 1 Km

200

16

Feral cats

☀r
20

30

manchots

Noddi terns cave

100

Bolivar channel

Beagle Lake

cove island

Flat island

Black lava Field
(not open to visitors)

PIROCO 1994

Punta Tortuga

On the west coast, slightly north of Tagus Cove, Punta Tortuga is a beach of dark sand, behind which is a mangrove swamp. One may observe the mangrove finch, similar to the carpenter finch but with a shorter and sharper bill.

The area was tectonically uplifted in 1975. In 1825, the American ship *Tartar,* anchored in Banks Bay, north of the site, and witnessed a volcanic eruption on Fernandina, 15 kilometres to the south. The air temperature rose to 50° C, and the sea temperature reached 40° C, so warm that the tar on the riggings began to melt. The eruption lasted for two weeks.

Tagus Cove

This small, U-shaped cove was a refuge of pirates and whalers. It is still a historical site, if one considers all the graffiti on the surrounding cliffs. Today, any kind of painting is forbidden and punishable. The name 'Tagus' was given in 1814 by a British navy ship of the same name, which came to look for tortoises and found some.

The landing site is awkward and rather slippery on the rocks. Behind the tuff formations bordering the cove, a wooden stairway, constructed by the Galápagos National Park in 1990, climbs up to a viewpoint. From there one discovers Darwin Lake down below. The brackish lagoon is perfectly circular, and is elevated above sea level by tectonic uplift. The white palo santos are everywhere around Darwin Lake, and turn happily green during the wet season. Darwin's finches are found in swarms, to the benefit of the feral cats that inhabit the area. The cats were studied by Mike Konecny in 1980; this American scientist partially lost his vision due to a viral disease as he attached radio collars around the cats' necks.

The trail goes halfway around the lake, then heads inland up to a ridge with a few spatter cones. From the viewpoint, one may appreciate the impressive landscape of Darwin volcano's lava flow (aa surface type) and, on a clear day, the wide silhouette of Ecuador and Wolf volcanoes to the north. A man with solid ranger shoes, would lose the sole of his boots after four kilometres of hard walking on the lava of this convict's country. The feral dogs that live in the area have developed the ability to cross the basaltic surface, thanks to horny pads under their feet, which protect them against cuts—a remarkable example of adaptation to the environment. The most extraordinary fact is that these dogs can drink seawater without any ill effect (see drawing, page 244).

It is possible to take a *panga* ride along the cliffs of Tagus Cove to observe pelican nests, blue-footed boobies, noddi terns in a marine cave, Galápagos penguins standing peacefully on a rock by the water, marine iguanas basking in the sun and lazy sea lions. Snorkelling and skin diving in Tagus Cove are interesting, especially at night, when one may see hornsharks on the volcanic gravel bottom and redlip batfishes (at greater depth).

Urvina Bay

West of Alcedo volcano, Urvina Bay was tectonically uplifted in 1954. Coral heads (nowadays white) were thrust five metres above sea level, as were six kilometres of coastline. A lateral eruption of volcan Alcedo occurred a few months later.

After a wet landing on a white sand beach, Urvina is a good site for seeing giant tortoises, big land iguanas and marine iguanas. Half an hour away from the beach along the shore, one may discover a few nests of flightless cormorants around a sheltered lagoon, where common egrets and great blue herons are also present (see drawing, page 248).

Elizabeth Bay

South of Urvina Bay and west of the Perry Isthmus, Elizabeth Bay is a marine site where landing is not allowed. As you pass by the small islets in the middle of the bay, you may sight Galápagos penguins, but they are as rare as flightless cormorants. A narrow channel penetrates farther inland, in a dense mangrove area with unusually tall trees, and opens up on a big lagoon with many arms. It is a haven for green turtles, golden rays and spotted eagle rays, small white-tip sharks. Marine turtle mate in the lagoon in November-December (see drawing, page 242).

Punta Moreno

This is a typical *pahoehoe* lava flow, southwest of Elizabeth Bay, with numerous cracks and water holes, formed when the roof of gas pockets under the lava surface broke in. A rich life has developed in and around these natural pools. One may see flamingos, Bahama pintails, great blue herons. Pelicans nest in the mangroves. Feral dogs roam the region and attack marine iguanas and sea lions.

Puerto Villamil

Principal centre of Isabela district, on the south coast of the island. It is one of the least inhabited islands, with a population of about 800 people, and an 'end-of-the world' feeling. The fishermen's village was founded in 1897 by Don Antonio Gil, an honorable citizen from Guayaquil. This is one of the most beautiful sites of the archipelago, with marvelous white sand beaches that stretch for kilometres. The historical past of Isabela is rich in fabulous and terrible stories. In fact, Turtle Bay (Bahia de la Tortuga) was used by pirates; buried treasure was hidden there, and some was discovered in 1974. Behind Villamil and along the coast, brackish lagoons are a refuge for flamingos, whimbrels, white-cheeked pintails, common stilts and gallinules.

Following the beach to the west, one passes by the cemetery of Puerto Villamil (one kilometre), with old graves and rotten crosses. The trail heads inland at the end of the beach, to the Muro de las Lacrimas, the Wall of Tears. It was erected from

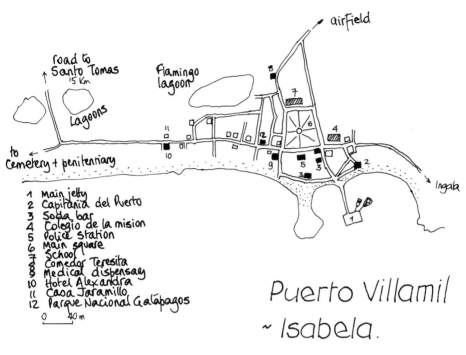

road to
Santo Tomas
15 km

Flamingo
lagoon

airfield

8

7

Lagoons

11

10

12

6

4

5 3

9

3

2

1

to
Cemetery + penitenciary

Ingala

1 Main jetty
2 Capitania del Puerto
3 Soda bar
4 Colegio de la mision
5 Police station
6 Main square
7 School
8 Comedor Teresita
9 Medical dispensary
10 Hotel Alexandra
11 Casa Jaramillo
12 Parque Nacional Galápagos

0   40 m

Puerto Villamil
~ Isabela.

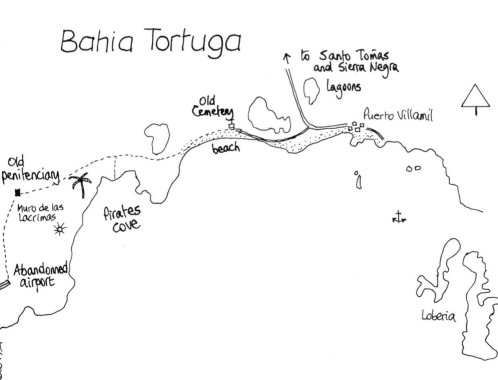

Bahia Tortuga

to Santo Tomas
and Sierra Negra

Lagoons

Old
Cemetery

Puerto Villamil

beach

Old
penitenciary

Muro de las
Lacrimas

Pirates
Cove

Abandoned
airport

Loberia

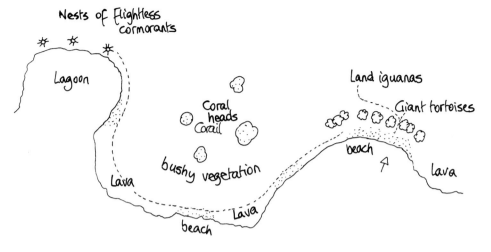

Nests of flightless cormorants

Lagoon

Coral heads
Corail

bushy vegetation

Lava

beach

Lava

Lava

beach

Land iguanas

Giant tortoises

Lava

Urvina bay

Punta Espinosa

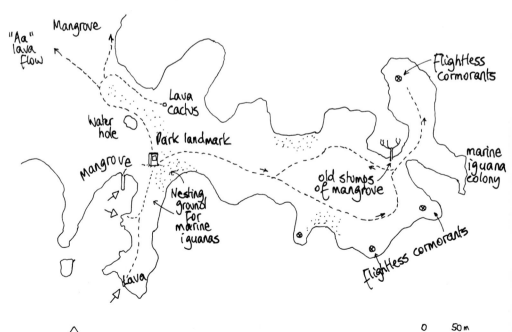

"Aa" lava flow

Mangrove

Lava cactus

Water hole

Park landmark

Mangrove

Nesting ground for marine iguanas

Lava

old stumps of mangrove

Flightless cormorants

marine iguana colony

Flightless cormorants

0   50 m

PIROCO 1994

big lava blocks by convicts of the penal colony. The penitentiary of Isabela was opened in 1944 at a foot of a desolated hill, in the arid zone, two to three hours' walk from Villamil. Following a mutiny that was mentioned in the press at the time, it was definitely closed down and blown up in 1959. More than 200 convicts had been forced to hard labour. Life was horrible there and the cruelty of the guards was legendary. This period will remain forever in the memory of Isabela. Of the penitentiary itself, the only ruins are a standing cylinder of rusted iron, and a huge wall of basalt, 50 metres long, five metres wide and eight metres tall. Behind the Wall of Tears, a trail climbs up the hill, from where you may best contemplate the desolation and perhaps feel a chill run up your spine. In the far distance, the bay of Villamil shines from the timeless surf that crashes on the beach, and the magnificent turquoise-blue waters in the midday sun are an exotic image that help dispel the unhappy past.

On the way back, notice the solitary coconut tree on the right. A pirate's treasure was discovered there 20 years ago by a mysterious Frenchman who left no trace of his passage but for a big hole with some rusted pieces of iron. Puerto Villamil, a small paradise lost, not yet open for tourism, is like the black sheep of the Galápagos. An airport was built more than ten years ago with a landing strip of white coral, but it was found later on that it was not practical because it was wrongly oriented in respect to the southeast tradewinds, and the site was abandoned.

On the beach at the end of the village, the little Hotel Alexandra is swept by the ocean wind like a deserted house. The last time it was used, two Japanese men changed the main hall into a sea cucumber depot for eight months before they disappeared with their smuggled goods. For lodging, ask the family of Natalia and Jorge Jaramillo, on the other side of the road. There are some *comedors* and food places in town (see map, page 247). To get to Isabela on your own, ask for '*la Lancha de Ingala*' (in Puerto Ayora, Santa Cruz Island), a ferryboat that goes to the inhabited islands once or twice a week, and which also transports mail and cargo.

SIERRA NEGRA VOLCANO

The local bus leaves for Santo Tomas in the highlands, at 7 am and 2 pm, and returns to Puerto Villamil at 4 pm (cost = $1 or 2,000 sucres) Sierra Negra Volcano The village of Santa Tomas, 18 kilometres from Villamil in the highlands, used to be the departure point for the ascent of Sierra Negra volcano. It was founded by Don Antonio Gil at the end of the 19th century, and has a population of 300 people. Cattle breeding and agriculture—there are plantations of coffee, oranges, grapefruits, papayas, guavas and avocados—are the main activities.

The road from the lowlands was constructed 20 years ago. A minibus makes the daily trip to the *parte alta*, from Puerto Villamil, but the new road goes up directly to the rim of the crater.

Otherwise, it's a three-hour walk from Santo Tomas. It is possible to hire horses, at $20 for the day (see Sr. Antonio Gil, at Hotel San Vincente, in Puerto Villamil*).

Sierra Negra is a huge caldera, ten kilometres wide, the oldest on the island. During the garua season the summit of the volcano is covered in mist; be prepared for rain. On the rim, the trail divides in two: Towards the west, it heads to Volcan de Azufre, an old sulphur mine that was exploited by the first settlers (10 kilometres, or three to four hours' walk); towards the east, the trail leads to Volcan Chico on the external slope of Sierra Negra, which erupted in 1979. The weather is often clear and good, once you reach the northern side of the caldera. You'll get excellent views of the Perry Isthmus, Elizabeth Bay and Alcedo volcano.

The Galápagos hawk, short-eared owl, vermillion flycatcher and large-billed flycatcher are common to Sierra Negra. Wild horses are sometimes seen. Camping is allowed, but fire is forbidden. Do not get lost. For refreshment there is a small bar on the road, just under the rim of Sierra Negra.

Hotel San Vicente (Sr. Antonio Gil) cafeteria-bar, 4 rooms, at $3.50 with private bathrooms. Horses for hire.

FERNANDINA

land surface: 642 square km
elevation: 1,494 m

Fernandina has an impressive volcano, one of the most active on the planet. Even though it is the youngest in the Galápagos, at least 12 eruptions have been recorded in the last 150 years. The caldera is six kilometres wide, with a depth of 900 metres. The lake that was once in the crater in 1946 disappeared in 1958 after two lava flows inside the caldera. In 1964, there was a new lake, but in June 1968, a memorable explosion blew up the caldera floor, which fell 300 metres. The personnel of Skylab mentioned a small eruption in December 1973, and the lava flow on the southeastern slope, inside the crater. The most recent eruptions were recorded in 1977, 1978, 1984, September 1988, April 1991 and February 1995. This last eruption maintained regular activity for over a month. Lava flows ran into the ocean from parasitic cones on the southwest towards Cape Hammond, creating a new cape three to four kilometres north-west of the former one.

The vegetation on the slopes of Fernandina belongs to the arid zone. At an elevation of 1,200 metres, the flora is reduced to islets of ferns, surrounded by lava flows. On the top of the volcano, high grasses and scalesia bushes are dominant (see drawing, page 248).

PUNTA ESPINOSA

The only visitor's site on Fernandina is on the northeast of the island, facing Isabela Island on the Bolivar Channel. Galápagos penguins and flightless cormorants are established, but rare. Disturbed by man, they tend to move their nesting sites regularly. The pahoehoe lava flows are bedecked by lava cacti (*Brachycereus*), which form yellow or dark green tufts with white spines.

Tectonically uplifted in 1975, the site of Punta Espinosa is also the home of a colony of sea lions and a few colonies of marine iguanas. Red and turquoise-blue crabs, *zayapas*, are everywhere. Land iguanas that came down from the volcano were once present in the bushes, but they seem to have disappeared. They are still numerous on the rim of Fernandina, however, where they dig burrows and lay eggs in the volcanic sand. The Galápagos hawk is common to the site, where it preys on snakes and marine iguanas.

CABO DOUGLAS

This site is not yet open to visitors, but will attract many visitors due to the considerable natural beauty. On a black basaltic shore (uplifted), one may observe a small colony of marine iguanas, a few land iguanas, Galápagos hawks and a big nest of twigs on a lava promontory, a few nests of flightless cormorants and a colony of fur sea lions. There is also a colony of blue-footed boobies.

THE 'PEPINOS' AFFAIR

The scandal of the exploitation of *pepinos*, or sea cucumbers, a delicacy to Chinese and Japanese palates, broke in 1992. Local pirate camps, encouraged by Japanese fishing ships, were established on the coast of Fernandina to collect sea cucumbers along the shoreline. Families with women and children lived illegally in this 'no man's land' to catch pepinos, which they dried in the sun on the lava rocks. Then they packed the merchandise in bags and placed the goods to local boats in Villamil and Puerto Ayora, which in turn delivered them to the Japanese fishing boats.

The sea cucumbers (*Isostichopus fuscus*) move on the rocky bottom at a depth of between 2 and 20 metres. They are ecologically important because they help to clean seawater by recycling organic waste. The ban on the fishing on *pepinos,* declared by President Borja in June 1992, was contested one year later by the Galápagos fishermen, who recognized the amount of money at stake. The illicit fishing went on, and about 1,000 pounds of pepinos was seized by the Equadorian authorities in one of the pirate camps, in November 1993. Thirty million pepinos were fished, dried or cooked on the coast of Fernandina in 1992. In 1994, striking fisherman pressured the government of the new president, Sixto Duran Ballen, to suspend the 1992 decree. Somehow they succeeded, because, as of July 15, 1994, the Ministry of Industry and Fisheries (MIIP) allowed lobster fishing for three months (July 15-October15), then sea cucumber fishing for three months (October 15-January15), then even shark fishing (January15-April 15), which has always been forbidden. For the Galápagos Marine Reserve, this is definitely 'Apocalypse Now' (see photo, page 174).

According to recent sources (March 1995), the local fishermen of Isabela have also been fishing Pacific sea horses (*Caballitos del Mar*) to sell to the Chinese for aphrodisiac medicine.

CHAPTER FIVE

THE LANDINGS

Whether you take an organized tour with an Ecuadorian travel agency or you decide to charter a boat from Puerto Ayora or San Cristobal with a few friends, once in the islands you'll have to get familiar with some practical advice and some new words.

You drop anchor in a turquoise-blue cove or in a wild bay with foaming surf. Then the *panga* will take you to shore. The pan*ga* is a small boat, comparable to a dinghy, accommodating up to 12 people, which is conducted more or less skillfully by the *pangero*.

The landing can be fun or it can be hell, depending on the difficulty of disembarking, and this depends on the season or your luck. It could be on a fine sand beach or on sharp coral rubble, on dry or wet rocks (with the wave and surf behind) or on a safe rocky quay where a few sea lions bask (and, of course, like Charlie, the big peevish male on South Plaza, they do not want to be disturbed). Simply imagine the paradisiacal setting, and this is where you step in. You do not get into heaven for free.

In short, you may experience a dry landing or a wet landing. You should have your shoes on or in hand, with your pants rolled up to your knees. In the latter case, shorts are definitely the most practical. If you disembark on a beach, do not forget about the wave behind you; if you are not careful, it could make you lose your balance with all your belongings (imagine your camera equipment in a bath of salt water). Consequently, you should sit on the side of the *panga* and put both your feet in the water at the same time, not one foot after the other. You may smile, but if you do not follow these directions you will find out what happens by which time it will be too late. Plastic bags may be useful for wrapping your camera to protect it from spray. In any case, the guide is there to warn you.

LIST OF THE LANDINGS

Island	Site	Type of landing
Santa Cruz	Puerto Ayora	dry
	Itabaca	dry
	Las Bachas	wet
South Plaza		dry, sea lions on wharf
Mosquera Islet		wet

Island	Site	Type of Landing
Santa Fé		wet
Floreana	Punta Cormorant	wet
	Post Office Bay	wet
	Black Beach	dry
Española	Gardner bay	wet
	Punta Suarez	wet
San Cristobal	Puerto Baquerizo	dry
	Cerro Brujo	wet
	Punta Pitt	wet
Genovesa	Darwin Bay	wet, coral beach
	Prince Philip's Steps	dry, but slippery rocks
Rábida		wet
Sombrero Chino		wet
Bartolomé	volcano climb	dry, but slippery rocks
	beach	wet
Santiago	Puerto Egas	wet
	Espumilla	wet
	Buccaneer's Cove	wet, watch for surf
Isabela	Tagus Cove	dry, but slippery rocks
	Puerto Villamil	dry
	Punta Moreno	dry, on rocks
	Urvina Bay	wet, watch for waves
	Punta Albemarle	wet, watch for waves
	Alcedo	wet
Fernandina	Punta Espinosa	dry, but slippery rocks

CHAPTER SIX
SCUBA DIVING

The underwater fauna is very rich in the Galápagos, and unusual by comparison to traditional dive sites, such as the Caribbean, Maldives, Red Sea, Indian Ocean, Philippines and Southeast Asia, where the warm tropical seas abound with colorful coral reefs. In the Galápagos, one finds more than 400 species of shore fishes, 32 species of corals, and 600 species of mollusks. Diving in Galápagos is not to be undertaken lightly. Some sites have strong currents, lava rocks and underwater ridges may be sharp and dangerous, and caves make enticing traps. One should never dive alone.

The Galápagos are still new to the sport. Even though a presidential decree of May 13, 1986, declared the Galápagos archipelago a 'Reserve of Marine Resources', very few laws were defined and implemented governing their proper exploitation. Nevertheless, one thing is certain: it is impossible to dive without a local dive guide, licensed by the Galápagos National Park and by the Ecuadorian Merchant Marine, who will look after you underwater, but who is not responsible for you in case of an accident.

No facilities are offered for the safety of divers. The closest decompression chamber is 1,000 kilometres away, at the Ecuadorian naval base in Guayaquil. Divers are informed that they dive at their own risk. A liability waiver will have to be signed before the cruise begins. In any case, you will have to show proof of your diver's certification, your logbook and a medical certificate.

There are three dive clubs in Puerto Ayora. Recommended are 'Scuba Iguana' at Hotel Galápagos, run by Matthias Espinosa and Jack Nelson and 'Nautidiving', at the Red Mangrove Inn, run by Polo Navarro and Vicente.

WATER TEMPERATURE
Despite their equatorial position, the Galápagos are considered to be a cold-water environment. Three main marine currents bathe the archipelago: two are cold (coming from the west and southeast) and one is warm (coming from Panama in the northeast).

The water temperature is influenced by the season: cold from May to December, warm from December to May. The sea surface temperature varies from 17° C to 27° C, and drops to 15° C sometimes to the west of Isabela.

In the Galápagos, temperatures are warmer in the northern islands, cooler in the central and southern islands, and cold west of Isabela and Fernandina. The exception occurs during Niño years, when the sea surface temperature averages 25° C to 30° C. Therefore, it is necessary to have a 5-mm wetsuit any time of the year. (See Part One, Chapter 2, for more details on seasons and temperatures.)

VISIBILITY

Water is generally clear during the cold season, but the sea surface is rough in August-September. In the warm season, water may be murky due to the presence of plankton on the surface, but it depends on the site.

CURRENTS

Mainly from east to west, they can be very strong. Underwater navigation with a compass is often necessary, and it is important to be cautious at all times.

DANGERS

There are no real dangers in the Galápagos; nevertheless, it is advised to avoid submarine caves. These can be long tunnels, sometimes labyrinthine, which can be rather dangerous because of the surf action.

Sharks are no real threat, and are not aggressive, as long as they are not provoked. An attitude of respect is recommended, and some distance has to be kept between the diver and the sharks. A refuge in the rocks or in the cliff should be nearby, just in case. Whitetips, grey reef or hammerhead sharks are usually inquisitive by nature. Although shy, they do not hesitate to come close to the diver, but at the last minute they turn at a right angle and disappear out of sight. Schools of Galápagos sharks, of up to 30 individuals, may circle you (eg Gordon Rocks). Fortunately, it doesn't mean that they have you in mind for a feast, for they usually vanish in a few minutes, with majesty and indifference.

If ever you notice a shark that wriggles or arches its back suddenly, then beware. This aggressive display is a warning preceding an attack. You should come up to the surface and leave the water quickly. There was a case in which a Galápagos shark bumped into a diver from the back (James Gribb, 1984)—not too nice. In March 1991, the guide Jonathan Green claimed he was attacked by a two-metre-long great white shark when he was skin diving at Playa Escondida, to the northeast of Pinzón Island. He kicked off the shark with his fins. The same year, again off Pinzón Island, a park guard was bitten in the thigh by a three-metre-long shark while in one metre of water.

Until now, sharks in the Galápagos have not attacked humans, for they have enough natural food to eat. This situation may change, triggering a series of accidents in the future.

There is one venomous snake on the islands. The yellow-bellied sea snake (*Pelamis platurus,* family Hydrophiidae), is dorsally black, ventrally yellow. About 85 cm long, this rare pelagic species appears in the warm season (especially during Niño years), when the sea surface temperature rises. It should not be approached, for its venom is more virulent than that of the cobra.

Among other pain-inflicting animals are the stingrays, which inhabit sandy bottoms in shallow water, and the scorpionfishes on the rocks. The long black spines of the crowned sea urchin can easily penetrate one's skin, and leave a numbness that may last or two or three days. The flower sea urchin (*Toxopneustes roseus*) should not be touched, for it is also venomous and may induce a high fever.

DIVING SITES   DEPTH

Classification:		
- Snorkelling	< 3 metres
- Skin diving	< 10 metres
- Scuba diving	+ 10 metres

CENTRAL ISLANDS

Diving around Santa Cruz	Snorkelling	Skin diving	Scuba
Isla Coamano (Academy Bay)		x	x
Punta Estrada (Academy Bay)	x	x	x
South Plaza (lagoon and cliffs)	x	x	x
Gordon Rocks		x	x
Itabaca canal (south Baltra)	x	x	
Mosquera Islet (east coast)	x	x	x
Nord Seymour (south coast)	x	x	x
(northwest caves)			x
Daphné Mayor			x
Daphné Minor			x
Santa Fé (northeast bay)	x	x	x

Around Santiago			
Bartolomé (pinnacle,	x	x	x
Cousin's Rock			x
Bainbridge rocks			x
Sombrero Chino (lagoon)	x	x	
Beagle rocks	x	x	x
Rábida (beach and west cove)	x	x	
James Bay (Puerto Egas and 'grottos')	x	x	x
Buccaneer's cove (rocky point)	x	x	x
Sullivan Bay	x		

EAST	Snorkelling	Skin diving	Scuba
Around San Cristobal			
Frigatebird Hill			
(Cove, Puerto Baquerizo)	x		
Kicker's Rock (Stephens Bay)			x
Punta Pitt	x	x	x
Roca Ballena			x
NORTH			
Genovesa			
Darwin Bay (beach)	x		
Darwin Bay (west reef)	x	x	x
Prince Philip's steps		x	x
Marchena			
Punta Espejo	x		
Punta Mejia	x	x	x
Wolf			
East coast			x
North Cove			x
Isla de la Fresa			x
Northwest cliff			x
Darwin			
Northeast coast		x	x
The Arch			x
Tower rock (west cove)			x
WEST			
Around Isabela			
Crossman Islands			x
Isla Tortuga	x	x	
Punta Moreno	x	x	x
Elizabeth Bay	x	x	
Tagus Cove	x	x	x
Punta Vicente Roca	x	x	x
Roca Redonda			x
Punta Albemarle	x	x	x
Alcedo beach	x	x	

WEST	Snorkelling	Skin diving	Scuba
Fernandina			
Punta Espinosa	x	x	x
Cabo Douglas			x
SOUTH			
Around Floreana			
Punta Cormorant (beach and rocks)	x	x	
Devil's Crown	x	x	x
Champion Islet		x	x
Enderby Island			x
Caldwell Island			x
Around Española			
Punta Suarez	x	x	
Gardner Bay (rocks)	x	x	
Gardner Island			x
Xarifa Island		x	x
OTHER			
Hancock Bank			x
McGovern Bank			x
Guy Fawkes Island		x	x
Punta Bowditch (Conway Bay)	x	x	

PART FOUR

THE GALAPAGOS NATIONAL PARK

CHAPTER ONE

ADMINISTRATION AND HISTORY

The Galápagos National Park is a public institution recognized by the Ecuadorian government. Its administration depends on INEFAN (1993), the Instituto Forrestal y Aereas Naturales, which in turn depends on MAG, the Ministerio de Agricultura y Ganaderia, the agriculture department based in Quito, capital of Ecuador.

There are about 15 national parks in Ecuador, which cover the Amazonian, Andean and coastal regions, but the Galápagos National Park is the first and most advanced in its administration, management and development. The first laws to protect the Galápagos were passed in 1934. Some islands were then declared reserves for a national park, with the exception of Santa Cruz, Floreana, Cristobal, the south of Isabela and Fernandina.

On July 4, 1959, all areas not colonized by man were declared a national park. The Charles Darwin Foundation was created in Brussels. The same year, to conserve and protect the unique Galápagos ecosystem and to promote scientific research. The Charles Darwin Research Station (CDRS) was established on Santa Cruz Island in 1960, with Raymond Lévêque as its first director.

The National Parks Department was created in 1968 within the Forestry Department. Two conservation officials were sent to the Galápagos and began the Ecuadorian administration. As the number of employees rose, it became necessary to construct the Galápagos National Park Service (SPNG) building.

In 1979, 60 park guards were on duty, supervised by five conservation officials. There were also an accountant and four university-trained professionals: the superintendent and his attendant, the chief of protection and the chief naturalist. The park staff is divided into two groups with specific functions. Four programs were introduced:

- eradication and control of animals and plants introduced by man.
- protection of the endangered native species.
- tourism management.
- education.

The budget of the Galápagos National Park comes directly from the Ecuadorian government, through the MAG. In 1978, it was estimated at $200,000, or six million sucres. The rest of the funds come from international organizations such as the WWF, the Frankfurt Zoological Society and private donations.

Use of the Park

Special Use Zones
On islands colonized by man, some areas of the National Park can be used by settlers and residents to extract products such as wood, sand and volcanic rocks. The hunting of introduced animals is also possible in some places, with a necessary permit.

Scientific Research
Scientists wanting to do research within the National Park must submit a detailed project to the director of INEFAN, to the park superintendent, to the director of the Darwin Station and to the secretary of the Darwin Foundation. The study has to deal with anything related to evolution or concerning conservation problems.

Tourism
Visitors to the National Park have to follow a number of rules made to protect the ecological integrity of the islands. Forty-eight visitor sites have been designed, with marked trails and open areas. Visitors are led by a guide, licensed by the Galápagos National Park, who will make sure the rules are respected.

These rules are set forth on decree 1306, published in 1971, which states the dos and don'ts. The entry fee to the National Park was of $6 in 1981, then $40 in 1989 and $80 for foreigners in 1993. The funds collected go to the management of tourism (30 per cent) and to INEFAN (70 per cent).

Mass tourism in the Galápagos started in 1969, with the arrival of the 58-passenger cruise boat *Lina-A*, of Metropolitan Touring. In the beginning of the 1970s, Ecuador became better known internationally, and the number of visitors increased in the following years: 1,200 in 1969, then 2,500 (1971), 3,000 (1972), 4,500 (1973), between 5,500 and 7,500 in 1974.

The *Lina-A* sank in 1975, without casualties, far off the coast of Ecuador. In 1977, two new cruise ships arrived in the archipelago: the M/N *Bucanero* of Gordon Tours and the M/N *Neptuno* of Macchiavello Tours. In 1980, Metropolitan Touring's M/N *Santa Cruz* replaced the *Lina-A*. The famous and unforgettable *Neptuno*, which, according to hearsay was under a curse and held together by paint alone, sank near Guayaquil in June 1984, drowning the unfortunate cook, who blew up with the kitchen.

It was replaced in 1987 by the M/N *Galápagos Explorer* of the Canodros agency (Guayaquil). The M/N *Bucanero* stopped operating in 1990. A new cruise ship arrived in the archipelago in September 1993: the M/N *Ambassador I*, with a capacity of 86 passengers, belongs to a Greek named Zacharias, of Islas Galápagos Turismo y Vapores (Quito).

Three big boats ply the Galápagos waters now, as well as another 100 smaller boats, yachts, sailboats. After being limited to 12,000 people (1973), then to 25,000 people (1981) by different Master Plans, the number of visitors to the Galápagos National Park is now out of control, and limits have become meaningless. The last Master Plan of Miguel Cifuentes (1985), former manager of the SPNG, forecast a new limit of 45,000 people per year. This limit was blown at the end of 1994, when the number of visitors exceeded 54,000 people. The economic pressure is such that the future looks hectic. Hotel construction has boomed in Puerto Ayora, Santa Cruz Island, for the last two years.

Annual flow of visitors to the Galápagos National Park (1974-1996)

Year	Total Visitors	Ecuadorians	Foreigners	% nationals	% foreigners
1974	7500				
1975	7000				
1976	6300	868	5432	13.78	86.22
1977	7788	1349	6439	17.32	82.68
1978	12299	1606	10693	13.06	86.94
1979	11765	2226	9539	18.92	81.08
1980	17445	3980	13465	22.81	77.19
1981	16265	4036	12229	24.81	75.19
1982	17123	6067	11056	35.43	64.57
1983	17656	7254	10402	41.09	58.91
1984	18858	7627	11231	40.44	59.56
1985	17840	6279	11561	35.20	64.80
1986	26023	12126	13897	46.60	53.40
1987	32593	17767	14826	54.51	45.49
1988	31248	14218	17030	45.50	54.50
1989	41899	15133	26766	36.12	63.88
1990	41192	15549	25643	37.75	62.25
1991	40746	14815	25931	36.36	63.64
1992	39510	12855	26655	32.54	67.46
1993	46818	10136	36682	21.65	78.35
1994	54000	12800	41200	23.70	76.30
1995	55782	15483	40303	27.75	72.25
1996	61500?	16100?	44500?	27.65	72.35

(source: Servicio Parque Nacional Galápagos, 1996)

The rise of the numbers in 1978 is explained by the arrival of the *Bucanero* and the *Neptuno* (with a capacity of 90 passengers each); the same applies in 1980 to the *Santa Cruz*. In 1986, a renewed influx of visitors followed the big fire that burned part of Isabela Island in 1985 and brought publicity to the islands.

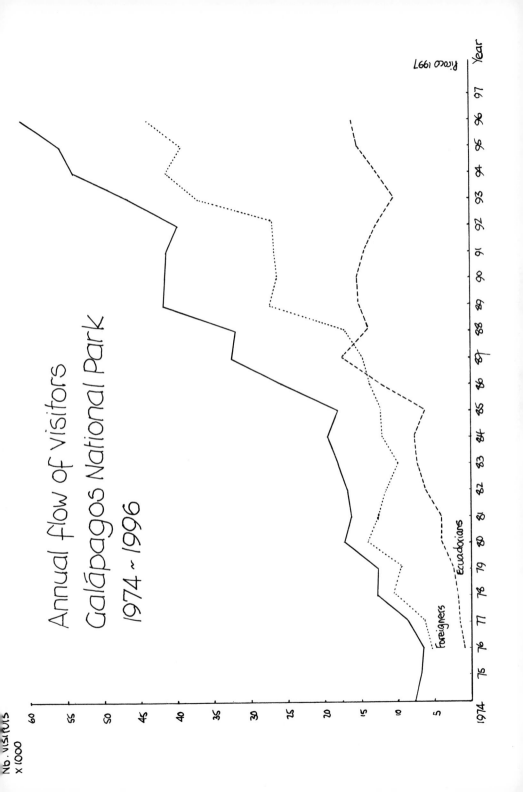

Annual flow of visitors
Galápagos National Park
1974 ~ 1996

Nb. visitors
x 1000

Foreigners

Ecuadorians

Ricco 1997

Year

About 3,000 to 5,000 people visit the Galápagos each month. In 1993, the heaviest months were January/February/March, then July/August and December.

As for Ecuadorian visitors, after their numbers peaked in 1987, when they accounted for 54.51 per cent of visitors, they have become gradually less interested in the islands, with only 12,000 people (27.50 per cent) visiting in 1993. The flow of foreigners, by contrast, is increasing, with 33,000 people in 1993, or about 72.50 per cent. By order and number of visitors, here are the 12 countries that send people to the Galápagos:

1	Ecuador
2	USA
3	Germany
4	Switzerland
5	Italy
6	Canada
7	South America
8	England
9	France
10	Holland
11	Israel
12	Japan

(source: SPNG and Carta Informativa CDRS, February 1988).

THE MASTER PLAN

Most of the natural and wildlife areas rapidly deteriorate if they are not managed properly. A number of objectives have been established for these natural areas, which includes designation as a national park. Consequently, the Galápagos Master Plan was divided in two parts, which sum up:

- the information concerning the resources of the area, culturally, historically, flora and fauna, and the human factor.
- procedures and goals of management, characteristics and qualities to preserve, not to mention the development of the local population.

The Master Plan for the protection and use of the Galápagos National Park was written in 1973 by a team of Ecuadorians and international experts. The Food and Agriculture Organization (FAO) already had 15 years' experience in South America. The plan, printed in 1974, is carried out by the park personnel and states seven main objectives:

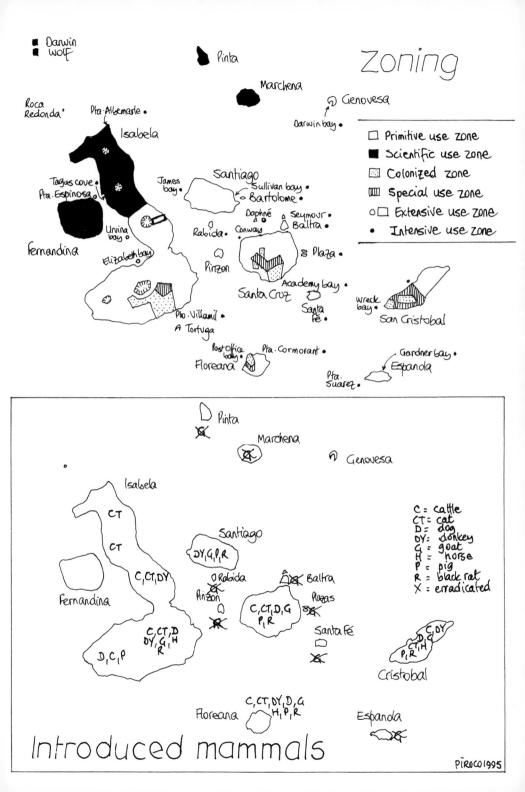

Zoning

Darwin ■
Wolf ■

Pinta

Marchena

Genovesa

Darwin bay •

Roca Redonda °

Pta. Albemarle •

Isabela

☐ Primitive use zone
■ Scientific use zone
▨ Colonized zone
▥ Special use zone
○☐ Extensive use zone
• Intensive use zone

Tagus cove •
Pta. Espinosa •

James bay •

Santiago

Sullivan bay •
Bartolome ○

Daphné
Seymour ○
Baltra △

Fernandina

Urvina bay •

Elizabeth bay •

Rabida ○
Conway

Plaza

Pinzon

Santa Cruz

Academy bay •

Santa Fé •

Wreck bay •

San Cristobal

Pto. Villamil •
A Tortuga

Post office bay •
Floreana

Pta. Cormorant •

Gardner bay •
Espanola

Pta. Suarez •

Pinta
✗

Marchena
✗

Genovesa

Isabela

CT

CT

C,CT,DY

Santiago

DY,G,P,R

○ Rabida
✗

Baltra
△ ✗

Pinzon
✗
○

C,CT,D,G
P,R

Plazas
✗

Santa Fé
✗

C,DY
CT,H
P,R

Cristobal

Fernandina

D,C,P

C,CT,D
DY,G,H
R

C = cattle
CT = cat
D = dog
DY = donkey
G = goat
H = horse
P = pig
R = black rat
X = erradicated

Floreana

C,CT,DY,D,G
H,P,R

Espanola
✗

Introduced mammals

PIROCO 1995

* Protection of the Galápagos ecosystem.
* Eradication or control of introduced species.
* Appropriate use for visitors.
* Providing information to visitors on what they can see.
* Educating for the local population.
* Encouraging economic development of the archipelago's residents
* Encouraging scientific research.

Another important point of the Master Plan is zoning. This technique allows division of the National Park into distinct zones for better management. Five zones were established (see map of Zoning, page 265):

Intensive Use Zones
There are about 25 of these particularly extraordinary touristic zones within the National Park. The plan recommends that a maximum of 90 people (four to five groups of 20 people with a guide) be authorized to disembark at the sites. Some of the areas are fragile, and control remains important.

Extensive Use Zones
There are about 16 of these zones, which are not as interesting as the intensive-use zones. A maximum number of 12 people may disembark on these sites. No large groups are allowed.

Primitive Use Zones
The majority of the land surface of the National Park. Sometimes affected by the presence of introduced species. These zones are nevertheless ecologically unique. A special permit is required.

Primitive Scientific Zones
These are kept for scientific research (eg Tower, Fernandina). No possible access to the casual visitor with no specialized interest.

Special Use Zones
Adjacent to colonized areas, these zones may be exploited by the residents, for wood, sand, volcanic rocks. Activity is nevertheless strictly controlled.

Among the numerous objectives of the park, as stipulated in the Master Plan, are the following:

* Eradication of introduced plants and animals; protection of the endangered species, touristic management. The transfer of organisms from island to island will be controlled and prevented.
* The park infrastructure will be more elaborate in the colonized areas, with construction of offices and staff quarters. A reception centre was built on Baltra for visitors, and a park guard station will be constructed in Puerto Egas (Santiago).
* A concession system will be established. Responsible tour operators may proceed with tourism within the archipelago, but they must comply with certain rules and pay a 10 per cent tax on their gross annual income. In exchange the SPNG will ensure the necessary protection to the tourism industry, and will supply ground services to the visitors.
* An area of two nautical miles will be added to the park's territory to ensure the protection of the marine environment. In this way, the interaction of the land and marine ecosystems will be protected. (The new Marine Reserve was established in 1986.)
* To enforce the Master Plan, the park personnel will be composed of 66 park guards, plus several technical advisers: carpenters and mechanics, six university-trained experts in education, protection and biology.

The aim of the Master Plan, however idealistic, is allow the people of the Galápagos to live in harmony with their environment, taking from nature only what they need, and disposing only of noncontaminating materials. Easy to say and hard to do.

All in all, man would not be a destructive organism (there are already too many in the islands) but, on the contrary, an introduced species that has found its place in the ecosystem of the Galápagos.

CHAPTER TWO

INTRODUCED MAMMALS
RULES OF PRESERVATION FOR THE VISITOR
ROLE OF THE GUIDE

INTRODUCED ANIMALS

The history of introduced mammals goes back 450 years, to man's discovery of the archipelago. Since then, the islands have been populated with herbivores, carnivores (cats and dogs) and omnivores (rats, mice and pigs), which all turned feral after a time. Dogs, pigs, goats and rats were brought by pirates as early as the 16th century. One of the worst introduced animals is the fire ant, which destroys the vegetation (see map of Introduced mammal).

Nowadays, at least 14 species of introduced animals are found in the Galápagos: 11 mammals, two birds, and one insect (see map, page 265).

The 14 Introduced Species

English	Spanish
Cow	Ganado
Goat	Cabra, chivo
Guinea pig	Cuy, cobayo
Donkey	Burro
Horse	Caballo
Sheep	Oveja
Black rat	Rata negra
Mouse	Raton
Pig	Chancho
Dog	Perro
Cat	Gato
Rooster	Gallo
Pigeon	Paloma
Fire ant	Hormiga colorada

GOATS (*Chivos*)

Mainly on Floreana, Santiago and Isabela. These unstable animals live in groups and often move from the coast to the highlands in the dry season.

Goats reproduce once a year in April-May, and have one or two young. These fierce herbivores are a plague upon the vegetation, for they'll eat anything, with the exception of two plants, *Vallesia* and *Castela galapageia*. Their predators are Galápagos hawks, dogs and feral pigs.

CATTLE (*Ganado*)

Found mostly on Isabela, where the population is about 1,000 individuals. They are a threat to the vegetation, but are also of economic value for their meat. Exportation has been considered.

HORSES (*Caballos*)

The threat is not so important, and no serious ecological impact is involved. Horses are found in the highlands of Isabela, Santa Cruz, Cristobal and Floreana.

DOGS (*Perros*)

Dogs turned feral on Santa Cruz and Isabela, where their population is estimated at 200 to 500. They gather mainly to the west of Cerro Azul volcano, where they decimate marine iguanas on the coast, and also on the slopes of Alcedo volcano, where they arrived recently after crossing the Perry isthmus. This barrier of basaltic lava, eight to 10 kilometres wide, has until now controlled their progression toward the north. Generally of a white colour with black spots, feral dogs hunt in small groups of two to three individuals. They attack cattle in the highlands and marine iguanas on the coast. On Santa Cruz Island, they are a serious threat to the Hawaiian petrel, which nests in the tropical zone. Feral dogs have been eradicated from Floreana and San Cristobal.

RATS (*Ratas*)

Recorded on Santa Cruz and on Santiago, they were eradicated from Pinzón (known once as the 'Island of the Rats') by a campaign of the SPNG, from September to November 1989. *Rattus*, the black rat, lives in the arid zone as well as in the humid zone. It reproduces in the hot season, with a breeding cycle of 27 days. Vegetables, insects, fruits, grains, turtle eggs and fledglings are part of its diet. The black rat is responsible for the disappearance of the Galápagos endemic rats, *Oryzomis* and *Nesoryzomis*, because of its competitiveness, aggression and spreading of disease.

The two native predators of the rats are the short-eared owl and the Galápagos hawk. Introduced predators are cats and dog. The black rat was eradicated from Bartolomé in 1976 by traps and poison.

PIGS (*Chanchos*)
Mainly on Santiago, but also on Isabela, where they dig up the nests of marine turtles. They also dig up a number of native plants.

CATS (*Gatos*)
Found mostly on Isabela, where they attack finches, boobies, lava lizards and even marine iguanas (Cartago Bay).

DONKEYS (*Burros*)
In the arid zone and in the highlands of Santiago and Isabela. Their population is estimated at 700 on Alcedo volcano, and 300 to 500 on Sierra Negra volcano.

The major problem of the Galápagos National Park is after all the eradication of goats, which is not an easy task. With time and numerous campaigns, some islands have been cleared of this plague: South Plaza (1961), Rábida and Santa Fé (1971). After a new introduction, Rábida was again cleared (1975); 4,000 goats were eradicated on Marchena (1976), then definitively (1979), as well as on Española (1978).

RULES OF PRESERVATION FOR THE VISITOR

The archipelago of the Galápagos belongs to those few places in the world that remain relatively untouched by human exploitation. The preservation of the environment is everybody's problem. Everyone may take part in it, by following some simple rules which will help to maintain the archipelago's fragile ecosystem intact. The future depends on you.

1. Be careful not to transport any live material to the islands, or from island to island (insect, seeds). If you have a pet, do not bring it to the islands. It will not be allowed.
2. No plants, rocks, animals or their remains, such as bones, pieces of wood, corals, shells, or other natural objects should be removed or disturbed. You may damage the island's ecological conditions.
3. Animals should not be touched or handled. A sea lion pup will be abandoned by its mother, for example, if she smells the scent of man on its young. The same applies to chicks of birds.
4. Animals may not be fed. It may alter their life cycle, their social structure and affect their reproduction.
5. Do not disturb or chase any animal from its resting or nesting spot. This is especially true for birds such as boobies, cormorants, gulls and frigates. The nests

should be approached carefully, keeping a distance of 1 to 2 metres. If disturbed, the bird will flee and abandon its egg or chick, which could die under the strong sun within 30 minutes.

6. All groups which visit the National Park must be accompanied by a qualified guide approved by the National Park. The visitor should follow the trail, marked with small black-and-white posts, and never leave it. If you do so, you may destroy nests without being conscious of it (eg marine iguanas nests in the sand).

7. Follow the guide; stay with him for information and advice. He is responsible for you. If he behaves badly or does not follow the rules himself, report him to the National Park.

8. Litter of all types must be kept off the islands. Disposal at sea must be limited to certain types of garbage, only to be thrown overboard in selected areas. Keep all rubbish: film wrappers, cigarette butts, chewing gum, tin cans, bottles, etc., in a bag or pocket, to be disposed of on your boat. Do not throw anything on the islands or overboard. It could end up at the coast or the beach, or eaten by sea turtles or sea lions. A sea lion may play with a tin can found on the bottom and cut its sensitive muzzle. Sea turtles may die from swallowing a plastic bag.

9. Do not paint names or graffiti on rocks. It is against the law, and you will be fined for it.

10. Do not buy souvenirs or objects made from plants or animals of the islands (with the exception of articles made from wood). Among such articles are turtle shells, sea lion teeth, black coral. This is the best way to discourage such a trade.

11. To camp, you need a permit from the National Park Service (Santa Cruz, Cristobal, Isabela). Do not make fires, but use a gas stove instead. Park suggestions may be useful.

12. Do not hesitate to show your conservationist attitude. Explain these rules to others, and help to enforce them.

The Galápagos National Park thanks you for respecting these rules. Think about others who come after you; they'll be grateful to you for your conservationist attitude.

THE ROLE OF THE GUIDE

The guides are trained by the Galápagos National Park with the help of the Charles Darwin Research Station. For many years, until September 1992, there were two categories of guides in the Galápagos: naturalist guides and auxiliary guides. Some were foreigners, multilingual, and with a scientific background; others were Ecuadorians, natives of the islands without any specific background. Some did not get along; the jealousy of others changed to racism, and eventually there developed a cold war between the guides of the Asociación de Guias and of the Agrupacion de Guias Interpretes, hidden behind the big smiles shown to foreign visitors. But it was common practice to be mean to each other, to denounce a guide at the National Park office for real or imaginary professional mistakes.

As is often heard in Santa Cruz, 'Pueblo pequeño, infierno grande', ie 'Small village, big hell.' Just as in the animal world, the human world submits to fierce competition in a struggle for survival and to irreversible evolution, which forces each individual to make a quick adaptation to this environment. Otherwise, he has to leave the islands. 'The survival of the fittest...' said Darwin.

Moreover, the galloping immigration of the last 15 years has not helped much: 5,000 people in the archipelago in 1980 swelled to more than 20,000 in 1994, and the numbers are on the rise, to such an extent that the authorities are now concerned about the future of the Galápagos.

In 1992, decree number 0434 of the Ministerio de Agricultura y Ganaderia, the Ministry of Agriculture, decided to establish a single organization of naturalist guides, divided in three parts: 'Guias Naturalistas (Naturalist Guides) I, II, III'.

Guia Naturalista I
A native of the islands or resident of the archipelago for many years, with a high school diploma, who has a sound knowledge of the region and speaks English. He must pass the course of Guia Naturalista I, and can lead a group of 10 visitors maximum.

Guia Naturalista II (ex-auxiliary)
Ecuadorian by birth or by naturalization, who has achieved a high school education or has a university background in biology or related fields, or in tourism. He has to be fluent in English, French or German, and must pass the course of Guia Naturalista II. He can lead groups of up to 16 visitors.

Guia Naturalista III (ex-naturalist)
Ecuadorian by birth or by naturalization, and, in the case of a foreigner, must have legal working papers. He has to show proof of a degree in biology or related fields, or in tourism. He must be fluent in Spanish, English, then French or German. He must pass the course of Guia Naturalista III, and may lead a group of 16 (in reality: 20) visitors.

The naturalist guides course takes place each year in September, for a period of six weeks. Priority is given to Ecuadorian nationals and Galápagos residents in registering for the courses, while 20 per cent of foreigners may be accepted to take the course for Naturalist Guides III. The candidate must pass the final exam with an 80 per cent grade in order to receive the guide's license of the Galápagos National Park. The license is valid for two years; the future guide must show proof of at least 120 days worked per year in order to keep his guide's status and the right to continue working.

Guides are responsible in the eyes of the law, and have many essential functions:
- To inform and educate visitors on the richness of the protected area and the natural history of the Galápagos, competently and with diligence.
- To be responsible and to control actions committed by the visitors, within the Galápagos National Park.
- To keep in touch with the administrative authorities, to signal the his group's whereabouts and to receive instructions.
- To carry a guide's license and identity papers, and to wear a uniform, if necessary.
- To be vigilant of the application of technical and administrative measures in order to protect the natural resources and the visitors.
- To cooperate with the control and with the patrol of the region to ensure conservation and rational use of the resources.
- To participate in the activities of observations, involving the collection of data on the ecological impact and other environment aspects.
- To provide interpretation for special groups.
- To report to the legal and technico-administrative authorities whenever necessary.

In conclusion, and in the eyes of visitors, the guide must make sure the rules are respected. In the intensive use zones, he has to keep his group on the trail. In the extensive use zones or open areas, all decisions are his responsibility and must prevent harm to the ecosystem. The guide may also interfere with another group in cases of questionable behavior. The Galápagos National Park has the right to sanction or even take away the license of a guide if he is convicted of a serious offense, whether he deserves a warning or suspension from work.

CHAPTER THREE

THE CHARLES DARWIN RESEARCH STATION

In 1957, UNESCO, in cooperation with the New York Zoological Society, Time Incorporated, and the Ecuadorian government, sent a mission to the Galápagos Islands for the purpose of conducting a study on flora and fauna, and also to look for an appropriate site for building a biological research station.

Two years later, in 1959, the centenary of the Theory of Evolution drew the attention of the International Congress of Zoology. A Galápagos committee was created under the presidency of Sir Julian Huxley. Thus was founded the Charles Darwin Foundation in Brussels, intended to preserve the environment and to favor scientific research with an aim toward conservation. The construction of the Darwin Station in Puerto Ayora was undertaken in the beginning of 1960, facing Academy Bay, with funds from UNESCO and Ecuador. The station was in operation two years later, but was officially inaugurated in 1964.

In 1965, the Ecuadorian government passed decree number 525 thus defining the boundaries of the National Park, so as to protect the giant tortoises and eradicate all feral goats. The first protection programmes started in 1968, with the creation of the Servicio Parque Nacional Galápagos (SPNG). In 1973, the Galápagos became a province of Ecuador for the second time in order to help the development and promotion of the archipelago. The INGALA, or Instituto Nacional Galápagos, was created in 1980 with the aim of developing the islands touristically, economically and for the producing for major projects such as airports.

The Charles Darwin Research Station, which celebrated its 30th anniversary in 1994, hosted a dozen directors, all European or American scientists; Chantal Blanton, the current, American director, was nominated in May 1992, after the terms of Daniel Ewans (1989–92) and Gunther Reck (1984–89). The research station has four main functions:

- to provide scientific information.
- to obtain funds from international organizations for conservation purposes.
- to help the National Park with education programs.
- to educate Ecuadorian students.

In 1986, the budget of the Darwin Station was US$600,000. In 1994, it was US$2 million per year. Visiting scientists with research projects must pay an indemnity for their expeditions and outings. Twenty per cent of the budget of the station is supplied by the Ecuadorian government. Another important donor is the Smithsonian Institution, which provides 20-30 per cent of the budget. The WWF was a serious contributor in the past, but gradually retired. The San Diego Zoo supports the giant tortoises projects. Other well-known donors include the Frankfurt Zoological Society. Private European and American societies also contribute modest funds to the CDRS.

ADVICE AND PRACTICAL INFORMATION

HOW TO GET TO THE GALÁPAGOS

By Plane
TAME (Transportes Aereos Militares Equatorianos)
      Avenida Amazonas y Avenida Colon
      Edificio Banco del Pichincha, 7mo piso
      P.O. Box 8736
      Quito, Ecuador
      Tel: 509392, 590375

It is also possible to make reservations through travel agencies in Quito and Guayaquil. Officially inaugurated on November 3, 1980, the Boeing 737 links Quito to Baltra Island in the Galápagos, Monday to Saturday. The flight stops over in Guayaquil—with or without a plane change—then proceeds to Baltra. The international return fare is US$374 (1994), US$328 for students with a student card. For Ecuadorians, the fare is 396,000 sucres return (US$203). For Galápagos residents, it's 201,000 sucres (US$103). A new low season fare has been offered by TAME at US$289 From January 16 to June 14 and from September 1 to November 30 (official since 1995).

		Quito	Baltra
UIO-GLPS	flight 191	9:30 am ..stopover Guayaquil 11:00 am.......	12:30 pm

		Baltra	Quito
GLPS-UIO	flight 190	12:30 am..........stopover Guayaquil................	5:30 pm

Since January 1986, it has been possible to fly straight to San Cristobal with SAN (Servicios Aereos Nacionales), based in Guayaquil. Daily flights except on Sundays. The international price is the same as on TAME, including the 25 per cent student discount for persons under 26 years of age with a student card. Starting from Quito, the return flight costs $297, but it is only US$264 from Guayaquil.

SAN	Avenida Colon 535 - Quito	Ave. Arosemena Km. 2.5
	Tel: 561995 - 562024	P.O. Box 09-01-7138 - Guayaquil
		Tel: 201516

		Quito	San Cristobal
UIO-GYE	WB821/800	11:00 am.....stopover GYE 12:00 pm.............	1:30 pm GLPS
		San Cristobal	Quito
GLPS-UIO	WB 801/832	1:00 pm.....stopover GYE 4:00 pm................	4:30 pm

There is an hour's difference between the mainland and the archipelago.

Visas
British and American citizens do not require a visa to enter Ecuador, as is the case for citizens of most countries. Since July 1993, French visitors must obtain a visa.

Exchanging Money
The currency in Ecuador is the *sucre*. It has been fluctuating since 1980, quite alarmingly, in fact, if one considers that US$1 was worth 30 sucres back then. In 1989, $1 = 500 sucres, and in 1995, $1 = 2,350 sucres.

There are two banks in the Galápagos, both are in Puerto Ayora (Santa Cruz Island) and in Puerto Baquerizo Moreno (San Cristobal Island): the Banco del Pacifico and the Banco de Fomento. It's possible to change money there, as well as in souvenir shops. But you would do better to change your money at the Quito airport upon arrival, at the banks of Avenida Amazonas or at the Casa de cambio (Casa Paz). You can also change back sucres into dollars at the airport before leaving Ecuador.

Spoken Languages
Spanish is the national language, but English is usually well understood in the Galápagos. Guides may also speak German, French, Italian and Dutch.

Electricity
110 volts in Ecuador as well as in the Galápagos, with American-type plugs. Europeans may be advised to bring along a plug adapter. On the Galápagos boats, you may also plug into 220 volts, 12 or 24 volt system, and recharge the batteries of your video camera without any problems.

Sun
Being right on the equator, the sun is very strong. Do not forget your hat, sun protection, lip balm. Burns may occur rapidly for those who are not protected from the very first day. You are well advised to put sunblock cream on your neck, behind your knees, on your calves and on your feet.

Clothes & Footwear
Light clothing like shorts and T-shirts is sufficient. Bring along a light raincoat or a rainjacket for protection during the garua and the showers of the hot season. A sweat-shirt or jumper will be necessary for cool and windy evenings on the boat, and for the high elevations of the Andes (Quito, 2,850 metres) and Ecuador. Sports shoes are the best for the islands, not to mention a pair of flip-flops (thongs) for walking in the shallow water or for disembarking on a coral beach.

Mosquitoes & Related Diseases

Mosquitoes are found in the hot season on the coast, in the mangroves of Puerto Ayora and in the islands. On the sea, where a breeze is always present, they are not a problem. There is no malaria in the Galápagos.

Besides seasickness, there are no risks of disease in the islands, even though some cases of cholera were reported after the 1992 epidemic in Ecuador. This bleak period is now over. Vaccinations against diphtheria and tetanus are recommended, however.

There is a small hospital and pharmacy in Puerto Ayora, as well as in Puerto Baquerizo Moreno (San Cristobal), and one dispensary is found in Puerto Villamil (Isabela). For any serious accident, returning to Quito or Guayaquil is strongly advised.

Photography

Kodak, Fuji and Sakura film are available, for slides or prints, in Puerto Ayora, Pto. Baquerizo and in Floreana (at Mrs Wittmer's place). Nevertheless, if you want to be sure of its freshness, it is better to bring your own supply from home, or, alternatively, from Quito or Guayaquil.

Hours of Sea Crossing

For small boats sailing at six or seven miles per hour.

		Nautical Miles	Hours
Puerto Ayora	-Punta Suarez (Española)	53	9
	-Puerto Baquerizo	40	7
	-South Plaza	17	3
	-Santa Fé		3
	-Bartolomé	45	8
	-James Bay (Santiago)	57	9
	-Puerto Villamil (Isabela)		8
	-Punta Espinosa (Fernandina)	140	22
South Plaza	-Bartolomé	33	5
Bartolomé	-James Bay	27	3-4
Bartolomé	-Genovesa	52	8-9
James Bay	-Rábida	16	2-3
James Bay	-Punta Espinosa	90	12-14
Punta Suarez	-Floreana	42	5-6

Historical Index

1535   Official discovery of the Galápagos, on March 10, by Fray Tomas de Berlanga, archbishop of Panama, on a boat that drifted off its course with the ocean currents. The first mass is celebrated on the islands.

1546   Arrival of Diego de Rivadeneira, who experiences the same trouble as Fray Tomas. He is the first to mention the Galápagos hawk and the flamingos.

1570   The Galápagos Islands appear for the first time on a world map, drawn by Abraham Ortelius. They are called *Insulae de los Galopegoes*.

1593–   Pirates use the Galápagos as a refuge and as a base to look for water and to collect
1710   turtle and tortoise meat. From there, they attack the Peruvian and Ecuadorian ports. Goats seem to have been introduced at this time.

1684   The pirate and cartographer Ambrose Cowley draws the first navigation map of the islands, as does William Dampier.

1685   The viceroy of Peru introduces dogs on some islands to eradicate goats, food of the pirates.

1790   The first scientific mission, led by the Sicilian captain Alexander Malaspina, sent by Charles V of Spain, lands on the island. The report of that expedition was lost.

1793   The British James Colnett makes a trip to the Galápagos to study the possibility of whale fishing. Start of the whaling industry, which will last until 1870. Some tortoise species are on the brink of extinction. James Colnett draws the first detailed map of the archipelago. The post office barrel is erected on Floreana by Colnett or Hathaway to facilitate communication with the United States and England.

1800–   Exploitation of the fur sea lions by North Americans and Europeans. The species
1900   comes close to extinction but some individual sea lions survive on Fernandina and Genovesa.

1801   The American captain Amasa Delano reports an eruption of Alcedo volcano or Darwin volcano when anchored at James Bay. He is the first to mention the lava lizard in the archipelago.

1807   Irishman Patrick Watkins is the first authentic settler in the Galápagos, being exiled on Floreana (unless he requested it). He grows vegetables, which he trades for whisky to the passing ships. Two years later, he steals a ship's boat and sails to the Ecuadorian coast.

1813   Arrival of the USS *Essex*. Darwin Porter, the captain, practically destroys the British whaling fleet in the archipelago. He makes many important observations on the natural history of the islands, but he is responsible for the introduction of goats to Santiago. He reports volcanic eruptions on Isabela and Fernandina.

1825   Captain Benjamin Morell of the *Tartar,* who came to look for sea lions in February, observes a volcanic eruption on Fernandina, from Banks Bay. Lava flows into the sea, heating up the water and air to such an extent that parts of the boat start melting.Two weeks later, the eruption was still not over.

1832   Ecuador, a young republic since 1830, takes official possession of the Galápagos Islands on February 12, and names them 'Archipelago del Ecuador'. The first colony— composed of soldiers exiled for having fomented a rebellion on the mainland— is founded on Floreana. General Villamil is the first governor. Domestic animals are brought to the island and will turn feral when the colony is abandoned some years later.Thirty-one ships stop over in Floreana during the following three years.

1835   Visit of Captain Fitzroy's HMS *Beagle* for five weeks, from September 15 to October 20. The young naturalist Charles arwin disembarks on San Cristobal, Santiago, Flo reana and Isabela. His observation will lead him to publish *The Origin of Species* 24 years later. Captain Fitzroy draws very accurate maps, which will be used until WW II.

1841   The American writer Herman Melville visits the Galápagos and will write a poetic book on the *Enchanted Islands.*

1846   The French boat *Genie* reports three huts at the foot of Cerro Ballena, south of Conway Bay. A trail to the top of Santa Cruz Island starts from there.

1859   Publication of *The Origin of Species.*

1861   Ecuadorian president Garcia Moreno declares the Galápagos 'Provincia', with Floreana as capital.

1872   Scientific expedition of Professor Louis Agassiz of Harvard University.

1875   First visit of Theodore Wolf, with a few scientists of the Quito Polytechnic School. He will make another trip three years later, and will publish a monograph explaining that the islands are of volcanic origin and were never linked to the mainland. The highest volcano of Isabela (1,707 metres) bears his name.

1885   The Galápagos are linked to the province of Guayas. The new authorities move to Puerto Baquerizo Moreno (San Cristobal).

1886   First school in San Cristobal.

1888   Manuel Cobos founds the penal colony of El Progreso (San Cristobal) after a first failed attempt in 1969. A sugarcane industry is established.

1890   Volcanic activity in the southeast of Santiago. The lava flows of Sullivan Bay may be from that period.

1891   Visit of Georges Baur, an American scientist who claims that the islands were connected to the mainland. For him, there is no other way to explain the presence of so many species on the islands.

1892   The archipelago gets the official name of Archipelago de Colon, after Christopher Columbus. Spanish names are given to the islands.

1897   Antonio Gil starts the colonization of Isabela, with the port of Villamil and the village of Santo Tomas in the highlands.

1904   Manuel Cobos is murdered by a Colombian convict (Sanbal).

1905–   Under the presidency of Rollo Beck, scientists of the California Academy of Science
1906   conduct studies and make numerous samples for one year. They take away with them the greatest collection of plants and animals ever made in the Galápagos. The last giant tortoises were collected on Fernandina, as well as a few specimens found on Rábida Island (which has never been a distinct subspecies). The fur sea lions are almost extinct, according to their findings.

1923   Visit of the American William Beebe, with the *Arcturus* expedition. His book, *Galapagos World's End*, a worldwide success, stimulates many expeditions, among which is the Norwegian colony of 1926.

1924–   First commercial exploitation of the salt mine of Puerto Egas in James Bay (Santiago).
1930   A second exploitation will be undertaken from 1960 to 1968.

1926   A group of Norwegians lands in the Galápagos, with the aim of fishing and agriculture. The company fails, triggering the return of many settlers, although a few remain on Santa Cruz and San Cristobal.

1930–   Appearance of the fire ant in the Galápagos, on the Bellavista road (Santa Cruz).
1934
1932   Drama on Floreana, with Dr Ritter, Dore Strauch, the Wittmer family and the Baroness von Wagner de Bousquet, with her two lovers Lorenz and Philipson. Disappearances, poisoning, strange deaths.

1934   First laws aimed at protecting the fauna of the Galápagos. Some islands become re serves or natural park. Some land iguanas are brought from Baltra to Seymour by a team of Americans of the Hancock Foundation, to find out whether the habitat of Seymour is favourable to the reptiles. (Curiously, that will save the species of Baltra, eradicated after the Second World War. The first flight over the Galápagos is made by two Americans, who came to help a yacht captain suffering from appendicitis in Tagus Cove (Isabela).

1935   Expedition of Victor von Hagen, who commemorates the centenary of Charles Dar win's journey and deposits a bust in his memory.

1941   The American Air Force takes over the islands and builds an air base on Baltra. They are partly responsible for the eradication of the land iguanas on the island, and for the bombing of Pinnacle Rock on Bartolomé, a perfect target for shells.

1954   Uplift of a coral reef at Urvina Bay, in Isabela.

1957   The American scientists Eibl-Eibesfeldt and R Bowman are sent by a few institutions to report on conservation, and to choose a site for the future research station.

1959   On July 4, the Ecuadorian government declares the Galápagos a national park, with the exception of the colonized areas. The Darwin Foundation for the Galápagos Islands is created in Brussels, on July 23. Victor van Straelen is the first president. Upon the centenary of Darwin's book, the penitentiary of Isabela is closed and blown up.

1960   Beginning of lobster fishing. Raymond Lévèque is the first director of the Darwin Station. Funds from UNESCO help to finance the first buildings of the station. Hotel Galápagos, of the American Forrest Nelson, opens up the same year in Puerto Ayora.

1961   Goats are eradicated on South Plaza. Frenchman André Brosset becomes the second director of the Darwin Station. The laboratory and the meteorological station are built the same year.

1963   David Snow becomes the third director of the Darwin Station.

1964   Grand opening of the Darwin Station on January 21, with many international personali ties. In May, Miguel Castro becomes the first official in charge of conservation and protection of the tortoise population. Roger Perry becomes the fourth director of the station.

1965   Tortoise eggs from Pinzón Island are brought back to the station to be incubated and for the young giant tortoises to be bred in captivity.

1968   Juan Black and Jose Villa, conservation officials, are sent by the Ecuadorian govern
        ment. They begin the administration of the Galápagos National Park, in October. During
        an intense period of activity, the caldera floor of Fernandina volcano drops down to 300
        metres (small eruptions within the caldera will follow in 1972, 1972, 1977, 1978, 1988
        and 1991).

1969   Mass tourism starts in the Galápagos with the arrival of the *Lina-A* of Metropolitan
        Touring, which will build many landing sites in the islands.

1970   The first 20 baby tortoises bred in captivity are freed on Pinza, their native island.
        Peter Kramer becomes the fifth director of the Darwin Station.

1971   Scholarships are given to Ecuadorian students to study at the Darwin Station. The
        giant tortoise named Lonesome George is found on Pinta Island.

1972   The *Beagle III* is inaugurated in March; it is the first boat of the Darwin Station, offered
        by the WWF (World Wildlife Fund). Engineer Jaime Torres is the first superintendent
        of the National Park. The Japanese boat *Chicuzen Maru* captures hundreds of turtles
        in Galápagos waters. Construction of the Van Straelen Hall at the station.

1973   Construction of the Puerto Ayora-Baltra road. Once again the Galápagos become
        'Province of Ecuador'. National and international experts write the Master Plan for
        the protection and use of the National Park.

1974   Craig MacFarland became the sixth director of the Darwin Station. Publication of the
        Master Plan.

1975   Seventeen five-year-old tortoises, bred in captivity, are released on Española, bring
        ing the total number of adults to 14 on that island. The feral dogs of Santa Cruz
        destroy the population of young tortoises of the reserve and hundreds of land igua
        nas of the northwest of the island. A breeding center will be established at the sta
        tion. The cruise ship *Floreana* (ex *Lina-A*) sinks 60 miles off the mainland, with no
        human losses.

1976   *Rattus rattus*, the black rat, is eradicated on Bartolomé, thanks to the experiments of
        the Darwin Station with traps and poison.

1977   Two new cruise ships arrive in the islands: M/N *Bucanero* and M/N *Neptuno*.

1978   The islands are declared a 'Patrimony of Humanity' by UNESCO.

1980   Arrival of the cruise ship M/N *Santa Cruz* (90 passengers) of Metropolitan Tour
        ing, and of the first B-727 of TAME Airline for the Quito-Baltra flight.

1982   Eruption of Wolf volcano, late August-early September, on Isabela. Unusual warming of the sea surface in the Galápagos. Dieter Plage and Friedmann Köster shoot a video for Survival Anglia Productions (English), for two consecutive years. First use of a ULM to fly over the archipelago.

1983   Memorable year of a disastrous Niño: nine months of rain until July. The Baltra road is flooded and cut off. Real streams appear and bridges are built in Bellavista. Sea surface temperature in Puerto Ayora reaches 30° C. The local population suffers from the humid heat, from colds and skin infections. Many couples divorce or separate. The number of sea lions, of marine iguanas and sea birds is decimated.

1984   In April, volcanic eruption on Fernandina. In May, arson fire at the administrative building of the Darwin Station. On May 28, fire on the boat M/N *Neptuno* of Macchi avello Tours, sinks off Guayaquil with the death of the cook.

1985   Big fire in the south of Isabela (March-April), on the slopes of Sierra Negra volcano, in the agricultural zone of Valle Alemania and in the National Park. A trench 62 kilometres long and seven metres wide is dug by the Ecuadorian army. Tortoises are evacuated on men's backs. Two Canadairs are sent from Canada to extinguish the fire, which lasts for 50 days. Covered on TV and in the international press. At the same time, the fishing boat B/P *Intrepido* of Captain Miguel Andagana disappears on March 6 and drifts for 74 days before it reaches the coast of Coast Rica. The six crew men survive on turtles, sharks and dolphinfish. In November: first course of Dituris, the Ecuadorian tourism office. Estimate of the number of visitors for 1985: 17,850 people (65 per cent foreigners).

1986   Opening on January 9 of the airport of San Cristobal by the vice-president. Creation of the Galápagos Marine Reserve by presidential decree on May 13, which extends 15 miles from the extreme points of the islands. In September: paving of Puerto Ayora. The new guides' hall of the National Park opens its gates for the naturalist guides course. The number of visitors to the Galápagos goes beyond 26,000.

1987   In October, arrival of the *Galápagos Explorer*, the new cruise ship of the company Canodros (SAN/SAETA), with a capacity to carry 90 passengers. New restrictions for the practice of scuba diving in the Galápagos. The dive guides must now have a diver's license from the Ecuadorian Merchant Marine. The number of visitors reaches 32,593.

1988   International Congress of Herpetology at the CDRS in May. It is decided to save the semen of Lonesome George, the last giant tortoise survivor of Pinta Island. The cargo boat *Iguana* (an old cruise ship) sinks in front of the CDRS in Academy Bay, in June. Around September 12-14, new eruption of Fernandina volcano: lava flows inside the caldera, displacement of the crater lake, fumaroles on the outer slope of the volcano. The number of visitors exceeds 31,200.

1989   The French cruise ship *Mermoz* (500 passengers) visits the archipelago twice, but the passengers cannot disembark on the islands of the National Park. Opening of the site of Punta Pitt on the eastern tip of San Cristobal. In May, the goats of southern Isabela cross the Perry Isthmus and climb up Alcedo volcano. A new Niño is preparing, with a noticeable change in life cycles. Gunther Reck resigns as director of the Darwin Station and is replaced by American Daniel Ewans. On July 4, the 30th anniversary of the Galápagos National Park is celebrated. In September and October, the blue-footed boobies abandon their chicks on a massive scale throughout the archipelago, but the albatrosses reproduce well. During the same month, black rats are eradicated on Pinzón Island. Illegal taking of shark fins by the Japanese becomes important. The number of visitors reaches 41,900.

1990   Creation of new trails on Santa Fé, Seymour and Rábida. Return of the cruiseship *Mermoz*. In March-April, the park guards of the Galápagos National Park go on strike for three months, asking for a salary raise. Disputes between the national guides of the Asociacion de Guias and those of the Agrupación de Guias Interpretes del PNG. Sergio Basan breaks the arm of Matthias Espinosa in Puerto Ayora with a club. In May-June, the French TV TF1 shoots two programs of 'Ushuaï a' with Nicolas Hulot and the author aboard the schooner *Cyprae*. Second use of the ULM to fly over the islands. Death of Marga Angermeyer, wife of Carl the painter and German pioneer. Foreigners cannot participate in naturalist guide's exam. In November: dramatic fire of the M/N *Bartolomé* at sea during the night. Five passengers and one crewmember sink with the boat and disappear. A wooden stairway is constructed at Tagus Cove by SPNG.

1991   A French team of XL Productions led by the author shoots two programmes: 'Les Animaux de Mon Coeur' ('Animals of My Heart') for French TV TF1, and 'Wildlife Sanctuaries', which will air on the Discovery Channel. In March, first report by Jonathan Green of an attack by a three-metre-long great white shark, at Playa Escondida (northeast Pinzón Island). March 21: earthquakes at Alcedo volcano, and in April, the eruption of Fernandina volcano. In June: 35 land iguanas are reintroduced to Baltra by the SPNG, after a 40-year absence. In July: opening of Banco del Pacifico in Puerto Ayora, on Santa Cruz Island. September 25: first historical eruption of Marchena Island, during the night, incandescent clouds and lava flows to the southwest. On October 19, Prince Henry of Luxembourg visits the islands. The Ecuadorian government extends for another 25 years the right of the Darwin Foundation to operate the Darwin Station. In December, Arturo Izurieta, former naturalist guide, becomes the new superintendent of the Galápagos National Park, after the scandal that ousted Fausto Cepeda. The telephone is connected in Puerto Ayora. The total number of visitors reaches 40,746.

1992   January: Daniel Ewans ends his term as director of the Darwin Station, and will be replaced by American Chantal Blanton in May. The Japanese commercial fishing boat *Kaiyo Maru,* with sophisticated electronic equipment, drops anchor at Academy Bay, in Puerto Ayora. On February 10, the *Donai,* an Ecuadorian fishing boat from Manta, is seized by the Ecuadorian navy patrol boat off Pinta with a load of 50 hammerhead sharks. Impounded, the sharks are found two days later on February 12 at the house of Copiano in Puerto Ayora, where they are slaughtered for illicit commercial purposes. The affair is reported in the international press (Europe and the US). The scandal of the exploitation of pepinos follows, with pirate camps established on the coast of Fernandina. In June: President Borja declares a ban on sea cucumber fishing. New Niño year, with warming of the sea and considerable rains, landslides above Santa Rosa (Santa Cruz). Construction in Puerto Ayora of the Thomas Fisher Science and Education Building, near the Darwin Station. A new wooden stairway is built at Bartolomé Island to stop the erosion of the trail and of the slope by the visitors (August). In September, a new system for the naturalist guide's course. Number of visitors: 39,510.

1993   Lobster fishing is banned for seven years until 2000. The National Park fee goes up to $80 for foreigners, and the port tax to $6. Blue whales are reported for the first time, by the research sailboat *Odyssey* south of Isabela (May), Fernandina, Cape Berkeley, Roca Redonda (David Day, personal communication). Telephone connections are now possible between the islands and the mainland. In September, arrival of the cruise ship *Ambassador I*, of the company Islas Galápagos Turismo y Vapores, of Mr. Zacharias in Quito. Pressure from Galápagos fishermen on the government of Sixto Duran Ballen, to suspend the ban on the fishing of pepinos. The American photographer Doug Perrine, takes underwater photos of hammerhead sharks caught in drift nets at Wolf Island (a letter is sent to the president of Ecuador). The number of visitors to the Galápagos reaches 46,818.

1994   The Department of Industry and Fisheries (MIIP) re-opens lobster fishing for three months (July 15 to October 15), pepinos fishing for three months (October 15 to January15), and shark fishing for three months (January 15 to April 15). One hundred and forty Japanese fishing boats are authorized to fish for tuna west of Isabela during the whole month of October, but must pay $20,000 each for the permit. Press campaign in Quito and Ecuador for the protection of the Marine Reserve. The number of visitors to the Park reaches 53,825.

1995   February: Death of Bernhard Schreyer an old German settler and owner of the schooner *Tigress*. February-March: Eruption of Fernandina Volcano and lava flows towards Cape Hammond. July: arrival of SPNG's new boat *Guadalupe River* to patrol the Marine Reserve. Goats found on top of Volcan Wolf. September: new tortoise center at Villamil (Isabela) named after Arnoldo Tupiza. After new law project made by Eduardo Velez and veto by President Sixto Ballen Duran, Pto.Ayora and Pto.Baquerizo go on strike for three weeks; assault of SPNG and CDRS offices. Army comes in. Introduction of goats on Pinta. Illegal fishing of pepinos and shark goes on. Eight boats from Manabi found at Roca Redonda, where a diver is attacked by a hammerhead shark. A Izurieta leaves Galápagos as Park's intendant. Number of visitors: 55,782.

1996   Chantal Blanton leaves as director of CDRS, replaced by Robert Bensted Smith (GB). M/N *Galápagos Explorer* hits the rocks in San Cristóbal and is sunk offshore. Road Itabaca-Pto.Ayoras asphalted. New dive centers: 'Scuba Iguana' (Hotel Galápagos) and 'Nautidiving' (Red Mangrove Inn). New president Abdala Bucaram prepares a law for protection of Marine Reserve, which is declared a 'biological reserve' by INEFAN in November. Number of visitors, up to 61,500.

Lexicon of the Fauna of the Galápagos

English	French	Spanish

SEABIRDS

English	French	Spanish
Common egret	Aigrette	Garza blanca
Waved Albatross	Albatros des Galápagos	Albatros de Galápagos
White-cheeked pintail	Canard Bahama	Patillo, pato
Flightless cormorant	Cormoran aptère	Cormoran no volador
Blue-footed booby	Fou à pattes bleues	Piquero patas azules
Red-footed booby	Fou à pattes rouges	Piquero patas rojas
Masked booby	Fou masqué	Piquero enmascarado
Magnificent frigatebird	Frégate magnifique	Fragata, tijereta
Great frigatebird	Grande frégate	Fragata comun
Great blue heron	Grand héron bleu	Garza azul
Lava heron	Héron des laves	Garza de lava
Yellow-crowned night heron	Héron de nuit	Garza nocturna
Oystercatcher	Huitrier	Ostrero, cangrejero
Galápagos penguin	Manchot des Galápagos	Pinguino de Galápagos
Swallowtail gull	Mouette à queue d'aronde	Gaviota colabifurcada
Lava gull	Mouette des laves	Gaviota de lava
Brown pelican	Pélican brun	Pelicano
Storm petrel	Pétrel des tempêtes	Golondrinas del mar
Hawaiian petrel	Pétrel hawaïen	Pata pegada
Redbill tropicbird	Phaéton, paille en queue	Rabijunco, pajaro tropical
Semipalmated plover	Pluvier semi-palm	
Audubon shearwater	Puffin d'Audubon	Pufino
Brown noddi	Noddi	Gaviotin
Sooty Tern	Sterne fuligineuse	Gaviotin
Royal Tern	Sterne royale	
Ruddy turnstone	Tourne pierres à collier	Vuelvepiedras
Whimbrel	Courlis	Zarapito
Common stilt	Echasse	Tero real
Flamingo	Flamant rose	Flamingo
Wandering tattler	Chevalier errant	
Sanderling	Becasseau sanderling	
Northern phalarope	Phalarope hyperboren	Falaropo

LAND BIRDS

English	French	Spanish
Smoothed-bill ani	Ani à bec doux	Garapatero
Galápagos hawk	Buse des Galápagos	Gavilan de Galápagos
Dark-billed cuckoo	Coulicou	Cuclillo, aguatero

ENGLISH	FRENCH	SPANISH
Barn owl	Effraie	Lechuza blanca
Yellow warbler	Fauvette jaune	Canario, maria
Short-eared owl	Hibou brachiotte	Lechuza de campo
Galápagos martin	Hirondelle des Galápagos	Golondrina
Galápagos mockingbird	Moqueur des Galápagos	Cucuve de Galápagos
Galápagos rail	Râle des Galápagos	Pachay
Painted-bill crake	Râle à bec rouge et jaune	Pachay
Galápagos dove	Tourterelle des Galápagos	Paloma de Galápagos
Large-billed flycatcher	Tyran à poitrine jaune	Papamoscas
Vermillion flycatcher	Tyran rouge	Brujo
Finches	Pinsons	Pinzones
Sharpbill Ground finch	Pinson à bec aiguisé	Pinzón de pico agudo
Carpenter finch	Pinson carpentier	Pinzón artesano
Warbler finch	Pinson chanteur	Pinzón cantor
Tree finch	Pinson des arbres	Pinzón arboreo
Small tree finch	- à petit bec	Pequeño pinzon arboreo
Medium tree finch	- à bec moyen	Mediano pinzon arboreo
Large tree finch	- à gros bec	Gran pinzon arboreo
Cactus finch	Pinson des cactus	Pinzón de tuna
Large cactus finch	Grand pinson des cactus	Gran pinzon de tuna
Mangrove finch	Pinson des paltuviers	Pinzón de manglar
Ground finch	Pinson de terre	Pinzón de tierra
Small ground finch	- à petit bec	Pequeno pinzon de tierra
Medium ground finch	- à bec moyen	Mediano pinzon de tierra
Large ground finch	- à gros bec	Gran pinzon de tierra
Common gallinule	Gallinule, poule d'eau	Gallinula comun
Purple gallinule	Gallinule violace	

REPTILES

Galápagos snake	Couloeuvre des Galápagos	Culebra
Gecko	Gecko	Salamanquesa
Marine iguana	Iguane marin	Iguana marina
Lang iguana	Iguane terrestre	Iguana terrestre
Lava lizard	Lézard des laves	Lagartija de lava
Black turtle	Tortue noire	Tortuga negra
Giant tortoise	Tortue géante	Galapago

MAMMALS

Feral donkey	Ane	Burro
Feral Cat	Chat	Gato salvage
Bat	Chauve-souris	Murcielago

ENGLISH	FRENCH	SPANISH
Wild horses	Chevaux sauvages	Caballos salvages
Feral goat	Chèvre sauvage	Chivo
Wild dog	Chien sauvage	Perro salvage
Fur sea lion	Otarie à fourrure	Lobo de dos pelos
Galápagos sea lion	Otarie des Galápagos	Lobo marino de Galápagos
Feral pig	Porc sauvage	Chancho
Galápagos rice rat	Rat de riz des Galápagos	Rata endemica
Black rat	Rat noir	Rata negra

FISHES AND MARINE LIFE

Galápagos garden eel	Anguille de jardin	Anguila de jardin
Yellow grouper	Bacalao, mérou jaune	Bacalao
Barracuda	Barracuda	Barracuda
Whale	Baleine	Ballena
Pacific amberjack	Carangue du Pacifique	Palometa
Slipper lobster	Cigale de mer	Langostino
Black coral	Corail noir	Coral negro
Shells	Coquillages	Conchas
Shrimp	Crevette	Camaron
Crab	Crabe	Cangrejo
Dolphin	Dauphin	Delfin
Blue lobster	Langouste bleue	Langosta azul
Red spiny lobster	Langouste rouge	Langosta roja
Green moray	Murène verte	Morena verde
Sea urchin	Oursin	Erizo de mar
Stingray	Raie à aiguillon	Raya de aguijon
Golden cownose ray	Raie dorée	Raya dorada
White spotted	Raie léopard	Raya aguila
Manta ray	Raie manta	Manta
Hornshark	Requin à cornes	Tiburon gato
White tip reef shark	Requin à pointes blanches	Tintorera
Blacktip shark	Requin à pointes noires	Tiburon aleta negra
Whale shark	Requin baleine	Tiburon ballena
Galápagos shark	Requin des Galápagos	Tiburon de Galápagos
Grey reef shark	Requin gris de récif	Tiburon gris
Hammerhead shark	Requin marteau	Tiburon martillo
Smooth hammerhead	Requin marteau lisse	Martillo
Scalloped hammerhead	Requin marteau à festons	Martillo
Tiger shark	Requin tigre	Tiburon tigre
Sea snake	Serpent marin	Culebra de mar
Tuna	Thon	Atun

APPENDICES

OCEANIC RESEARCH AND 'HOT SPOTS' IN THE GALÁPAGOS

Studies were conducted in the eastern Pacific Ocean, off the North American, Mexican and South American coasts, to explore the east Pacific mid-oceanic ridge and the transformation faults located along the ridge. During the summer of 1977, the American scientific submarine *Alvin* dived on the ridge at the latitude of the Galápagos islands. The fault is an extension of the southeast Pacific ridge, almost parallel to the equator, and separates the oceanic Cocos Plate (to the north) from the Nazca Plate (to the south). This is the tectonic hinge of the Central America/South America system. Westward and beyond the East Pacific Rise is the Pacific Plate.

Given these facts, we may conclude that the Galápagos archipelago is located on an important tectonic joint, which explains not only its volcanic nature, but also the fact that it is a hot spot, with quasi-permanent seismic and volcanic activity.

In the Galápagos rift, the spread of the plates is about eight to ten centimetres per year, while it is only 6.2 centimetres at the tip of Baja California, but 13.7 centimetres per year north of the equator and 17.5 centimetres per year at the latitude of Easter Island. That is to say that the Pacific Ocean opens up toward the south.

The dive of *Alvin* has observed hot springs, sulphur deposits and a very intense and localized life. The interest in the *Cyamex* dives, at a depth of 2,600 to 2,800 metres, mainly concerned with geological features, was then doubled. The scientists noted a biological and geological analogy with the dive of RITA (Riviera-Tamayo), which was made in 1979 in the rift (on the ridge) at the southern tip of Baja California. The geological conditions are the same, ie a rift spreading at an average of six to ten centimetres a year. The physical conditions and bathymetry are identical, and the temperature of the water is 2° C. Here, too, extremely hot springs, more or less active, bring about profuse sea life. Twenty new species have been reported, but in the Galápagos, a unique mussel was discovered which does not exist in the RITA zone.

These hot springs are not so frequent in the Atlantic, where if present, they are weak. This is due to the fact that the Atlantic mid-oceanic ridge has reached old age, which is evidenced by reduced activity, a slow speed of expansion, a thermic flux which is not so high and a more conspicuous hydrothermal metamorphism.

In contrast, proof of volcanic activity is spectacular in the Pacific. The French oceanographic ship *Jean Charcot* conducted a survey in March and April of 1980 between Ecuador and Easter Island, at 115° west longitude, where very localized gas emanations could portend a powerful submarine eruption. Such a deep-sea eruption was observed in 1991, 10° north of the equator, off the coast of Mexico, by the submersible *Alvin*.

Hot springs, loaded with black material, create true chimneys, with deposits of sulphur and other minerals. These fragile pipes are two or three metres high and made of sulfides of iron, tin, copper, lead, silver and gold. The temperature of the hydrothermal vents reaches 360-380° C. Basaltic landscapes of pillow lava and basalt columns were also observed.

The Americans found important thermal activity in the zone of the Galápagos. This prolific life is a real 'oasis of the deep', where giant tube worms of the species *Riftia pachyptila* (three metres long, and two to three centimetres wide) swarm, and where bacteria may survive at temperature up to 402° C.

All actual and recent volcanic zones are closely associated with seismic zones, which does not mean that one phenomenon is the cause of the other, but that both arise from a common origin. The latter resides in the movement of the lithospheric plates. The main volcanic and seismic zones coincide perfectly with the mobile joints of these plates.

Oceanic Ridges

Seismologic and oceanographic studies show that these are distension zones from which the expansion of the oceanic floor is made. These are characterized by a mean thermic flux (1.82 micro cal/cm2) which is superior to the mean thermic flux of the earth (1.5 micro cal/cm2) and which can reach up to 8 micro cal/cm2 in some areas called 'hot spots', the most active areas of the globe.

From the petrochemical point of view, it seems that in the stage of intense activity (fast expansion and high thermic flux) corresponds tholetic lava flows (subalkaline basalts), poorly or not at all affected by hydrothermal metamorphism of the oceanic floor. This is the case of the southeast Pacific.

Oceanic Archipelagoes

These are a chain of islands or submarine volcanoes, which are only active at one of their extremities. The volcanic formations getting older towards the other end. This is the case in the Galápagos. Some create a single chain from a 'hot spot' located far away from any ridge. Others are placed symmetrically on each side of a hot spot located on a ridge, eg Tuamotu-Easter Island, in the southeast Pacific (see map of the Hot Spots, page 15).

An abnormally high thermic flux creates a 'plume'. This magmatic plume is right on the hot spot, at least at the emerging ones. When such a plume hits a lithospheric plate, it pierces it like a laser beam. If the plate moves on the asthenosphere, the plume will leave its track on it, ie a chain of islands or a chain of submarine volcanoes. The farther they are from the point of origin, the older they are.

DISTRIBUTION OF THE LAND BIRDS ACCORDING TO VEGETATION ZONES

Mangrove Zone

Common
Herons
Yellow warbler
Small ground finch
Mockingbird

Present
Mangrove finch
Medium ground finch
Dark billed cuckoo
Small tree finch
Dark-billed cuckoo
Large-billed flycatcher
Short-eared owl

Arid Coastal Zone

Small ground finch
Medium ground finch
Cactus finch
Galápagos dove
Mockingbirds
Yellow warbler
Vegetarian finch

Large ground finch
Vegetarian finch
Carpenter finch
Large-billed flycatcher
Galápagos martin
Barn owl

Transition Zone Common

Small ground finch
Medium ground finch
Cactus finch
Small tree finch
Yellow warbler
Galápagos dove

Large ground finch
Carpenter finch
Warbler finch
Dark-billed cuckoo
Vermillion flycatcher
Short-eared owl

Tropical Humid Zone

Common
Warbler finch
Tree finches
Large-billed flycatcher
Vermillion flycatcher
Dark-billed cuckoo
Yellow warbler
Short-eared owl

Present
Small ground and medium ground finches
Mockingbirds
Carpenter finch
Barn owl

Herbs and Fern Zone

Galápagos rail
Galápagos martin

Small ground and medium ground finches
Short-eared owl

HUMAN POPULATION OF THE GALÁPAGOS

In 1980, the resident population of the Galápagos was about 5,000 people. Ten years later, it had doubled. In 1995, it was estimated that the population had reached 20,000. Most immigration from the mainland is made of Ecuadorian Indians and 'mestizos' (mixed blood) who consider the Galápagos the new El Dorado, a touristic paradise where it seems easy to make money. But there is no such heaven, and problems become more apparent as time goes by and new settlers arrive: water and electricity problems (the power plant cannot meet the demands), problems of garbage disposal and pollution, poor medical and surgical facilities, disrespect for the rules of the National Park and abuses of all kinds, illegal fishing in the Reserve of Marine Resources, economic pressure, and so on.

INHABITED ISLANDS IN 1986   Number of Inhabitants

Santa Cruz	Baltra	San Cristobal	Isabela	Floreana
3,632	50	2,752	729	65
7 primary schools 1 high school	air and naval base	8 primary schools 1 high school	3 primary schools 1 college	1 high school

The migration from the continent was then comprised of 54 per cent men between 20 and 35 years, looking for work, and 15 per cent women. On San Cristobal, 66 per cent of the population is not native to the Galápagos; on Isabela, it is 50 per cent; and on Santa Cruz, 90 per cent. The number of cars in the islands increased from 88 in 1980 to 186 in 1986.

The population of Santa Cruz Island was around 10,000 people in 1994, and Cristobal's around 8,000 people.

TABLE OF MAPS AND ILLUSTRATIONS

" Flightless cormorant "

PIROCO 19

INDEX

"Great Frigates"

Glossary

Andesitic .... From the name Andes. This type of volcanic material is found in the volcanoes of the South American mainland, above the subduction zone of the eastern Pacific, and due to a mix of granitic and basaltic materials. Grey in colour with small white crystals.

Caldera .... Huge craterlike depression formed by the subsidence of the upper part of a volcano following a series of dramatic collapses.

Dimorphism .... Two distinct forms of the same species.

Hornito or .... Pocket of gas escaping from the still-molten lava. When the flow
driblet cones encounters a pocket of moisture, the water is turned into steam and bubbles up through the flow. Patches of lava are flung into the air and pile up to form small chimneys less than one metres high.

Medio-oceanic ...... A chain of undersea mountains found at a depth of 2,500
ridge or mid metres below the ocean surface, resulting from the opening of the
-oceanic ridge oceanic crust, and from where magma expands constantly, pushing oceanic plates toward the continents. Known as the East Pacific Rise in the eastern Pacific Ocean.

Orthogonal .... Parallel fractures lines at right angles in a crisscross design.
fractures

Oviparous .... Egg-laying, as opposed to giving birth to live young.

Ovoviviparous ...... Giving birth to live young hatching from eggs held inside the body without receiving nutrients from the mother.

Pelagic .... Organisms living in open ocean waters, rather than close to the shore.

Plate tectonics ...... A theory that was initiated by Alfred Wegener in 1929, and then known as the 'drifting of the continents'. Later on perfected by the French Prof. Xavier Le Pichon in 1969, who renamed it 'plate tectonics'.

Scoria cones .... Or cinder cones. Explosive ejection of large amounts of solid volcanic rock thrown into the air, which deposit as tephra.

Subduction .... When the sea floor is forced under the continent, the oceanic plate goes under the continental plate in the subduction zone.

Tephra .... Solid fragments of different sizes from explosive volcanic eruptions.

Thermic flux .... A flow of temperature due to the 'magmatic soup' which circulates under the oceanic crust (creating convection currents), and which can be high, medium or low, according to its intensity. A hot spot is the result of a high thermic flux. It is calculated in micro calories per square centimetre.

Transformation .... A type of plate boundary that occurs where two plates are moving
fault past one another, with little or no destruction of plate material. Occurs along the mid-oceanic ridge and the Galápagos rift.

Viviparous .... Bearing live young, which have received nutrient from the mother.

BIBLIOGRAPHY

ANGERMEYER, Johanna. *My Father's Island*, Viking Penguin, 1989, London.

BOYCE, Barry. *Traveler's Guide to the Galápagos*, California.

COLLIN-DELAVAUD, Anne. *Guide de l'Equateur et des les Galápagos*, Ed. La Manufacture, 1993, Paris.

CONSTANT, Pierre. Notes des 'Cours de Guide Naturaliste 1980-82-86',Galápagos National Park Service, Puerto Ayora.

CONSTANT, Pierre. *Marine Life of the Galápagos—a guide to the fishes, whales, dolphins and other marine animals*, Paris, 1992. Ed Pierre Constant. (Distributed in the USA by Sea Challengers, 4 Sommerset Rise, Monterey, California.)

DARWIN, Charles. *Voyage d'un Naturaliste de la Terre de Feu aux îles Galápagos*, Ed Maspero, 1979, Paris.

GRANT, Peter. *Ecology and Evolution of Darwin's finches*, Princeton University Press, 1986.

HARRIS, Michael. *A Field Guide to the Birds of Galápagos*, Collins, London/Taiplinger, New York, 1974.

HICKMAN, John. *The Enchanted Island: the Galápagos Discovered*, Anthony Nelson, 1985, England.

JACKSON, Michael. *Galápagos, a Natural History Guide*, University of Calgary Press, 1985, Canada.

LA TORRE, Octavia. *La Maldicción de la Tortuga*, Quito, 1992, Ecuador.

MACBIRNEY and WILLIAMS. *Geology and Petrology of the Galápagos Islands*, Geological Society of America, 1969.

MOORE, Tuy de Roy. *Galápagos, Islands Lost in Time*, Viking Press, 1980, New York.

MOORE, Tuy and Alan. *Guia del Parque Nacional Galápagos*, SPNG, 1980.

PERRY, Roger. *Galápagos, Key Environments*, Oxford, Pergamon, 1984.

STRAUCH, Dore. *Satan Came to Eden*, New York and London, 1935.

THORNTON, Ian. *Darwin's Islands: a Natural History of the Galápagos Islands* Natural History Press, Garden City, New York, 1971.

TREHERN, John. *The Galápagos Affair*, Jonathan Cape, 1983, London.

VONNEGUT, Kurt. *Galápagos*, Dell Publishing, Doubleday, 1985, New York.

WITTMER, Margret. *Floreana, Poste Restante*, Anthony Nelson, 1989, London.

ABOUT THE AUTHOR

Pierre Constant was born on December 3, 1954, in Boulogne sur Seine (near Paris), France. A student at the University of Pierre and Marie Curie - Paris VI, he earned a DEUG degree in biology-geology in 1975, then a master's in geology from Grenoble and Paris (1977-79). At the same time, he followed courses at the School of Anthropology in Paris (1977-78). Nevertheless, an unquenchable thirst for travelling has held him since 1974. The US, India, Central and South America, Pakistan and Nepal were his first travel experiences, followed later by the Philippines, Thailand, Japan, Malaysia, Papua New Guinea, Taiwan, Namibia and Madagascar.

The mirage of the Galápagos struck him in 1980. Having been selected by an English marine consultant (Julian Fitter), he signed a contract with an Ecuadorian company (represented in England), and was sent to Ecuador, where he attended the naturalist guide's course for the Galápagos National Park on Santa Cruz Island. He then worked in Ecuador for two years, in the Galápagos Islands and the Amazon jungle. Back in France, he published his first book, *L'Archipel des Galápagos* in 1983, and has become the French specialist on the Galápagos Islands for the last 13 years.

He organized expeditions and cruises for the agency Explorator, based in Paris (1984-86), then on his own ever since. Invited to radio and television programs in France and Switzerland (1983-84), he has also been a lecturer in different settings, including the 500-passenger French cruise ship *Mermoz* of the Compagnie Française des Croisières Paquet (1989), sailing from the Caribbean to the Galápagos. Constant organized two television programs of 'Ushuaïa' for the French TV TF1, leading Nicolas Hulot to the Galápagos (1990); he then organized the shooting of two video programmes: 'Animals of My Heart' (TF1) and 'Wildlife Sanctuaries' in the Galápagos, for XL Productions (1991), which aired on the Discovery Channel around the world. In 1992, he led a group of students of the Ushuaïa Foundation for a discovery and scientific mission in the islands.

Immersed in the underwater world of the Galápagos since 1984, Pierre Constant took up underwater photography and produced a new book (in English), *Marine Life of the Galápagos, a guide to the fishes, whales, dolphins and other marine animals (1992)*, in Hong Kong. The following year, he published a 1994 calendar of Galápagos marine life.

As a photojournalist, Pierre Constant has also published articles and reports on various countries, in travel and diving magazines, such as *Les Nouveaux Aventuriers, Iles Magazine, Voyager Magazine, Grands Reportages, Oceanorama, Apnea* and *Subaqua*, as well as in the American magazine *Ocean Realm*, and the Hong Kong-based magazine *Action Asia*.

Any person interested in the organization of trips and cruises in the Galápagos Islands, diving trips, filming trips or any other relevant subject may write to the author at the following address:

Pierre Constant   8 rue Erlanger, 75016 Paris - France
Phone: 331–42248983 or 331–45837351   Fax: 331–45837362